Big Promises, Small Government

Big Promises, Small Government

Doing Less with Less in the BC Liberal New Era

GEORGE M. ABBOTT

UBCPress · Vancouver · Toronto

29 28 27 26 25 24 23 22 21 20   5 4 3 2 1

Printed in Canada on FSC-certified ancient-forest-free paper (100% post-consumer recycled) that is processed chlorine- and acid-free.

Library and Archives Canada Cataloguing in Publication

Title: Big promises, small government : doing less with less in the BC Liberal new era / George M. Abbott.
Names: Abbott, George M., author.
Identifiers: Canadiana (print) 20200214179 | Canadiana (ebook) 20200214225 | ISBN 9780774864879 (softcover) | ISBN 9780774864886 (PDF) | ISBN 9780774864893 (EPUB) | ISBN 9780774864909 (Kindle)
Subjects: LCSH: Taxation — British Columbia — History — 21st century. | LCSH: Finance, Public — British Columbia — History — 21st century. | LCSH: British Columbia — Economic conditions — 21st century. | CSH: British Columbia — Politics and government — 2001-
Classification: LCC HJ2460.B8 A23 2020 | DDC 336.200971/1—dc23

Canadä

UBC Press gratefully acknowledges the financial support for our publishing program of the Government of Canada (through the Canada Book Fund), the Canada Council for the Arts, and the British Columbia Arts Council.

This book has been published with the help of a grant from the Canadian Federation for the Humanities and Social Sciences, through the Awards to Scholarly Publications Program, using funds provided by the Social Sciences and Humanities Research Council of Canada.

Printed and bound in Canada by Friesens
Set in Bodoni and Baskerville 10 Pro by Apex CoVantage, LLC
Copy editor: Deborah Kerr
Proofreader: Alison Strobel
Indexer: Margaret de Boer
Cover designer: David Drummond

UBC Press
The University of British Columbia
2029 West Mall
Vancouver, BC V6T 1Z2
www.ubcpress.ca

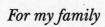

For my family

Contents

Tables

Foreword

THE 2001 BC election was uniquely one-sided. The BC Liberals, under leader Gordon Campbell, captured 57 percent of the popular vote and won seventy-seven of the seventy-nine seats in the provincial legislature. The New Democrats, after a decade in power, were reduced to the remaining two seats, losing official party status.

Buoyed by that overwhelming mandate, Premier Campbell and his Liberals set out to remake the provincial government and its structure, programs, and finances. The launch point was a 25 percent tax cut that was supposed to pay for itself but didn't. The fallback was a desperate effort to balance the budget with drastic cuts in programs, services, and government offices.

Overreaching, the Liberals squandered much of the goodwill reflected in that extraordinary mandate. Four years later, the voters delivered a stinging rebuke. The Liberals lost some thirty seats to the New Democrats, whose party headquarters on election night seemed more like a victory celebration than the depressing affair at Liberal headquarters.

The Liberals held enough seats to remain in power, and they would go on to win three more elections. But they and the province would continue to be dogged by the fallout from that botched and bitter first term – how they came into office with a mandate for the ages and threw it all away, mostly through their own doing, in a mere four years.

George Abbott was a minister in that first-term BC Liberal government, saddled with a ministry, Community, Aboriginal and

Women's Services, which absorbed much of the bruising. In a joke not all that far removed from where those programs stood in the new government's priorities, it was known as "the ministry of lost causes."

In a landmark study of those years, Abbott tells the story of what went wrong, how it went wrong, and where many of the wrong-headed ideas came from in the first place. He argues that from day one, the size of the victory clouded Campbell's judgment.

He wrote this book, not just for history, but as a cautionary tale for public servants and voters alike. Politicians, says Abbott, "are expected to arrive in office wholly equipped for their roles, having convinced their electors that they and their party have all the answers to the problems of the day." Too often they are freighted with election promises and a sense of the clock ticking on their mandate that compels them to do the rough stuff in the first eighteen months of their term, whether the plans are workable or not.

The book displays many of the good qualities that Abbott brought to public office – diligence, reflection, and a keen wit that lightened many a moment on the floor of the legislature.

He manages to tell the story without violating his oath of secrecy as a cabinet minister. "Respecting that oath ... proved less challenging than I anticipated," he writes. He relies largely on material from the public record, including media reports, legislature debates, and the exchanges in Question Period.

But as a minister who survived the storms clinging to the wreckage, he also knew where to look to help tell the story. He sought out and granted anonymity to some senior public servants from those years. This invites a parlour game for those of us who covered the government, as we try to guess the identities of "Respondent J" and others.

Abbott continued to serve in cabinet during the second and third terms of Liberal government. When Campbell resigned in 2010, he sought the party leadership, finishing third in the contest won by Christy Clark, and retired soon after.

Though Abbott makes a point of citing the accomplishments that he admires from his years in office, he does not pull any punches about the things he did not admire. Witness this characterization of the premier whom he served at the cabinet table for almost ten years: "Gordon Campbell despised indecision and was particularly impatient with long debates on matters on which he had already formed his conclusions. He preferred to act before doubters and naysayers could crowd his path."

The Campbell stubbornness is especially highlighted in the most discouraging eighth chapter in this book, where, as Abbott says, the consequences "c[a]me home to roost" in the Ministry of Children and Family Development, custodian of thousands of children in care.

The ministry embarked on a top-to-bottom reorganization at the same time as it was trying to manage a 23 percent budget cut, a combination that was as unworkable as it was ruinous. The incredible thing is not just that the Liberals tried it in the first place but that they stuck with it as long as they did.

Even after the debacle had been fully chronicled and exposed by an independent review, Campbell balked at delivering a full-blown apology, instead contenting himself with weasel words about how the government had "taken on too many challenges" and "maybe asked too much of front-line public servants."

Abbott's verdict is withering: "The pace and magnitude of expenditure reductions were driven, first, by the faulty belief that the tax breaks would pay for themselves regardless of the economic environment in which they were introduced and, second, by the self-imposed balanced budget imperative for 2004–05. Sustainability of vital programs finished, at best, a distant third in the pecking order."

This book can be read as both an ugly slice of political history and an academic case study in public policy failure. But at the end of it, Abbott also reminds us that there were real victims in all this, and they included some of the most vulnerable citizens in the province.

— **Vaughn Palmer**

Acknowledgments

I AM GRATEFUL to many people for assisting me in pulling this project together. In particular, I want to thank Colin Bennett, Jamie Lawson, Evert Lindquist, and James Tully from the University of Victoria. This venture would not have been launched, never mind completed, without their inspiration and advice. I had the good fortune to hold elected office for thirty-five years. The New Era was resoundingly my least favourite period in political life, and I was not initially enthusiastic about taking a deep dive into the topic. Happily, they convinced me that my misgivings simply made telling the story all the more important. Their early advice with respect to content and organization was remarkably helpful, as were their later suggestions for improvement. My thanks to Allan Tupper of the University of British Columbia for his advice and support. I am appreciative of advice around the efficacy of tax cuts from Brant Abbott at Queen's University.

I also enjoyed the benefit of draft reviews from former public servants and cabinet ministers of the New Era. Their wisdom, observations, and insights were very valuable and much appreciated (just as they were back in government), but acknowledging them personally here would be inconsistent with the objective of maintaining strict anonymity for interviewees. I was frequently surprised by the interest (and sometimes even passion) that former civil servants demonstrated regarding the New Era project, enabling me to provide a far more precise and detailed account of the period than would otherwise have been possible. Their courage, energy, and wisdom also allowed me and other politicians to survive the New Era, and I thank them for it.

Many thanks to the UBC Press editorial team – Randy Schmidt, Megan Brand, and Deborah Kerr – for their advice and support. I'm also appreciative of the insights and suggestions provided by the anonymous manuscript readers from UBC Press.

Special thanks to Vaughn Palmer for writing the foreword to this volume. Vaughn has been authoring pithy and insightful columns for the *Vancouver Sun* and other newspapers for decades. In what follows, I frequently mention those insights and quote passages from his columns. I'm honoured to have more of his retrospective thoughts provided through his foreword.

My friends and colleagues at Circle Square Solutions were steadfastly supportive throughout this project. In particular, I want to thank my friend and business partner, Anna Nyarady, who has offered more than a few examples of courage and determination in recent years, and my friend, senior associate, and former deputy minister Bob de Faye, who – despite being stuck with me in three different ministries – continues to work with me today.

And lastly, I thank my family. We do not get to choose our parents, but I was entirely fortunate in my luck of the draw. My mother and father, Irene and Malcolm Abbott, were always supportive of chasing dreams while securing a good education. In the composition and completion of the manuscript, my wife, Lesley, patiently answered my many questions about the mysteries of Word and word processing. Our children – Megan, Brant, and Wade – have long since ascended into adulthood, but I remain appreciative that, despite the ignominy of a politician father, they are such balanced, thoughtful, and capable people. My political gene will perhaps re-emerge in my grandchildren – Raiden, Alissa, Serena, and Owen – but I won't wish it on them. I do hope that someday, in a political science course of their own choosing, they will read this book and say: "Oh, so that's what Grandpa meant by 'what a long strange trip it's been.'"

Chronology of Key Events

2001

17 May	BC Liberals decisively win provincial election.
25 May	Gordon Campbell announces appointment of BC Fiscal Review Panel.
5 June	Premier and cabinet are officially sworn in.
6 June	Campbell and Finance Minister Gary Collins announce a 25 percent cut for all personal income tax brackets.
25 June	Campbell issues mandate letters to cabinet ministers launching core review, deregulation, and other processes.
27 June	Campbell advises cabinet that getting costs under control tops the government agenda.
23 July	BC Fiscal Review Panel issues its report.
30 July	Collins issues an Economic and Fiscal Update in the legislature, predicting 3.8 percent economic growth.
29 August	Campbell replaces MLA Val Roddick as chair of the core review committee.
4 September	Collins advises media that his growth forecast was "down a full point, perhaps more."

11 September	Terrorist attack on New York and elsewhere in the United States.
18 September	Collins provides "message to ministries": "Global economy is slowing ... bring deficit down and get spending under control."
3 October	Open Cabinet in Penticton. Collins advises that all ministerial budgets excluding Health, Education, and Advanced Education will be cut an average of 35 percent.

2002

18 January	Deputy Ministers' Council discussion of 270-day plan.
12 February	Throne Speech confirmation of 25 percent cut to all ministries, excluding Health, Education, and Advanced Education.
19 February	Budget Speech confirms $4.4 billion deficit and 0.6 percent economic growth, introduces sales tax and Medical Services Plan premium increases.
17 May	Campbell advises ministries of need to conclude program reviews or face newly created External Panel.
27 June	Child, Youth and Family Advocate Paul Pallan releases his final report entitled "Rethink the Reductions: Children and Youth Need More."

2003

12 February	Campbell's televised "Heartlands" address emphasizes transportation infrastructure in the Interior and rural British Columbia.
4 June	Campbell announces a $122 million infusion into the Ministry of Children and Family Development budget.
23 July	Campbell announces that the Coquihalla concession will not be privatized.

2004

10 and 17 February   Throne and Budget Speeches extoll the
                     "Spirit of 2010" Olympics themes and
                     balanced budget.

24 February   Auditor General Wayne Strelioff releases
                     report on Ministry of Human Resources
                     disability review.

2005

8 and 15 February   Throne and Budget Speeches extoll "Five
                     Great Goals for a Golden Decade."

May   Liberals re-elected, with a reduced majority.

October   A storm of controversy arises from report on
                     the death of Sherry Charlie and exposure
                     of failure on child death reviews, leading to
                     appointment of Ted Hughes to lead review.

2006

7 April   Hughes report includes scathing criticisms of
                     the impact of 2001 budget cuts and difficulty
                     of completing service delivery reforms in that
                     environment.

Big Promises, Small Government

PART 1

SETTING THE STAGE

1

The New Era in Brief

"This is the story of how we begin to remember."
– Paul Simon, "Under African Skies"

THE BC LIBERAL New Era began with high hopes and a massive victory at the polls. Although Gordon Campbell's Liberals were widely expected to win the provincial election of 17 May 2001, the scale of their triumph – seventy-seven of seventy-nine seats – was unprecedented in British Columbia. High hopes were fostered by the party's electoral manifesto, *A New Era for British Columbia*. It promised a future of "vision, imagination, hope and prosperity," in which the Liberals would "act boldly and decisively to open up government, to rebuild our economy and to lead the way to a New Era full of promise and potential for you and your family."[1]

New Era offered over thirty pages of promises such as a public health care system that would "guarantee all patients the care they need, where they live and when they need it" and "a top-notch education system for students of all ages."[2] *New Era*'s lofty promises, and a campaign strategy aimed at reassuring nervous voters, offered little hint that a BC Liberal government would mean doing less with less. But beneath the relentless optimism of the *New Era* document lay tension between big promises and small government. The 1996 version of Gordon Campbell had vigorously and repeatedly promised smaller government, including pledges to "roll back government's share of the economy by

5

15%" and to "cut the number of MLAs from 75 to less than 60."[3] Had Campbell embraced a more expansive role for government in 2001?

The potential tension between Campbell's larger government promises and his smaller government aspirations emerged in 2001 pre-election interviews with journalist Frances Bula. She described him as an "introverted extrovert who believes in both an activist government and a smaller government."[4] When asked by Bula to describe himself politically, Campbell "paused for a long moment" searching for the right turn of phrase. "Zen federalist," he responded, presumably tongue-in-cheek, but loath then as always to use traditional labels of left and right, liberal and conservative, in describing himself. Asked to further clarify, he stated (probably more in earnest): "Zen federalism means you do less and by doing less, you actually do much more. If they [government] did a few things that everybody wants them to [and did them] well, there'd be far more benefits than trying to do everything."[5] In short, government could do more with less if it just focused on services of vital public importance and dispensed with the wasteful or redundant.

Big Promises, Small Government is the story of how the dream of doing more with less was transformed into the harsh reality of doing less with less. It focuses on the New Era from the election of 2001, which ushered in the Liberal government, to the Throne Speech of 2005, which signalled its profound shift from austerity and retrenchment to a more expansive social agenda headlined by "Five Great Goals for a Golden Decade."

In 2001, Campbell sought nothing less than the immodest goal of remaking government.[6] The initiatives he unleashed in the wake of the election were largely unprecedented – for the province but not for the world. Campbell and his government drew policy inspiration from many sources, national and international. The ideas and experiences that propelled the remaking of government wind like strands of DNA across both time and space, then find expression in the *New Era* document's thematic content, as well as in post-election processes.

Campbell's remaking of government got under way quickly. One day after being sworn into office, the newly minted premier announced a 25 percent personal income tax cut, potentially relinquishing over $1 billion in tax revenue. He believed, on the basis of the experience of other jurisdictions, that a tax cut would generate economic growth and induce concomitant revenues. The day-one tax cut proved to be, in Christopher Pollitt's words, prescription before diagnosis: implementation of important public policy reforms without the benefit of thorough analysis, typically by politicians who are driven by ideological zeal.[7]

A tax cut was anticipated, but its timing and magnitude surprised some observers.[8] *New Era* mentioned a "dramatic tax cut" at least ten times.[9] However, unlike *The Courage to Change,* the BC Liberal platform of 1996, which had promised a 15 percent drop in personal income taxes, *New Era* did not specify what its "dramatic tax cut" would entail. This lack of specificity was consistent with Campbell's comments before and during the 2001 campaign. As he told Vaughn Palmer on 26 October 2000, he "won't know how dramatic a tax cut is possible until the Liberals get an unhindered look at the state of government finances."[10] Campbell's pre-election caution promptly surrendered to post-election ideological zeal.

Premier Campbell formed his conclusions about the state of the books remarkably quickly. The first act of the new government – or more precisely of its premier and finance minister – was to define "dramatic" as a 25 percent drop in personal income tax, a revelation that came less than twenty-four hours after inauguration. Seven weeks later, the finance minister added another billion in corporate and related tax cuts. In taking these steps, the government may also have deliberately or inadvertently defined its public image for years to come. Although the tax break was undoubtedly popular among many British Columbians, few understood that it would come at a very high cost.

Some may have believed the claim, prominent in the *New Era* document and tirelessly repeated on the campaign trail, that provinces "like Ontario have proven that lower personal income tax rates lead to *higher* revenue – not less."[11] However, unlike in Ontario during the latter 1990s, where very strong economic growth masked tax-cut revenue losses, British Columbia's tax cuts failed to "pay for themselves," at least in a timely way. World economic conditions and events quickly extinguished any prospect of a magical made-in-BC turnaround.

Within months of taking office, the new government found itself in a $4.4 billion fiscal hole.[12] It faced a dilemma of its own making: it was boxed in by its commitments to decrease taxes by more than $2 billion, to balance the budget in 2004, and to exempt the Health, Education, and Advanced Education budgets from reduction (as *New Era* promised). Those three ministries comprised some 70 percent of the overall provincial budget, leaving billions in savings to be found in the 30 percent of government that was not Health, Education, or Advanced Education.

The dramatic day-one tax cut proved to be a defining moment in the New Era. Lofty *New Era* aspirations "full of promise and potential" quickly surrendered to the New Era reality of austerity and retrenchment. Ontario's tax cut siren song of "higher revenue – not less" faded all too soon, prompting a host of questions: Why were the cuts less effective (at least in terms of paying for themselves) than the government had anticipated? Were they the wrong policy at the wrong time, destined to fail amid weakening local and world economies? And would their failure have a negative impact on vital social programs?

The prime authors of the cuts, Premier Gordon Campbell and Finance Minister Gary Collins, appeared to nurse a genuine belief in their efficacy. That confidence was fostered by apparent successes elsewhere, particularly in Ontario, where the tax cuts of the late 1990s coincided with a period of very strong economic growth averaging 4.7 percent per year. In stark contrast, British Columbia's 2001 cuts were introduced during a period of steeply declining energy and commodity revenues and negligible growth, which improved only marginally over the next two years.[13] Given this, were the cuts something more than an instance of prescription before diagnosis? Were they designed to produce a budgetary crisis – a "burning platform" – whose ultimate purpose was to diminish the size of government?[14]

Certainly, nothing in the *New Era* document suggests that this might be the case. As well as promising to cut taxes, it made more than two hundred platform commitments across a broad range of policy areas – social and environmental, as well as economic – involving substantial operational and capital expenditures.[15] It was far from a recipe for smaller government. The document offered a generous and expansive vision for social programs while concurrently slamming the New Democratic Party (NDP) government for mismanagement. It contended that children had particularly suffered under the NDP. Children and families deserved more and better programs, such as early identification of at-risk children, subsequent prompt intervention, enhanced preventative drug and alcohol efforts, and improved "training, resources and authority for front-line social workers."[16] *New Era* gave no hint that radical cuts might be on the horizon for social programs.

Premier Campbell took *New Era* commitments seriously; the first task of every ministry was identifying its role in fulfilling them. The document was framed and mounted on the wall of the cabinet room, immediately adjacent to the premier's chair. Ministers and deputies were frequently and pointedly reminded of their progress, or lack thereof, on their New Era commitments. Failure to fulfill those commitments was not an option, but success confronted multiple barriers, the most daunting of which were budget reductions flowing from tax cuts that failed to pay for themselves.

A "no excuses" pursuit of success was demanded, notwithstanding the ongoing tension between smaller government aspirations and larger government promises. At the quantitative level, the relationship between electoral platform and policy agenda appeared powerful and direct. Campbell regularly pointed to progress on, or completion of, a high percentage of *New Era* promises.[17] At the qualitative level, the reality of the New Era was a stark departure from the optimistic vision in the *New Era* document, whose uniformly cheery character offered no warning of the harsh retrenchment that would soon arise.

Christopher Pollitt and Geert Bouckaert suggest that in public policy "different kinds of objectives will sometimes trade off
against each other ... Decision-makers are obliged to decide what
they think is most important – they can seldom hope to have everything at the same time."[18] Cover to cover, *New Era* promised British
Columbians that they could have everything at the same time. Confronted by the reality of tax cuts that failed to deliver as expected,
the social agenda articulated in *New Era* gave way to its economic
agenda. With their budgets slashed by 40 to 45 percent, resource
ministries such as Forests and Agriculture were hit particularly
hard, but even this measure could fill only a small portion of the
$4.4 billion budget hole. The focus then turned to social ministries,
producing a second and stark example of prescription before diagnosis: the belief that social ministries could manage deep budget
and staffing cuts without any serious impacts to the disadvantaged
and vulnerable British Columbians whom they served.

As a consequence of steeply declining resource revenues in 2001,
British Columbia was headed for an approximately $2 billion
deficit, with or without tax cuts. Under such straitened circumstances, did the magnitude of cuts and their application across
tax brackets really matter?[19] Indeed they did, especially given the
stated exemption of Health, Education, and Advanced Education
from budget cuts and the demand for a balanced budget in 2004.
Ultimately, three social ministries were forced to make sweeping
cuts in their services, the magnitude of which were in direct cor-
relation to the tax cuts that exacerbated the province's budgetary
woes. The decrease in taxes did not pay for itself in rebound revenues prior to 2004, so reductions in government services would
be required to fill the breach.

As ministries struggled to meet daunting budget targets, they
encountered another powerful example of attempting to have
everything at the same time: a process barrage – core review,
deregulation, outsourcing, regionalization, devolution of service
delivery, and much more – that was largely drawn from other
jurisdictions through their experience with the tenets of New
Public Management (NPM), a managerial doctrine whose roots

are in Margaret Thatcher's Britain. NPM espouses a reduced role for government, particularly in programs and services that might ostensibly be delivered more efficiently by the private sector (or through private-sector-style strategies). Once again, participation was obligatory, as was achievement of process goals.

The process parade kicked off with Premier Campbell's post-inaugural mandate letters of 25 June 2001, which set out his priorities and vision for government and how, specifically, each minister would work to achieve them. The parade was quickly joined by the "90-day agenda," which begat the "6 month agenda" and the "270-day plan," each containing its own mind-bending deliverables to be rendered despite staff and budget cuts.[20]

Confronted by seemingly endless and intractable problems, ministries looked nationally and internationally for policy experience that might provide them with solutions. Gordon Campbell's British Columbia was not the first jurisdiction to boldly launch a remaking of government or to boldly redesign the complex subsystems – such as health, social services, and resource management – that comprise it. Much could be learned from the rest of the world and quickly – no small concern given the rigid deadlines that applied to many processes. But policy transfer produced mixed results, generating more than a few vital lessons for government.

The New Era was an intense and demanding time for many politicians and public servants. I was among the ranks of the former, a minister in Gordon Campbell's cabinet throughout the period and now author of belated reflections on those tumultuous days. The New Era story is one of miscalculation, frustration, and angst but also one of perseverance, innovation, and – particularly among civil servants – courage and professionalism in the face of remarkably intimidating challenges.

Gordon Campbell's New Era Leadership in Context

The New Era story unfolded within a challenging economic environment, soon exacerbated by broader geopolitical turmoil; it was also shaped by its institutional setting.[21] In Westminster-style parliamentary systems, premiers (just like prime ministers) hold great power, and Gordon Campbell's emergence as the dominant (and often dominating) figure of the New Era should come as no surprise. Premiers arrive with a vision of what government can or should do. They use their many levers of power to impose their will: they hire and fire ministers and deputies, they set agendas through mandate letters and throne speeches, they design and fill critical cabinet committees, and much more. The extensive literature in this area suggests that centralization of power is increasingly the norm across parliamentary institutions, whether in Victoria, Ottawa, or Westminster.[22]

The New Era offers a remarkable story of Premier Campbell's drive for power and control. He used his authority not only to direct the political agenda but also to mould government processes and institutions. He immediately set the direction for his government with his announcement of the 25 percent tax cut. He followed up with mandate letters to cabinet ministers, laying out his ambitious reform agenda. Mandate letter content was provided as information, not as a subject for debate. Cabinet ministers were effectively boxed into that agenda, a fact of life that was less than subtly reinforced by a 20 percent holdback on ministerial stipends. Failure to achieve the goals set out in ministerial mandate letters within prescribed timelines would have immediate financial (as well as unstated political) consequences.

Change was not unidirectional. Institutions and processes also shaped Campbell's perspective throughout time. In retrospect, when viewed across his full decade in power, Campbell is a difficult politician to categorize. For example, some of his public policy initiatives in the environmental and social spheres are inconsistent with the neo-liberal label that he sometimes bears.[23] He was, at best, a climate change agnostic in 2001, but seven years later his government introduced North America's first revenue-neutral carbon tax. Similarly, when he took office, he firmly opposed the Nisga'a Treaty and advocated for a populist referendum on treaty rights (one of several policies strategically adopted from the Reform BC party in 2001). By 2005, in contrast, he was personally leading the drive for a provincial New Relationship agreement with First Nations and for a federal-provincial-Indigenous Transformative Change Accord.

Were these profound shifts something more than short-term, strategic politics? Campbell not only learned through his voracious reading, but he also listened and learned during his many public and private interactions with First Nations leaders and Indigenous citizens, as well as with academics who were alarmed by climate change.[24]

Some elements in the Campbell ideology (such as Indigenous relations and concern for climate change) shifted over time, whereas others (such as the advocacy for tax cuts in 1996, 2001, and 2010) remained consistently neo-liberal. The ideological perspective he brought to bear on government in 2001 was shaped by the experience of other jurisdictions, notably those of Alberta, Ontario, and New Zealand. That perspective regarding tax cuts, smaller government, and NPM-style processes would in turn fundamentally shape the New Era. Viewed solely through a New Era lens, Campbell fits the neo-liberal label much more comfortably. The austerity and retrenchment triggered by the 2001 tax cuts left scant room for public policy innovations beyond those necessitated by demands to do more with less.

Campbell's core beliefs and objectives were far from new, a premise I explore in subsequent chapters. His expectations for government were honed by the experiences of leaders such as Alberta's Ralph Klein and Ontario's Mike Harris. In 2001, Campbell was simply the latest exponent of "a jolt to the system" as an essential element in the rebalancing or remaking of government in the wake of freer-spending reformist liberal or social democratic administrations. His deputy minister, Ken Dobell, articulated (in what he thought was an in camera setting) the obligatory character of the painful jolt: "We're 10 years behind everybody else. We have the misfortune to be doing it [budget reduction] now, but nevertheless we have to do it."[25]

In 1993, Klein had condemned the "uncontrolled spending" of his predecessor, Don Getty.[26] Two years later, Harris promised a hard-edged remaking of the Ontario government, following five years of New Democratic Party leadership. In both cases, claims of lavish spending signalled severe spending cuts. Similarly, the *New Era* critique of the BC NDP's ostensibly profligate spending was soon followed by austerity and retrenchment.

The remaking of governments in Alberta, Ontario, and British Columbia hinged on three key elements: the size of the tax cut, the economic environment in which it was introduced, and the subsequent distribution of budgetary pain that was required to produce a balanced budget. British Columbia's 25 percent tax cut was greater than both the two-stage 15 percent cut that Campbell had promised in 1996 and the 10 or 15 percent that he called for in 1998.[27] It was also larger than anything suggested in the 2001 campaign. The *New Era* document specifically promised that British Columbia would have the lowest tax rate of any Canadian province for the bottom two tax brackets, deliverable during the first term in office, along with a "dramatic tax cut" that it never defined.[28] Furthermore, Ontario's tax cuts were spread over time, whereas British Columbia's entire package of approximately $2 billion in tax reductions was fully implemented in 2001. Even more importantly, Campbell's cuts were introduced into a precariously weak economic environment, in striking contrast to that of Ontario during the late 1990s.

Ontario could argue in 2001 that its cuts had fuelled its record economic growth of the late 1990s. British Columbia's cuts clearly did not; nor did they pay for themselves in the pinched economic circumstances of the early 2000s. New Era budgetary challenges were worsened by the platform promise, as noted above, to exempt Health, Education, and Advanced Education from any expenditure reductions. In contrast, Ralph Klein's bitterly controversial inclusion of Health and Education in across-the-board cuts in Alberta several years earlier had diffused the pain throughout the entire government. The failure of New Era tax cuts to deliver rebound revenues, in combination with the exemption of Health and Education, drove dramatic cuts to large social ministries and, subsequently, to the often disadvantaged clientele whom they served.

A host of vital and interrelated questions arise from the New Era experience: Did a coherent ideological framework support the Campbell vision? Did the rapidity, intensity, and complexity of the reform agenda move some New Public Management (NPM) processes from being mutually supportive to becoming mutually contradictory, hence undermining prospects for success? And did the scope and intensity of change undermine the quality and sustainability of provincial public services?

Gordon Campbell contemplated nothing less than a fundamental remaking of government, aided by process tools drawn from NPM, which was notable both for the breadth and speed of reforms. He attempted to implement all mandated changes simultaneously: delivering *New Era* promises despite budget cuts, reforming service delivery amid severe staff layoffs, and much more as detailed below. The economic situation of the day proved incompatible with this approach, and Campbell was obliged (as Pollitt and Bouckaert would have predicted) to decide what changes he thought were the most important. In doing so, he sacrificed his *New Era* social agenda to protect his New Era economic agenda. This outcome had profound implications for the lives of those who operated inside government.

Reflections on Life inside Government

Political scientist Rod Rhodes enjoyed the rare opportunity, as an academic, of spending time within the senior reaches of the British government. "Observation," he argues, "is conspicuous for its absence in the political science armoury of research methods." His book, *Everyday Life in the British Government,* seeks to relieve that absence.[29] As a cabinet minister from 2001 to 2012, I also enjoyed a first-hand opportunity to observe and participate in public policy construction. However, unlike Rhodes, I am not a conventional participant-observer. I did not enter political life with the intent of writing a book on the subject. My focus during the New Era was day-to-day survival while leading a large ministry with an expansive mandate and a daunting budget cut.

Rhodes chose the role of participant-observer as a proactive research method. Although I maintained a personal journal throughout my time in office, my account of the New Era is largely retrospective; my conclusions are shaped by knowledge and evidence that I gathered more than a decade later. Politics has always been an object of fascination for me, both personally and academically. I was fortunate to teach political science prior to spending seventeen years in provincial politics, before returning to it in 2013 as a late-onset doctoral student. What I read and learned as a student moulded my understanding of the New Era experience.

I was struck by the similarity between Rhodes's observations and those I gleaned as a cabinet minister. For example, he notes that "most ministers had close relationships with their Permanent Secretary," a benefit that I too enjoyed with my deputy ministers throughout my tenure in government. Rhodes highlights the roots of such relationships in observing that "distinctions between policy and management, politician and civil servant, are meaningless when confronted by the imperative to cope and survive."[30] The daily grind of tackling frequent and sometimes intractable problems brings politician and public servant together toward a common goal: the resolution of those problems in ways that meet the expectations of the Premier's Office.

Coping and surviving through the New Era was no small feat. I served as Community, Aboriginal and Women's Services minister through much of that period, a new and expansive ministry that comprised all or portions of seven former NDP ministries.[31] It was home to two ministers of state, twenty-four New Era commitments, and dozens of programs that excited detailed scrutiny in the Campbell drive for smaller government. The New Era demanded high levels of candour, trust, respect, and collegiality between minister and deputy.[32] I was privileged to enjoy such a relationship.

David Cameron and Graham White also capture the relationship between minister and deputy minister as "a state of mutually dependent professional intimacy; neither can do his or her job properly without the other's assistance and support."33 Not all New Era ministers were willing or able to cultivate such relationships, a reality that is probably true everywhere. As part of New Zealand's package of 1980s reforms, the appointment of deputies by the prime minister was replaced by appointment of chief executive officers through a public service central agency. As Martin Lodge and Derek Gill suggest, that shift does not appear to have altered ministerial relationships: "Some chief executives saw their main role as providing their minister with strategic 'free and frank' advice and being in a 'partner' role, others saw a change in their role toward an executive-type 'do as you are told' understanding."34 Ministerial character and style, rather than title and mode of appointment, appear to be the prime determinants of these relationships.

My experience across seventeen years as an MLA and twelve as a cabinet minister leads me to conclude with Thea Vakil that "BC's senior public servants hold strong traditional Westminster-based values concerning public servants' commitment to serve the public good, be respectful to the government of the day, behave responsibly and be willing to be held accountable and above all, take pride in public service integrity."35 But in these same respects, the BC Liberal New Era proved an extraordinarily challenging period for civil servants.

Despite the host of pressures recounted below, they transformed – sometimes with, sometimes without, supportive ministers – a complex and occasionally contradictory political agenda into coherent public policy. They "may live in the era of new public management," Rhodes writes, "but long-established patterns of behaviour exist."36 Similarly, Evert Lindquist, John Langford, and Thea Vakil note that the post–New Era public service of British Columbia "may be directed, lean, and constrained, but it is not politicized and, in our view, remains competent, professional, and merit-driven."37

The New Era proved to be a very long four years for deputies and at least some of their ministers. Advocates of smaller government may have thrived in their pursuit of that goal, but for others the New Era was a period of puzzlement, frustration, ambiguity, and uncertainty. My account of its unfolding uses ministerial experience both to enrich the narrative and to offer a unique perspective on the "black box" of government policy making. Such experience can also come with certain downsides, among them lingering emotional baggage and hindsight bias. Fortunately, personal experience and observation can be complemented by the range of methodologies and sources detailed below.

Why write a book on the New Era? My aim is not just to provide an honest and compelling account of an intense and controversial period in BC history but also to identify some vital political and public policy lessons that it taught. Continuing education and mentoring are commonplace for public servants, but far less so for politicians. The latter are expected to arrive in office wholly equipped for their roles, having convinced their electors that they and their party have all the answers to the problems of the day. Alas, the New Era demonstrated that politicians are not immune to periodic miscalculation and misjudgment.

I hope that current and future politicians and public servants can learn from my account of New Era adventures and misadventures. For example, tax cuts remain a frequent visitor to the political stage, particularly among parties of the centre-right. Aspiring policy makers would be well advised to heed the cautions offered here. Among the most critical of such lessons is that failures in tax policy reform can all too quickly translate into the attrition of social services. Learning from this painful episode in our recent history, to paraphrase George Santayana, may help us to avoid repeating it.

Methods and Sources Employed in the New Era Story

The New Era story offered below is supported by evidence and argument from a broad range of sources. Interviews with former public servants were among the most fruitful of these. Although nearly two decades have elapsed since the New Era began, it still excites emotions. Former public servants, by and large, were more than willing to tell their stories, which are drawn from what was (for many) the most difficult period in their professional lives. All interviews were conducted on the basis of strict anonymity; direct quotes are used but never attributed to an identifiable source.

My account also draws on the experience of cabinet ministers. Ministerial quotes come largely from media interviews, the annual Estimates debates of the legislature, and its daily Question Period.

Media stories and columns provided colourful and often insightful comments and analyses. The legislature's press gallery frequently exposed the inevitable shortcomings and unintended consequences of public policy initiatives. In the age of omnipresent mainstream and social media, very few government "secrets" remain secret for long. Like all ministers, I took an oath of confidentiality prior to service in cabinet. Respecting that oath (as indeed I have done in this book) proved less challenging than I anticipated. Important or controversial issues discussed in cabinet or caucus during the New Era almost invariably found their way into the public realm.

Estimates debates proved a very rich source of information and insight, as ministers confronted the challenges of the New Era. In Estimates, they are joined on the benches by senior public servants, and it is customary to take at least a few minutes for consultation on questions tendered. Prodded by Opposition or private-member questions, ministers provide an account of their responsibilities and headaches – usually carefully but occasionally candidly. In contrast to Question Period, Estimates offer a less adversarial and more detailed explanation of what ministries are attempting to achieve and through what means. One consequence of a very small Opposition (only two of the seventy-nine MLAs) was that the Liberal MLAs had extensive opportunities to ask questions of their ministers. In an atmosphere of ostensibly "friendly fire," ministers sometimes provided surprisingly frank answers to questions from their colleagues, in contrast to their more carefully couched responses to the Opposition.

Exchanges during Question Period (QP) also contributed to the narrative, though less substantively than those from Estimates. Both government and Opposition parties expend a great deal of time and energy on preparing for QP. Stakes are high, and theatrics often abound. The Opposition attempts to demonstrate the government's utter failure to deliver on its promises, whereas ministers attempt to portray the Opposition attack as ill-conceived, inconsequential, and hypocritical. The press gallery pays close attention to their interaction. A successful QP (particularly from the Opposition's perspective) can deliver a lead story for the six o'clock news or a banner headline in the papers. However, as others have pointed out, QP is "question period, not answer period." QP answers are typically less substantive and thoughtful than those furnished in Estimates.

Governments emit almost continuous signals about what is on their agenda, and the associated documents frequently tell the story. Mandate letters from the premier to incoming ministers are one of the first indicators of the government's agenda and the processes envisioned to realize it. The 2001 mandate letters from Premier Campbell were new to British Columbia (but not to Canada). They were an early signal of the looming barrage of processes that lay at the heart of the New Era. Ministers are appointed at the pleasure of the premier, whose ability to dominate the agenda is highest in the days immediately following cabinet formation. Viewed collectively, mandate letters reflect the premier's vision, goals, and priorities – in Gordon Campbell's case, a detailed "plan of action" in combination with ministerial marching orders.

Other government documents provided vital clues. Throne and budget speeches detail what the government considers or acknowledges as core challenges. The speeches also set out suggestions about how the government intends to meet those challenges, though typically at a high level of abstraction. Words are carefully chosen to convey precisely what the government wishes to convey. Subtle nuance, and even calculated ambivalence, may also be employed to mask discordant messages or awkward compromises among leaders or factions. Similarly, government press releases – despite their frequently self-laudatory content – can flag new priorities or shifts in direction.

The passage of time has allowed us a small window into cabinet discussions and decisions. Cabinet minutes, typically very brief but occasionally informative, are protected for fifteen years (via freedom-of-information and protection-of-privacy laws), so those from the early days of the New Era are now available on the Internet. They are used at several points in my narrative to illustrate the character of cabinet discussions and the relationship between Campbell and his ministers. Briefing and communications notes provided as "Advice to the Minister" (and again protected from public exposure for fifteen years) were a useful complement to the minutes.

Reports generated by the auditors general and other independent officers of the legislature proved very valuable, particularly in assessing the experience of social ministries. The New Era was a controversial and challenging time for independent officers. Two of them – the children's commissioner and the child, youth and family advocate – were eliminated early in the New Era (a move characterized by the Opposition NDP as governmental silencing of critics). All officers were subject to substantial budget cuts, but their various reports were nonetheless professional, respectful, and well evidenced.

Among non-government documents, party platforms from the 1996 and 2001 elections proved essential in understanding the New Era. Deeply disappointed by the 1996 election results, the Liberals attempted to win over Reform BC's base by adopting select portions of the Reform platform. Party platforms are also important to the administrative side of government. In 2001, senior public servants carefully assessed the *New Era* document as they prepared for the probable transition to a Liberal government, and fortunately so. The fulfillment of *New Era* commitments was a critical measure of success for every minister and deputy. Failure to tick off a *New Era* box was a failure of courage, replete with both pecuniary and political consequences.

Publications and articles from non-government organizations such as the conservative Fraser Institute appeared to influence government policy intermittently.[38] Conversely, papers produced by the Canadian Centre for Policy Alternatives – though typically ignored or disparaged by the Campbell government – offered pithy and critical analyses of Liberal policies, particularly in the social policy realm.[39]

My exploration of the New Era was also assisted by a tremendous body of literature around politics, political agendas, public management, and public policy development. An emerging body of scholarship on BC politics and government focuses on the decade of Gordon Campbell's premiership.[40] This book aims to enrich that pool. It does not offer a formal literature review but instead cites important learnings from the relevant literature.

British Columbia is often described as a small, open trading economy; it is similarly a small and open trading jurisdiction in the world of public policy. Governments and ministries often face a long list of policy challenges and, as was commonly the case in the New Era, short time frames in which to find or develop solutions. Other jurisdictions may have dealt with similar challenges, and their answers can sometimes inform responses in the recipient jurisdiction (via lesson drawing and policy transfer).[41] The case studies of social ministries presented here illustrate the use of policy transfer – sometimes successfully, sometimes not – in the New Era. Context and compatibility of political cultures are among the key determinants of their success or failure.

Policy inspiration is derived from both endogenous (domestic to British Columbia) and exogenous (external to the province) sources. Prominent among these was New Public Management (NPM) – or local variants of it – which were influential in the construction of both the *New Era* document and New Era change processes. NPM fostered many characteristic New Era ideas, approaches, and goals: tax cuts, deregulation, private-sector-style management, competitive outsourcing, and much more.[42] As detailed in Chapter 2, the phrase "smaller government" does not appear in *New Era,* though the 1996 Liberal platform, *The Courage to Change,* included it several times. However, its absence in 2001 did not indicate that it was off the menu. The robust body of NPM literature from New Zealand, Great Britain, and elsewhere enables us to better understand Gordon Campbell's drive for smaller government.

Summary of Chapters

Part 1 of *Big Promises, Small Government* examines contextual elements that shaped the New Era: political, ideational, and institutional. Chapter 2 assesses the evolution of the BC Liberal Party between the elections of 1996 and 2001. That evolution was reflected in the doctrinal content of party platforms and in Campbell's concerted coalition building, which was largely aimed at shoring up support on the party's right flank. Key influences here included Reform BC, the federal Reform Party, and Mike Harris's Progressive Conservatives, through the use of their 1995 platform *The Common Sense Revolution.* The example of Ralph Klein's Alberta also significantly influenced both the institutions and processes of the New Era. Alberta provided strategies in Campbell's political game plan and was also a rich source for the institutional elements that helped shape the New Era. Finally, this chapter assesses the character and content of the Gordon Campbell approach to politics and his use of speed, intensity, and crisis as political weapons.

The role of New Public Management (NPM) and of policy transfer in shaping and guiding the New Era is discussed in Chapter 3. The interaction of speed, focus, and financial resources in addressing complex public policy problems is also considered. The chapter examines the comparative experiences of the Ministry of Health Planning and the Ministry of Children and Family Development in the regionalization of their operations. That episode prompts the question of whether inadequate resources and fragmented focus can exacerbate the risks of rapid political and institutional reform. Chapter 3 also discusses the role of New Zealand and its 1980s government restructuring in shaping BC Liberal views on the pace of policy reform.

Part 2 focuses on policy and process. Chapter 4 examines the genesis of the post-election tax cut, the debate that preceded its announcement, and its implications for public policy and programs. Here, I address a key question: Was the cut a leap of faith grounded in ideology, or was it a burning-platform pretext for the harsh medicine of smaller government retrenchment? Perhaps it was both. Textual analysis of throne and budget speeches helps inform my conclusions. The chapter also assesses why the BC experience of the early 2000s was so different from that of Ontario in the late 1990s.

Chapter 5 discusses the many and varied processes engaged in the New Era and their genesis in the world of NPM and elsewhere. All were ostensibly geared toward downsizing government. Among the most prominent and time consuming was a core services review, chaired by Premier Campbell and largely modelled on the federal government's 1994–97 "Getting Government Right" program review. Some processes aimed to reinforce the *New Era* narrative that the NDP government was bloated and wasteful. Others flowed from budgetary deficits that were produced, in considerable measure, from tax cuts that failed to pay for themselves. Chapter 5 also explores the Heartlands Economic Strategy of 2003, an unofficial retreat from some controversial aspects of remaking government.

Part 3 examines the consequences – often unanticipated – of public policy shifts in the New Era. Chapters 6, 7, and 8 provide three case studies involving large and socially sensitive ministries – Community, Aboriginal and Women's Services; Human Resources; and Children and Family Development. Although these ministries varied in size, scope, and range of responsibilities, each one offered experiences that were reflective of social policy challenges amid the austerity of the New Era.

Other ministries encountered pressures, some of a comparable character, but the stories of these three are especially important because each had a compelling (and potentially contradictory) mission set out in the *New Era* document. Each ministry struggled to fulfill that mission within budgetary parameters, and each one faced demands for reorganization of service delivery along NPM lines within a highly charged environment. All attempted to utilize and sometimes adapt NPM tools to achieve their own mandates, and all were severely challenged by the confluence of change processes in the New Era.

The book concludes with Chapter 9, which draws lessons from the New Era – particularly at the critical intersection of tax and social policy. As demonstrated in the pages ahead, a defining feature of the New Era was the frequency and intensity of the change processes initiated by the government, such as core review, deregulation, budget and staff reductions triggered by tax cuts, and reorganization of service delivery. The New Era has much to teach us, and most of its lessons are sombre ones. Nevertheless, more than a few must be gathered and visited for a final time. As Robbie Robertson sings in "Somewhere Down the Crazy River," a potential theme song for the New Era, "this is sure stirring up some ghosts for me."[43]

2

Roots of the Narrative

"Everyone you know's been through it,
You bite the bullet then you chew it."
— Roy Orbison, "The Only One"

GORDON CAMPBELL AND his BC Liberals captured over 57 percent of the popular vote in the 2001 election, a remarkable victory even before the first-past-the-post system translated that result into seventy-seven of seventy-nine seats in the legislature. The strategy and tactics employed by Campbell to generate this massive win had their roots in his crushing defeat in the 1996 election. In that contest, despite winning the largest share of the popular vote, the Liberals fell several seats short of the incumbent New Democrats.[1] Although the populist Reform BC won only 9.3 percent of the vote, that proved the decisive margin between victory and defeat for the Liberals.

Campbell was determined that history would not repeat itself in 2001. His campaign was largely predictable, particularly given his 1996 experience: maximize the breadth of voter appeal, minimize the NDP's faint hopes of resurgence, and avoid leakage of support on his party's right flank. The dominant lines of the 2001 campaign were laid out in the *New Era* platform – all calculated to advance pragmatic coalition building and shed the vulnerabilities exposed in 1996. In short, foster public confidence in the Liberals as the safe choice and the ideal antidote for a "decade of decline" under the NDP.

The *New Era* Narrative

Part of the challenge facing public servants (and indeed some BC Liberal ministers) as they reviewed their designated commitments in the *New Era* plan was reconciling its apparently contradictory visions. It promised to "minimize undue government intervention in people's lives," but taken as a whole, it certainly did not offer a coherent or credible prescription for smaller government.

The document was larded with over two hundred often expansive and expensive commitments – among them more computers in schools, "incentives to make computers and Internet access more affordable for all families," more funding for arts and athletics, doubling the First Citizens' Fund, increased research grants to post-secondary institutions, and the installation of five thousand new intermediate- and long-term–care beds for the frail elderly – reflecting a reformist liberal rather than a neo-liberal zeal.[2] Viewed from this perspective, Jean Chrétien's reformist liberal *Red Book* seems as powerful an exemplar for *New Era* as Mike Harris's neo-liberal *Common Sense Revolution* of 1995. Unlike the *Red Book,* however, *New Era* did not offer even tentative costing for the approximately $2 billion worth of promises that filled its pages.

The mismatch of Reform-style "minimize government interference" with $2 billion in new spending commitments reflected a strategic hedging of bets (or a calculated ambivalence) by a Liberal Party that was still stinging from its unexpected defeat in 1996. Unlike the *Courage to Change* platform document of 1996, *New Era* tried to be all things to all voters. It aimed to reassure the skeptical voter while simultaneously presenting the incumbent NDP government as a wasteful and irresponsible free-spender. The Liberals had spent ten long years as the official Opposition, plenty of time to construct this narrative, strategically expressed through the *New Era* platform.

Strategic narratives are common to all politicians and political parties, not just the BC Liberals. In *Policy Paradox,* Deborah Stone analyzes the art of their construction, primarily in the American context, but the essential elements of political persuasion readily transfer across time and space, including to British Columbia in the early twenty-first century. *New Era* made extensive use of what Stone calls the story of decline, which runs as follows: "In the beginning, things were pretty good. But they got worse. In fact, right now, they are nearly intolerable. Something must be done."[3]

New Era devoted most of its thirty-five pages to promising everything from higher paycheques to enhanced Internet connectivity. Interspersed among them were six pages that documented the story of decline, with headlines such as "A Decade of Incompetence," "Health Care Is in Trouble," "Where Has Your Money Gone?" and predictably "A Decade of Decline." Despite the NDP's purported doubling of debt, *New Era* intoned, "everywhere we look, the quality of services has gone down." Hospital wait-lists were growing and students lacked textbooks, while "your money has been squandered on everything but better public services." Children and the vulnerable suffered as "the human toll of the NDP's waste and mismanagement."

Fortunately, something could be done: "Don't let anyone tell you we can't improve critical government services. We will stop the NDP's legacy of waste and act quickly to better and more effectively manage your tax dollars."[4] A full page was devoted to the $463 million wasted just on the fast ferry project, contrasted with the array of public services that such money could buy (including, ironically, "construction of 7 new rural hospitals").[5] Remediation of the NDP's supposed economic and social damage would be achieved by a pain-free prescription of tax cuts, deregulation, effective and efficient service delivery, and elimination of $2 billion in waste and duplication. The *New Era* document offered a relentlessly optimistic vision of the province's future, interspersed with caustic criticism of the NDP.

Shoring Up the Right Flank Brings Platform Content Shift

The content of *New Era* is closely linked to the evolution of the BC Liberal Party in the 1990s. Its 1996 platform, *Courage to Change*, employed what Norman Ruff describes as a "hard policy edge."[6]

For example, welfare recipients would receive "a hand up, not a hand out," because "it is time to stop paying people who are able to work to stay at home."[7] As Table 1 reveals, *Courage to Change* strongly reflected the content and rhetorical flavour of Mike Harris's *Common Sense Revolution,* which dates from the 1995 Ontario election. Cameron and White describe Harris as "a conviction politician with clear, hard-edged policy commitments," including to "'hot-button' issues such as welfare reform."[8] In 1995, Ontario voters would have expected a dose of bitter medicine from Harris, who was determined "to change the way government does business" despite "gut-wrenching changes both inside and outside government."[9]

Unlike *Common Sense Revolution,* the BC Liberal platform of 1996 failed to produce the desired electoral result. During the election, as Ruff notes, the Liberals "absorbed much of the old Social Credit vote" but still fell six seats short of the New Democrats. They widely believed that the 9.3 percent of the vote captured by

TABLE 1
Comparative party platforms

Common Sense Revolution (1995)	*Courage to Change* (1996)
"We will reduce the number of MPPs from 130 to 99"	"We will cut the number of MLAs from 75 to less than 60"
"Require all able-bodied [welfare] recipients either to work, or to be retrained in return for their benefits"	"Require all welfare recipients who are able to work to take training and work experience to receive their benefits"
"This plan will cut your provincial income tax rate by 30%"	"We will vote to cut provincial income taxes by 15 percent"
"This plan guarantees full funding for health care, law enforcement, and education"	"Honestly balance the budget, without cutting health care or education"
"Sell off some assets, such as the LCBO [Liquor Control Board of Ontario] and surplus government land, to the private sector"	"Sell those crown corporations and government agencies that are commercially viable"

Sources: Ontario Progressive Conservative Party, *The Common Sense Revolution* (N.p.: Ontario Progressive Conservative Party, 1995), 2, 8, 9, 17; BC Liberal Party, *The Courage to Change,* v, 6, 9, 13.

Reform BC had robbed them of victory.[10] A split vote on the right flank was only part of the story. Campbell also got some painful schooling from NDP premier Glen Clark on just how quickly political tides can be turned by the shrewd exposure of party platform loose ends and unanswered questions. As Vaughn Palmer notes, Clark's attacks "were so effective that at times it seemed as if Campaign 96 revolved around Opposition promises rather than the government's record."[11] Campbell was shaken by the loss and determined to minimize the chances of its recurrence.

Soon after the 1996 election, Campbell recruited Martyn Brown away from Reform BC, then MLA Richard Neufeld later in the term. Reform BC leader Jack Weisgerber declined to follow but did the next best thing by providing an unequivocal endorsement of Campbell, prominently featured in *New Era:* "If I could turn back the clock I would change the role that I played in the last election. I'm not going to make that mistake again. I'm going to do everything in my power to help ... BC Liberals form the next government."[12] Campbell took policy sustenance from Reform BC's 1996 *Voters' Warranty,* most significantly a commitment to a referendum on First Nations treaties.[13] *New Era* also captured other Reform BC staples, such as rejecting gun control, legislating a fixed election date, and – most prominently – opposing the sale of BC Rail.[14]

Two planks in *Courage to Change* sparked particular public blowback in northern and rural British Columbia, where Reform BC enjoyed its greatest strength. The first was a pledge to "cut the number of MLAs from 75 to less than 60."[15] With predictable assistance from the NDP, critics argued that this measure would directly punish the least populous areas of the province, most notably the North, giving voters one more reason to support rural-based Reform BC rather than the Vancouver-centric Liberals. The second plank was to sell the "crown corporations and government agencies that are commercially viable." Critics interpreted this promise as a plan to sell BC Rail to commercial interests that had no accountability to the North, something that Reform BC explicitly opposed in its *Voters' Warranty.*[16]

The Liberal platform of 2001 worked to minimize such vulner-abilities. *New Era*'s style and content reinforced the critical priority given to the strategic absorption of Reform BC's leadership and membership. It made no reference to diminishing the number of MLAs and stated flatly that a Liberal government would "not sell or privatize BC Rail."[17]

Support for personal income tax cuts was consistent between 1996 and 2001 but with one key difference: *Courage to Change* prom-ised a 15 percent tax cut, whereas *New Era* merely pledged a "dra-matic" tax cut, without specifying what it would be. Will McMartin suggests that this "dodge enabled Campbell to avoid repeating a key mistake from 1996. Then, the 15 percent income tax reduc-tion was offset by an identical 15 percent decrease in government spending so as to balance the budget, a tacit acknowledgement that tax cuts had a cost." By 2001, McMartin argues, the Campbell Liberals knew that linking tax cuts with reductions in government expenditures was "a losing electoral proposition," hence the *New Era* assertions that tax cuts would pay for themselves.[18]

One commitment that remained consistent from 1996 to 2001 was "protection of health and education funding." The genesis of that promise extends well beyond Harris's Ontario. Chris Rudd observes that budget-slashing New Zealand governments of the 1980s and 1990s "were keen to advertise their increased spending in the areas of health and education. This was viewed as produc-tive investment whereas spending on [social services] benefits was unproductive." He notes that New Zealand's Labour minister of social welfare boasted in 1990 of cutting benefits by $800 million, "hardly something the ministers of Health or Education would wish to claim for their portfolios."[19] The same would certainly hold true for British Columbia.

In attempting to be all things to all people, the *New Era* doc-ument was relentlessly cheery about the prospects of British Columbia – subject of course to election of a BC Liberal govern-ment. Certainly, no one would describe it as hard-edged. And it studiously avoided the phrase "smaller government," unlike *Cour-age to Change,* which used it at least seven times. This shift was

tactical rather than principle-driven. Mentioning smaller government would have opened avenues of attack from the NDP that
Campbell hoped to keep closed. Similarly, *New Era* commitments
to "protect BC Hydro ... under public ownership" and to "maintain the longstanding ban on bulk water exports" were designed
to safeguard the populist right flank, as well as to reassure the
broader public.[20]

The document is defined as much by what it excludes – any
reference to welfare reform or sale of Crown assets – as by what
it includes: planks specifically tailored to draw support from
federal and provincial Reform, plus a $2 billion commitment in
health, education, social services, and infrastructure. Nor did
the tone of the Campbell campaign suggest that hard-edged
leadership and severe retrenchment were imminent. As Campbell stated, "I am not tearing up any [labour] agreements,"
and "we're not planning massive lay-offs in the civil service."[21]
The *New Era* document presented a uniformly upbeat outlook
for the future: British Columbians would be spared from such
hard choices by a combination of strong leadership, elimination of wasteful spending, and a revitalized economy – spurred
on by the vital tonic of tax cuts. Reducing personal income
tax rates had produced higher tax revenues across Canada and
"throughout the world."[22] Why would British Columbia be any
different? Perhaps for several good reasons, as discussed in
Chapter 4.

Lessons from the Federal Realm

The early and remarkable success of Reform BC's more prominent
federal cousins was not lost on the BC Liberals. The Reform Party
of Canada's populist brand resonated well and generated early
electoral success across much of British Columbia. The *New Era*
document deliberately and extensively reflected federal Reform-
style populism (as found, for example, in Reform's *63 Reasons to
Support the Reform Party of Canada,* produced in 1995). Some similarities at the core thematic level are noted in Table 2.

TABLE 2

Common themes, Reform Party of Canada and BC Liberals

Reform Party of Canada	BC Liberal Party
"[We support] eliminating unnecessary intrusions into the lives of individuals and businesses"	"Liberating our economy and minimizing undue government intervention in people's lives"
"We support legislation that would compel the government to balance the budget"	"[We will] pass *real* Balanced Budget legislation"
"We believe that Canada would work best as a federation of equal provinces and equal citizens"	"Stand up for the equality of all Canadians and all provinces"
"We want freer votes and less party discipline in the House of Commons"	"Introduce free votes in the Legislature to allow all MLAs to vote freely on behalf of their constituents"

Sources: Reform Party of Canada, *63 Reasons to Support the Reform Party of Canada* (Calgary: Reform Party of Canada, 1995), 3, 4, https://www.poltext.org/sites/poltext.org/files/plateformesV2/Canada/CAN_PL_1995_RP_en.pdf; BC Liberal Party, *New Era,* 4, 8, 11 (emphasis in original).

Similarities occur in a host of areas, among them recall and initiative legislation, debt and deficit elimination, and tax reduction.[23] A long-term staple of the *New Era* plan was a fixed election date that had among its earlier proponents the Reform Party of Canada.[24] More immediate similarities can also be found with Reform's federal successor, Canadian Alliance. Alliance was not only the most aggressive of federal contenders on tax cuts in the 2000 election, but it also called for the elimination of business subsidies and for a tougher stance on fighting crime, both of which found expression in *New Era.*

Campbell was careful *not* to take on some of the socially conservative elements in Reform/Alliance platforms. The Liberal caucus, both pre- and post-2001, was home to disparate political views. As Vaughn Palmer noted, the BC Liberal Party was a "centre-right coalition of [federal] conservatives, liberals and supporters of other parties," which was prone to "deep disagreements between the centrists and some of the rightists on social issues, particularly abortion."[25] During the latter years of the NDP government, the

Campbell Liberals had been embarrassed by free votes on same-sex marriage, which exposed the social policy divide within their ranks.[26] Prior to the 2001 election, Campbell emphasized that the abortion policy would not be open to "free votes" or a public referendum.[27] He was pragmatic but typically progressive on social issues and always keen to avoid controversies that might uncover his party's internal disagreements on social policy.

Alberta Proves a Rich Source of Inspiration and Institutions

In his post-election program, Campbell drew lessons, first and foremost, from Alberta's initiatives in restructuring and downsizing government. Ralph Klein led his Alberta Progressive Conservative (PC) Party to victory in June of 1993 and promptly announced his intention to curb the "uncontrolled spending" of his PC predecessor, Don Getty.[28] Alberta's Throne Speech stated that the "core of this strategy is tax and regulatory reform," including, in its first phase, a "deregulation action plan" in every department of government. Klein's austerity drive promised to "reorganize, deregulate, and streamline government" and to "balance our provincial budget within four years."[29] No ministry was spared from the consequent budget cuts, which ranged from 12 percent in Education to 47 percent in Municipal Affairs, an average of 17 percent across all departments.[30]

The Alberta experience was quickly put to use in the New Era. Jim Dinning, Alberta's provincial treasurer during the restructuring, and Rod Love, Klein's long-time adviser and chief-of-staff, were influential before and during the BC Liberal transition to power. Paul Taylor, Dinning's former deputy, assisted in the transition and then assumed the post of deputy minister of finance in 2001. The Alberta example shaped the Campbell government's approach to the management of change; it also inspired certain processes and institutions, some of which are discussed below.

The BC Liberal DNA featured at least a few strands from America, some via Alberta. For example, Barry Cooper points to David

Osborne and Ted Gaebler's *Reinventing Government* as a source of inspiration in Klein's Alberta. Osborne and Gaebler are American authors and political consultants whose work on public service delivery reform reflects principles of New Public Management. Some themes and language from Osborne and Gaebler also resonated in the BC Liberal New Era. Table 3 charts some key similarities in style and content between *Reinventing Government* and Gordon Campbell pronouncements.

Some phrases drawn from Osborne and Gaebler, such as "government should be steering, not rowing" and (particularly in Health discussions) "funding outcomes, not inputs," enjoyed wide usage in the New Era.

Another comparison is noteworthy. On the distinction between user fees and taxes, Osborne and Gaebler ask: "What is fairer than

TABLE 3

Comparison of *Reinventing Government* and the Gordon Campbell narrative

Reinventing Government	Gordon Campbell narrative
"Putting resources directly into the hands of the intended recipient of services so that they can make choices based on quality and price"	Among the premier's "core values" was "choice: to afford citizens the opportunity to exercise self-determination"
"Entrepreneurial governments ... measure outcomes and reward success"	Among the premier's stated principles: "Results oriented and client focused"
"Entrepreneurial governments ... are leveraging private-sector actions to solve problems. They steer more than they row"	"Collaborative partnerships within the public sector and the broader provincial community"
"Entrepreneurial governments push control of many of the services out of the bureaucracy and into the community"	"Greatly reduced direct delivery: local delivery, outsourcing, shared services, and private sector sponsorship"

Sources: David T. Osborne, "Reinventing Government," *Leadership Abstracts* 6, 1 (January 1993): abstract, 2, 3; British Columbia, Premier's Office, "2001/02 Annual Report: A New Era Update," 4, https://www.bcbudget.gov.bc.ca/Annual_Reports/2001_2002/premier.pdf; British Columbia, Premier's Office, "Core Services Review: Themes and Issues," PowerPoint presentation, 4 October 2001, 2.

a system in which those who benefit from a service and can afford
to pay for it do so, while those who don't benefit don't have to
pay?"[31] The application of such thought was evident in the New
Era with the 2002 decision to meet unexpected costs by substantially hiking medical services premiums and raising the sales tax
(from 7.0 to 7.5 percent), rather than reconsidering personal tax
rates.

Further, Cooper states, the "logic of *Reinventing Government*
also indicated that the goal of public policy is not simply to balance budgets but to restructure government using the budgetary
process as leverage."[32] The New Era relationship between tax cuts
(and subsequent budget cuts) and the goal of smaller government
(through core review) is further explored in Chapters 4 and 5. The
phrase "smaller government" may have been absent from *New Era,*
but it was certainly not forgotten.

Processes and Institutions That Helped
Shape the New Era

In his effort to remake government, Gordon Campbell embraced
ideas, beliefs, processes, and institutions that were embedded
in other times and other jurisdictions. The New Era produced a
lexicon of words and phrases – some local, some exogenous – to
describe processes and institutions in British Columbia. Seven of
them are discussed below.

Ministers of State
On 5 June 2001, Premier Campbell introduced a cabinet of twenty-
eight, the largest in BC history, including seven ministers of state,
a novelty in the province but not in Canada.[33] Both Community,
Aboriginal and Women's Services (MCAWS) and Health had two
ministers of state, whereas Children and Family Development
(MCFD), Competition, Science and Enterprise (MCSE), and the
Premier's Office had one each.[34]

Peter Aucoin describes ministries of state as "horizontal policy
ministries," meaning "portfolios with mandates for developing

policy for designated subjects that fall within the scope of several portfolios but without being given any authority to intervene in the administration of these operations."[35] Five of the seven new ministries of state readily match Aucoin's description; the ministers of state for intergovernmental relations and for deregulation had pan-governmental mandates but no greater authority than their peers.

Aucoin's description is consistent with the theory that underpins ministers of state, as set out in Campbell's mandate letters: "Consideration has been given to the depth and breadth to which any Minister can reasonably be expected to have adequate command over a very diverse range of programs, policies and issues ... The nature of high profile, project specific assignments warrants this designation."[36]

The premier also set out ground rules for ministers of state in a letter of 25 June 2001. Again, the goal of achieving "lean and efficient government" dictated that ministers of state would be supported by caucus staff but would not have "independent staff within the bureaucracy assigned exclusively to them."[37] In short, ministers of state would not have their own deputy but would have access to their minister's deputy and assistant deputy ministers (an opportunity that some fully exploited).

Aucoin offers a valuable insight on ministers of state: "Beyond perhaps the initial burst of cabinet support that greets each new portfolio, a mandate to coordinate the work of other portfolios does not carry a great deal of weight unless cabinet heavyweights, including the prime minister, have agreed that the subject constitutes a corporate priority."[38] As noted in Chapter 5, Premier Campbell was never reluctant to put his personal stamp on the deregulation initiative.

Government Caucus Committees

Campbell described Government Caucus Committees (GCCs) as "an important part of the cabinet decision-making process ... not a legislative decision-making process." As he explained, the GCC was new to British Columbia but was "very similar to the model that is used in the province of Alberta."[39] Largely populated by and chaired by backbench MLAs, GCCs in concept operated as a pre-screen for ministerial initiatives that had not yet secured cabinet endorsement. Campbell described decision making this way: "Policy initiatives are brought to the ministers' offices. They may decide it's time to bring forward those issues to Agenda and Priorities [a powerful cabinet committee chaired by the premier]. They come through the government caucus committees. The Chairs report to the cabinet. The cabinet makes decisions after robust conversations about the direction we would like to go."[40] GCC meetings were closed to the media and the public. The New Era featured five GCCs, which dealt with the areas of communities and safety, economy, government operations, health, and natural resources. They were reduced to two after 2005.

The BC Fiscal Review Panel

Appointed by the premier-in-waiting on 25 May 2001, the BC Fiscal Review Panel comprised seven members from the business community, including four accountants. It was chaired by Gordon Barefoot, a chartered accountant who had served on a similar review in Alberta, launched by Ralph Klein in 1993.[41] Journalist Norman Spector suggested that the panel and its business predominance were yet another import from the Klein Alberta playbook.[42] In Will McMartin's view, "Campbell's appointment of the panel followed an old political tradition in British Columbia, whereby newly elected governments attempt to discredit their defeated predecessors for alleged fiscal incompetence and misconduct."[43] Notwithstanding the *New Era* commitment to a "comprehensive audit of the Province's finances," the panel noted at the outset that its report was "not an audit" but rather a review based on information "from the professional public service and the public."

The panel "found the current accounting policies, financial reporting and capital planning processes of the province substantially sound," although the outgoing NDP government's $1.1 billion surplus was built on "a legitimate but one-time gain of $1.4

billion due to the change of public sector pension plans to a joint trusteeship basis." This accounting surplus, in combination with "windfall gains due to high and volatile energy prices that are unlikely to be maintained over the next few years," signalled pending deficits.

With expenditures pegged to rise between 6.0 and 7.4 percent in the following years, the panel projection was that the fiscal years 2001–02 and 2002–03 would see deficits of $3.0 and $3.8 billion. It revealed this projection on 23 July 2001, one week before the government announced that corporate taxes would also be cut, adding an estimated $800 million to pending deficits. "Unlike some other jurisdictions," the panel noted, "British Columbia's relatively low debt gives it a capacity to run deficits in the short run while a 'made-in-BC' solution" was implemented. Very significantly, though suggesting that fundamental change was required, the report argued that "cuts to key services should not be the solution."

The portion of the report most widely utilized by the government was its conclusion (number six of ten) that "projected deficits indicate a structural fiscal imbalance that represents a serious threat to the financial health of the province. While we are not in an immediate financial crisis, government is operating in a fundamentally unsustainable manner."[44] The panel delivered its conclusions six weeks after Campbell and Collins concluded that a 25 percent tax cut was the right thing to do, notwithstanding the economic storm clouds subsequently flagged by the panel. From the nuanced conclusions of the panel came the Liberal narrative of a spendthrift NDP government imposing a "structural deficit" that demanded strong measures if the provincial economy was to be saved.

Ministerial Assistants

Another page from the Ralph Klein playbook was evident in the provision of political aides, namely ministerial and executive assistants (commonly known as MAs and EAs). Shortly after assuming the premiership, Klein attempted to distance himself and his new government from the "free-spending" administration of Don Getty, to which he himself had recently belonged, by reducing the staffing of ministerial offices from over 1,500 to 360. As Barry Cooper points out, "ministers in the Klein Government evidently would have to get by without a phalanx of aides and outriders to clear their way."[45] Similarly, Campbell attempted to distinguish his government from that of the NDP by downsizing the political staff. "We intend to be a lean and efficient government," he declared in mandate letters. Ministers' offices would have one ministerial assistant and one executive assistant, and administrative support staff would "be kept to a minimum."[46] Among the casualties were executive assistants in ministerial ridings.

Mandate Letters

Premier Campbell's mandate letters of 25 June 2001 appear to be the first issued in British Columbia, but certainly not in Canada, Britain, or the Commonwealth. His letters laid out priorities and pending processes in considerable detail: core review, deregulation, service plans, and participation on GCCs and cabinet committees. They also established his rules of the road for ministerial participation in processes, including a remarkably blunt warning that there "will be *no* tolerance for deviations from the accepted process protocols."[47] Donald Savoie suggests that "mandate letters run counter to the collective nature of cabinet decision making. How can priorities be established and major tasks identified even before Cabinet has held its very first meeting?" One potential answer is that the letters reflect the premier's expectations of cabinet; in the case of profound disagreement, a minister "is free to leave or to resign on the spot."[48] Remarkably few ministers, often after striving for years to reach cabinet, choose that option. The power relationship is clear from the start, and ministers are boxed in to the premier's agenda, as set out in the letters.

Campbell's mandate letters also reminded ministers that all "Deputies and Assistant Deputy Ministers and equivalents are appointments of the Premier." That is the convention in most Westminster-style parliamentary democracies. However, the letters also specified that ministerial assistants would be hired by, and report to, the premier's chief-of-staff. This relationship may be less common outside British Columbia. In *Modernizing Government Accountability,* Peter Aucoin and Mark Jarvis describe political aides as appointees who serve at the pleasure of their minister.[49]

Open Cabinet

Open Cabinet added another process pressure to ministerial lives. The first of many Open Cabinet meetings was held on 27 June 2001, and they continued every week or two thereafter until 2002, when they moved to monthly intervals. According to Will McMartin, thirty Open Cabinet meetings took place during the first forty-four months of the New Era; in December 2004, he reported in mock alarm that none had been held for over two months, a signal that enthusiasm for these events was fading.[50] Norman Ruff also noted the gradual decline of Open Cabinet: "Increasingly, new initiatives came directly from the Premier's Office, and no Open Cabinet meetings were held after January 26, 2005."[51]

Many of the Open Cabinet presentations in 2001 involved ministerial reports on "strategic shifts" derived from core review consideration. Open Cabinet also provided "occasions for policy information updates and policy announcements" on a range of issues from deregulation of liquor sales to restructuring of health authorities. By 2005, in Ruff's reckoning, Open Cabinet had "outlived ... its limelight utility for government messaging."[52] Columnist Les Leyne was appropriately skeptical of whether Open Cabinet was reflective of closed cabinet discussions: "If the open cabinet forum was a safety-conscious industrial worksite, Campbell would be able to post a sign at the gates: 'Nine full days without a major disagreement.'"[53] Vaughn Palmer dismissed Open Cabinets as "expensive infomercials."[54] No public expressions of regret at their demise after the 2005 election can be found in the written record.

Public Affairs Bureau

Under the BC NDP government (1991–2001), the communications arm was labelled Government Communications and Public Engagement. In Alberta, the Klein government's communications arm was known as the Public Affairs Bureau (PAB); after becoming premier in 1992, Klein took on direct responsibility for PAB.[55] After the 2001 election, Campbell moved quickly to rebrand Government Communications as the Public Affairs Bureau and, like Klein, to move it into the Premier's Office.[56] In the language of New Public Management, Campbell described PAB as a "new service delivery framework," complete with a "client feedback mechanism" and "performance targets."[57]

PAB was one more element in the centralization of power in the Premier's Office, as Campbell's mandate letters made very clear: "Implementation of the government's political agenda will be coordinated by the Communications Director in the Premier's Office."[58] Soon after, Campbell's new deputy minister responsible for government communications advised, "effective immediately ... directors of communications will report directly to me."[59] Henceforth, all advertisements and press releases required prior vetting from PAB.

According to Campbell, PAB was a shared service that was administered by the Premier's Office, not a manifestation of control from the centre: "Development of a shared service across government is a well-known management technique ... This is a service that is being provided to ministries. It is a coordinating role so that government is acting in unison and is reinforcing the various objectives that we have ... [to] make sure we are speaking with a unified, concerted voice in the province."[60] Communications directors, like deputies and ministerial assistants, were first and foremost responsible to the Premier's Office, not ministerial offices.

Centralization of communications in the Premier's Office generated complaints from reporters about tardy responses, as they strove to meet their deadlines. Vaughn Palmer pointed out that the delay had "nothing to do with the news outlet making the request. It is the ultimate result of Premier Gordon Campbell's rigid centralization of communications, plus his notion that politicians, not communications staffers, should do all the talking."[61]

In the New Era, the push for control from the centre was strongest during the first few months. The speeches of ministers were to be approved beforehand (a stipulation that did not persist), their interactions with the media were to be regulated (a practical impossibility, given co-location of press and politicians in the legislative buildings), and events were to be co-ordinated and approved (a requirement that lives on through the "corporate calendar").

Centralized control over important levers of power would enable Campbell to steer the New Era as he chose. As Keith Baldrey argues, he had "a one-man band approach to governing ... He has a hard time giving up control."[62] New funding for the Premier's Office reinforced the drive for control. Budgets tendered in Finance Minister Collins's Economic and Fiscal Update of 30 July 2001 revealed a five-fold staffing increase in the Premier's Office to 198 and a seven-fold increase in its budget to $21 million.[63] On 22 August 2001, just weeks into office, Campbell advised the legislature: "We thought it was important that we have a number of government-wide initiatives led by the Premier's office so it didn't again become one ministry having an argument with another ministry."[64] Such thinking had already prompted the move of the intergovernmental relations secretariat, the public affairs bureau, the chief information officer, and the Crown agencies secretariat into the Premier's Office. Each came with its own deputy or assistant deputy minister. As Palmer observed, "all those consolidations serve to further centralize power in the premier's office."[65] But what did Gordon Campbell intend to do with that power?

What Prompted Campbell's Frenetic Pace?

Naomi Klein offers a thought-provoking analysis of political exploitation of crises and disasters in *The Shock Doctrine: The Rise of Disaster Capitalism*. She looks in particular at economist Milton

Friedman and the impact of his ideas. Friedman believed that successful political reforms must be undertaken quickly: "A new administration has some six to nine months in which to achieve major changes; if it does not seize the opportunity to act decisively during the period, it will not have another such opportunity."[66] As further discussed in Chapter 3, the notion of reform as a time-limited opportunity resonated powerfully in the New Era. The immediate and dramatic tax cut, the ninety-day agenda, and the process barrage initiated by mandate letters were all reflective of a premier in a hurry.

Friedman's "three-part formula of deregulation, privatization and cutbacks" was also well represented in the New Era program. As detailed in Chapter 5, processes such as core review were structured to diminish the size of government: ministries were required to present a compelling case if a program were to be preserved, but little more than notification was needed to eliminate it. In the New Era, at least 33 percent of regulations in every ministry were presumed to be unhelpful or unnecessary and therefore demanding rescission. Adding a new regulation (even in pursuit of a *New Era* commitment) necessitated that an existing regulation be expunged.[67] Campbell also demonstrated an enduring personal affection for tax cuts. One of his last acts, on 28 October 2010, was to propose a "hail Mary" 15 percent cut. A few days later, he announced his departure from the premiership.[68]

Friedman also argued that "only a crisis – actual or perceived – produces real change. When the crisis occurs, the actions that are taken depend on the ideas that are lying around." A crisis enables "politically impossible" ideas to become "politically inevitable."[69] Some aspects of the Campbell record suggest that he exploited political opportunity through crisis. His 2001 tax cuts were initiated amid strong signals of a weakening economy. He appeared untroubled by their failure to pay for themselves. As he explained, periods of deficit and economic restraint were "exactly the time when you should be looking at what the critical services are that government provides."[70] The $4.4 billion deficit supplied a burning platform for programmatic sacrifices via core review.

In 2009, when Campbell was confronted by the "deepest reces-sion since the Great Depression," his first instinct was again deep cuts and retrenchment, an initiative that was soon truncated by introduction of the Harmonized Sales Tax (HST) and a corre-sponding $1.6 billion federal transition grant.[71]

Did Campbell also exploit the supplemental crisis produced by the terrorist attacks of 9/11? The tax cuts of 6 June and 30 July, in combination with revenue declines since 15 March, had already created a burning platform in the shape of the $4.4 billion defi-cit. No added crisis was needed. Processes whose goal was smaller government – core review, deregulation, and so on – were well under way three months before 9/11. Did it further embolden the budget-cutters? Perhaps, but only to the extent that it exacerbated the growing fiscal deficit.

Campbell used crisis to advance his ideological agenda, but he was not a typical neo-liberal ideologue as set out in *The Shock Doc-trine*. His burning platform aimed to focus services on "those who really needed them." Diminishing services was a way to smoke out the freeloaders and ne'er-do-wells who theoretically exploited the generosity of the state under the NDP.[72] He drove smaller govern-ment as a political strategy and as a means to an end, but not as an ideal end-state. Rather, smaller government created a "foundation for achievement" on which a stronger economy and more sustain-able public services might be built.[73]

The premier certainly took on some neo-liberal attributes when political or economic circumstances suggested it, but a portrait of "Campbell as Friedmanite" would not be sustained by the historical record. As mentioned above, *New Era* is far from a recipe for laissez-faire small government. It promises costly and expansive new programs, along with a progressive social agenda, including more, better-trained, and better-resourced social workers. As detailed in Chapter 4, Campbell readily sacrificed his *New Era* social agenda to protect his New Era economic agenda, but the former was never entirely lost and would re-emerge in the "Five Great Goals for a Golden Decade" of 2005.

Campbell's pattern of political choices across time is far too diverse and inconsistent to sustain any single characterization. Crawford Kilian aptly describes Campbell as a "policy wonk and voracious reader."[74] Indeed, the books he consumed often stoked the enthusiasms of the policy wonk, from health care to climate change, and from education to Indigenous relations. When his government enjoyed strong revenues during the abbreviated Golden Decade (2005 to late 2008), he was far more a reformist liberal like Dalton McGuinty than a neo-liberal like Mike Harris. The Golden Decade brought substantial reinvestment in social services, public education (through programs such as StrongStart and full-day kindergarten), and Health (through programs such as ActNow BC and the Wait Times Reduction Strategy). His embrace in 2008 of a carbon tax to fight climate change puzzled both his political foes in the NDP and other Canadian premiers of the centre-right: Where did *that* Gordon Campbell come from?

Gordon Campbell: Neo-Liberal, Reformist Liberal, or Hybrid?

The character, tone, and content of the *New Era* platform offered, as argued above, a mix of neo-liberal and reformist liberal elements. Gordon Campbell as politician offered a similar mix of these elements. J.R. Lacharite and Tracy Summerville suggest that his "policy record appears to reflect a considerable measure of both pragmatism and ideological zeal." Although both Campbell and the New Era were heavily influenced by the 1990s experiences of Alberta and Ontario, "there was more to Campbell's legacy than a desire to transform BC into a simple replica of the Klein and Harris regimes."[75] What the public saw from 2001 to 2005, notwithstanding the extraordinary efforts of ministries to fulfill the reformist liberal *New Era* commitments, was the severe retrenchment measures of a neo-liberal.

Campbell's belief that personal and corporate tax cuts would spawn made-in-BC growth amidst the recessionary trends of North American and world economies shaped not only the unfolding of the New Era but also the public's sense of Campbell as a political leader. Unrelenting budget-driven retrenchment did not leave much room for reformist liberal zeal. Had the Five Great Goals initiative been launched in 2001, it would have been laughed out of the core review and budget target review rooms (or perhaps even forcibly expelled).

As Lacharite and Summerville also suggest, Campbell was "a very complex politician."[76] He demonstrated both pragmatism and skill in bringing much of Reform BC into the Liberal fold prior to the 2001 election. The BC Liberals were (and are) a coalition of federal Liberals and Conservatives, and Campbell met the challenge of maintaining a united public face across a large and diverse caucus during the dark days of the New Era. Like his party, he himself was a political hybrid: when his instincts or the fiscal situation suggested retrenchment, he was a small-government conservative, but he was a social progressive on issues such as abortion, same-sex marriage, and safe-injection sites.[77]

Kevin Ginnell effectively summarizes Campbell's managerial proclivities, as "1) a penchant for hard work and even over-achievement; 2) an ideological tendency (leaning to the right) tempered by a more pragmatic, and at times, progressive streak; and 3) a quixotic inclination to intensify focus on an issue, or set of related issues, and then eventually drift off to other policy areas."[78] When Campbell was mayor of Vancouver, his support of "progressive social issues, such as the construction of abortion clinics in Vancouver, the hosting of the Gay Games, and the development of AIDS protocols, suggests a pragmatic and adaptable leader rather than an ideologue driven by a set of unrelenting neoliberal values."[79] A strong case can be made for both, but an assessment based only on the New Era years would undoubtedly conclude that Campbell was the latter.

Campbell was drawn to big ideas and lofty goals. He enjoyed bold successes, such as the New Relationship agreement with First Nations, the Great Bear Rainforest Agreements (2006), the 2010 Winter Olympics, and the carbon tax, along with some notable failures, such as the 2001 tax cuts, the standoff between the

Community Charter and the Significant Projects Streamlining Act (detailed in Chapter 6), and the 2010 HST.[80] But despite being a big-picture guy, he was prone to correcting his ministers on the smallest of details, which earned him a reputation for micromanagement. For example, a cabinet minute of 5 September 2001 notes (more diplomatically than Campbell himself), "the Premier reminded Ministers that Powerpoint presentations should be brief, numbered and not used as speaking notes."[81]

Campbell had a long memory for any perceived disloyalty and was never inclined to forgive or forget such a failing. In his view, loyalty was personal, not partisan. The BC Liberal Party was simply a vehicle for delivering his vision of government. In other circumstances, a Social Credit or Conservative Party would have been equally useful in attaining his goals. His wife, Nancy, came very close to capturing her husband's outlook and orientation, though perhaps inadvertently: "Gordon doesn't like politics, he likes government." Her description, as Vaughn Palmer remarked, "was an accurate summation of her husband's policy wonk tendencies."[82] Campbell was never able to match the smooth and relaxed public demeanour of a Bill Vander Zalm, Glen Clark, or Christy Clark – and he knew it. Politics was the price he gladly paid for getting to the prize of driving policy and governance.

He was generally an effective player on the national stage. Moving the intergovernmental relations secretariat into the Premier's Office in 2001 did not signal a re-emergence of federal-provincial tensions, characterized by Philip Resnick as the "politics of resentment."[83] Throughout the twentieth century, BC premiers had frequently employed the strategy of attacking federal policies "to gain domestic electoral advantage and to direct attention away from troublesome issues."[84] Campbell largely avoided sectional and partisan quarrels, as well as unhelpful Ottawa bashing. He played best with his equals on organizational charts. During his darker moments, he was inclined to lash out at cabinet ministers who failed to meet his expectations, but he was calm, constructive, and collegial in the federal-provincial realm, typically seeking ways to reach agreement rather than battling for political advantage.

Campbell showed remarkable leadership in bringing British Columbia and Canada forward on Indigenous relations through the Kelowna Accord of 2005, a sharp but commendable departure from his spirited opposition to the Nisga'a Treaty a few years earlier. And, after getting religion on climate change in 2007, he demonstrated national leadership by introducing the carbon tax (another initiative that would have been utterly abhorrent in 2001). Campbell's more notable achievements were largely post–New Era, which is not surprising given that the period's imperatives of expenditure reductions and balanced budgets left little space for progressive initiatives not otherwise specified in the *New Era* document.

Campbell's approach to politics and government was founded on the belief that great successes flow from bold and decisive actions. Hesitation equated with weakness and uncertainty, which could only mar results and ensure that the government failed to do what really needed to get done. His determination to stick to the agenda during the New Era meant, in reality, sticking to the fiscal and economic agenda, not to the social agenda articulated in *New Era*. As one former official argued, his steadfast devotion to tax cuts, balanced budgets, and the economic side of the ledger reflected an ideologically based inability to see that "there are things you can do in the short term that are reversible in the short term, but other short-term goals can produce decades of social and environmental damage."[85]

Some of that single-mindedness was chronicled in *Vancouver Sun* articles written by Frances Bula on the eve of the 2001 election. At one point during an on-the-record dinner interview, Campbell "enthused about the miracle that tax cuts will work on the economy with the fervour and rhetorical sophistication of a vegetable-slicer-dicer pitchman." For Bula, the pitch apparently wore thin: "When you hear the familiar phrase, as I did heading into our third hour of dinner conversation, 'I don't think tax cuts will work, I know they'll work!' it's time to turn off the lights. The boyishly engaging and offbeat Gordon Campbell vanishes – poof! – to be replaced by a machine."[86]

The pitchman's fervour was on full display just five weeks later, as Campbell announced his day-one tax cut. Would it blow a billion-dollar hole in the budget, as provincial treasury officials suggested? Of course not, international experience shows that the bigger the cut, the bigger the revenue growth. However, as anticipated rewards became adverse consequences, Campbell refused to acknowledge the connection between deep tax cuts and deep budget cuts. When Opposition leader Joy MacPhail attempted to establish a causal link between budget cuts and core review outcomes, Campbell implied that the results were precisely as planned.[87] He gave not the slightest hint that the tax cuts had fallen short of expectations. To Bula, the "public" Campbell was "one who seems utterly incapable of admitting a fault," a trait that came to the fore as the tax cut saga unfolded.[88]

The election of 2001 offered some of the best and worst moments in the leadership of Gordon Campbell. He had won a huge victory by absorbing much of Reform BC and uniting the right. He had addressed the weaknesses of the 1996 campaign and created a *New Era* platform that would maximize public appeal. He ran a strong campaign that reduced the previously formidable NDP to a mere two seats.

The magnitude of that victory appeared to cloud his judgment. As detailed in Chapter 4, his 25 percent tax cut was dismissive of negative economic indicators and consequent threats to the budget. His haste to remake government saw the *New Era* social agenda sacrificed for the New Era economic agenda. In the rarefied air of a massive victory, British Columbia was not a small jurisdiction comprising less than 1 percent of trade in North America; it was an exemplar to Canada and the world of how a resource-rich and inspired province, freed from constricting taxes and regulations, could light its own way and shape its own destiny. Misjudgment would have serious consequences.

The Liberal government faced a myriad of complex and often intractable problems during the New Era, some of its own making.

Chapter 3 examines global components that helped shape the period. The Campbell government drew ideas, institutions, and processes from outside as well as inside Canada. Among the most prominent of those – though seldom formally recognized as such – was New Public Management.

3

Global Components and a Made-in-BC Solution

"We are all just prisoners here, of our own device."
– Eagles, "Hotel California"

DURING THE NEW ERA, anyone who mentioned New Public Management to a BC cabinet minister would probably have been met with a blank stare.[1] However, all ministers were well versed in stories of Klein's Alberta, Harris's Ontario, and even David Lange's New Zealand. Those jurisdictions had all been the object of extensive caucus discussions in the years preceding the 2001 election, sometimes featuring out-of-province guest speakers. Stories of decline and the need for strong medicine to address it were common. The BC Liberals were firmly – and in some cases fervently – convinced that the road to prosperity was paved with tax cuts, deregulation, balanced budgets, competitive outsourcing, privatization, and smaller governments that steered but never rowed, all consistent tenets of New Public Management (NPM).[2]

Among BC Liberal politicians, the experience of exogenous (external) jurisdictions was rarely characterized as having anything to do with New Public Management. Instead, it was described in terms of "streamlining," "rebalancing," or "restructuring" government (normative slogans being, then as now, more powerful weapons in political battle than academic constructs). However, NPM itself was not new to British Columbia; some of its elements had featured in the Social Credit governments of Bill Bennett and Bill Vander Zalm two decades before the New Era. Philip Resnick describes how Social Credit's 1983 budget included themes of privatization, deregulation, and centralization of spending controls "with direct analogies to practice, both in the U.K. and the U.S."[3] Social Credit's privatization of highways maintenance in the 1980s offered a potent provincial example of public service delivery reforms that were employed elsewhere in the world.[4]

The New Era was made in British Columbia, but it was built from global components. The Campbell prescription, J.R. Lacharite and Tracy Summerville argue, took "its cue from, and advantage of, well-established pro-market maxims and policy reforms advanced by progenitors like Margaret Thatcher (UK) and Ronald Reagan (US)."[5] As Mark Evans notes, NPM "struck a chord with governments of the radical right," such as those of Thatcher and Reagan, "who blamed 'Big Government' for global economic downturn and were seeking to roll back the frontiers of the state to redress market failures."

The Thatcher "revolution" caught the attention of the world: "Indeed, in relation to market reforms, the UK became a net exporter of administrative innovations first to the Commonwealth and later to developmental states."[6] Those innovations were revised and enriched by subsequent international, national, and provincial experiences, particularly (for New Era purposes) in New Zealand, Alberta, and Ontario.

Some elements of New Public Management were evident in NDP governments of the 1990s. For example, Lacharite and Summerville point to the Glen Clark government's encouragement of public-private partnerships.[7] And Katherine Teghtsoonian casts a critical eye on the "insertion of corporate management practices and discourses into the workings of government." In her view, equity and social justice goals were being displaced by business plans and three-year performance plans that were "couched in terms of performance indicators and targets."[8] The new BC Liberal government, she suggests, intensified a shift that was already under way.[9]

The Liberal fondness for the content – if not necessarily the label – of NPM was an extension and elevation of ideas and practices that had enjoyed long currency in the province. The overwhelming election win of 2001 set the stage for an uninhibited remaking of government. In that remaking, to quote Lacharite and Summerville's memorable words, Campbell "rode the wave of a legacy that had already hit the shore."[10]

New Public Management offered themes and approaches that fit well in the New Era. For example, Christopher Hood identifies two key elements that are common to both NPM and the Liberal agenda, "*slow down or reverse government growth* in terms of overt public spending and staffing" and "shift toward *privatization* ... with renewed emphasis on 'subsidiarity' in service provision."[11] Campbell's demand for smaller government fuelled not only core review, but also privatization (BC Rail and the Coquihalla toll concession) and devolution (BC Safety Authority and the Land Title and Survey Authority). "Subsidiarity" was the belief that services should be delivered by the government or entity that was "closest to home" rather than by central government. It was implicit in Campbell's early conception of a Community Charter and in devolution of functions such as safety services.[12]

British Columbia's version of NPM was an amalgam of national and international experience. John Alford and Owen Hughes suggest that NPM "was not a monolithic set of practices but had variants from one jurisdiction to another."[13] It did not offer a precise and consistent prescription for reform, but rather "a bundle or 'shopping basket' of measures, in the main mutually supportive but occasionally mutually contradictory."[14] Janine O'Flynn identifies central and recurrent themes in the NPM shopping basket. For example, "the way in which government was viewed, constructed and arranged was firmly rooted within an economic frame and, from here, policy rhetoric focused on the notion that small government was superior and that government failure must be addressed in order to maximise efficiency."[15]

O'Flynn's focus is largely on the Australian experience, but her description is perfectly apt for the BC New Era. Table 4 sets out common normative themes of NPM that found expression in the *New Era* document.

TABLE 4
Common normative themes of New Public Management and
New Era

Themes of NPM	Themes of *New Era*
Separation of policy and administration	"Merit Employment legislation to restore a professional public service" (three citations)
Deregulation	"Cut the 'red tape' and regulatory burden by 1/3 within three years" (two citations)
Achieving private-sector-style competition	"Restore open tendering on government contracts" (three citations)
Improved accounting	"Pass *real* Truth in Budgeting legislation that ensures all provincial finances are fully, accurately and honestly reported under Generally Accepted Accounting Principles" (two citations)

Sources: Gruening, "Origin and Theoretical Basis of New Public Management," Table 1, "Characteristics of the New Public Management," 2; BC Liberal Party, *New Era,* 4, 8, 10, 15, 30 (emphasis in original).

Perhaps most importantly, the New Era drive for smaller government, which lay at the heart of the Campbell "revolution," was fuelled by the tenets of New Public Management and strongly reflected in the core services review.

NPM Wins Official Blessing but No One Has Time to Study It

Although NPM was little known in political circles, its link to the New Era was neither random nor retrospective. The Campbell government drew heavily from NPM theory and practice, explicitly so in the senior public service. The "Deputy Minister Performance and Development Plan" for 2002–03, for example, directed that the study of NPM and attendance at one or more major conferences on alternative service delivery were among "key development goals."[16]

Alas, study and reflection were incompatible with the hectic pace of the New Era: "For most [deputy ministers], there was precious little time to examine and understand the roots of what was happening. All DMs were immediately thrown into the maelstrom of 30, 60, 90-day deliverables," one former deputy observed. "For all the exhortations of the Premier and his staff to get us to think 'outside the box,' the reality was we were hard-pressed to think at all. The imperative was to 'do,' not to 'think' and most certainly not to 'question' the strict orders we had been given."[17] Gernod Gruening cites "freedom to manage" (for public servants without onerous political control) as an "undisputed characteristic" of NPM.[18] However, the rapidity and intensity of the Campbell reform agenda not only left scant opportunity for the study of NPM, it also created an environment in which "rather than loosening or even relinquishing the levers of control, the implementation of NPM reforms had the opposite effect."[19] The New Era process barrage was intense, omnipresent, and utterly consuming.

The already daunting challenge of reconciling the 25 percent tax cut with delivery of existing programs and *New Era* commitments was exacerbated by post-election processes laid out in Campbell's mandate letters of 25 June 2001. These entailed core review, preparation of "Alberta-style" three-year service plans, deregulation, alternative service delivery, consultations and complex planning for devolving functions, and reporting to the Agenda and Priorities Committee, Government Caucus Committees, and Open Cabinet.[20] The process parade was quickly joined by the "frantic" ninety-day agenda, which, as the premier's deputy minister Ken Dobell described it, "was Looney Tunes in many ways to deal with the government's agenda."[21]

The BC experience reflected that of other jurisdictions, also working from the NPM shopping basket – "a confusing welter of changes goes on simultaneously, among which it is difficult to distinguish ephemeral and hyped-up innovations from those that are fundamental and longer lasting."[22] Christopher Pollitt and Hilkka Summa's description of NPM reforms in Thatcher's Britain and Lange's New Zealand could easily be applied to the New Era: "Driven through short time scales," "pace of change was high and opposition was steam-rollered more often than placated," "too far too fast," "scope of reform was broad and doctrinal content high," and most significantly "the *process* of change was an intense and often painful one."[23] How did Gordon Campbell's devotion to getting things done become too far too fast?

When Speed Becomes Haste

Speed, haste, and demands to "have everything at the same time" were recurrent elements in the New Era story. Former public servants whom I interviewed for this project routinely cited the pace of change as the primary obstacle to achievement of goals, particularly in combination with budget and staffing cuts. Their experiences suggest that speed can be compatible with the successful resolution of complex problems but that the prospects of success will be inhibited by inadequate resources and/or fragmented focus.

In 2001, the ministries of Health Planning and Children and Family Development (MCFD) both undertook ambitious and challenging processes to reform their regional service delivery.[24] An Open Cabinet presentation of 12 December 2001 from Health Planning Minister Sindi Hawkins proposed a "streamlined regional health system" that would "save and renew public health care."[25] She argued that the current fifty-two health authorities were "poorly structured and organized." Moreover, they were "not financially sustainable," causing "duplication and inefficiency."[26] Her proposal to create five regional health authorities and one provincial health services authority was subsequently approved by cabinet. Remarkably, the Ministry of Health Planning announced later that day not only the revamped health governance model, but also the appointment of six board chairs, who would lead the new "accountable corporate governance boards" that were soon to follow.[27] Within six months of taking office, the government had radically transformed the health care delivery system, a speedy achievement of Friedmanesque proportions!

The MCFD core review presentation of 7 November 2001 emphasized "community" and "community delivery" of services (further detailed in Chapter 8), but regionalization was always part of its decentralized model, particularly after the new health authorities paved the way for MCFD to follow suit.[28] Up to 2,800 MCFD staff, primarily child protection workers, were slated for transfer to the new authorities. Atop the five regional authorities would be a permanent provincial authority (mimicking the Health Planning model), with a board appointed by government, "enabling the provincial authority to develop a coherent and corporate approach to delivering a broad range of services."[29] MCFD Minister Gordon Hogg promised that plans for regionalization would be complete in 2003, with full implementation of the new service delivery model in 2004. However, those plans remained on hold long after Hogg left MCFD in January 2004.[30]

What accounts for Health Planning's swift success in comparison to MCFD's long-running struggles with regionalization?[31] Part of the answer may lie in resourcing. In their study of policy innovation in the federal bureaucracy, James Desveaux, Evert Lindquist, and Glen Toner link policy achievement to the provision of "necessary financial resources and the latitude to develop policy."[32] In the case of British Columbia, Health and Health Planning enjoyed lifts of $1.1 billion in both the 2001–02 and 2002–03 budgets.[33] On the other hand, Hogg reported "$55 million in unfunded cost pressures" in August 2001, exacerbated by a subsequent 23 percent budget cut to be delivered at the latest by February 2004. Health and Health Planning possessed the financial resources to implement their new regional model without widespread resistance. MCFD's proposed model was unsurprisingly viewed with suspicion because of its concurrence with severe budget cuts.[34]

The premier and cabinet provided Health Planning with ample latitude to develop policy around regionalization. The operation of fifty-two service delivery agencies was predictably deemed incompatible with a more disciplined and cost-effective health care delivery. Their replacement by a much smaller number of provincially appointed "corporate" boards was seen as an essential precondition to getting control over health care spending. In MCFD's case, regionalization involved a transfer of authority away from central ministerial control and into structures that were closer to and more sensitive to community voices. The Ministry of Finance and Treasury Board were at best agnostic on the MCFD plans; the former needed caseload and budget reductions from MCFD, and diffusion of control was potentially inimical to that goal.

Desveaux, Lindquist, and Toner also suggest that the "difficulty in producing comprehensive responses to problems may be due less to policy and political errors and more to organizational factors." In some cases, they argue, new capacity must be "created and structured to take up the challenge."[35] Health Planning followed that recipe: it was a new ministry whose top priority was the design and implementation of a "streamlined regional health system," a mission that was generously funded and fully staffed. On the other hand, MCFD was shedding staff (including assistant deputy ministers) rather than adding new capacity. As one former official pointed out, MCFD did create planning committees, but they "all got bogged down early in multiple process issues. We in the ministry headquarters were also deeply embroiled in the budget nightmare so things were very stretched." Momentum was further dissipated with the realization that "it would be extremely difficult to move services out with less funding."[36] MCFD's focus on regionalization was constantly fragmented by the urgency to extinguish budget-induced fires. Organizational factors were indeed at play in its failure to achieve its goals, but the decision to impose unrealistic and unrealizable budget cuts on a caseload-driven ministry lay at the heart of that failure.

Health Planning enjoyed the opportunity to focus on a vitally important but well-defined goal, whereas MCFD was hamstrung by the premier's demand for everything at the same time. As the next section demonstrates, the government borrowed from New Zealand on the scope and speed of change, as well as its experience with New Public Management.

New Zealand Invades British Columbia through Alberta

The BC Liberals drew both political and policy lessons from New Zealand. That small nation bears a remarkable resemblance to British Columbia, demographically and historically, and it had a significant impact on the political and administrative sides of the BC government. Table 5 compares the NPM aspects of New Zealand's public policy, as identified by Jonathan Boston and his colleagues, with Campbell's mandate letters and other directives to ministers.

Like British Columbia, New Zealand learned from the experiences of Britain, the United States, and other jurisdictions. However, its trajectory of decline and its playbook for economic recovery were consistent with and complementary to the emerging BC Liberal narrative.

TABLE 5

Comparative New Zealand and BC New Era reforms

New Zealand	British Columbia
Emphasis on corporate goals, performance targets, and measurement	"Service plans that include measurable performance standards and targets"
"A preference for private ownership, contracting out, and contestability in public service provision"	"Maximum reliance upon competitive choice in so far as the public interest and consumers are protected"
"Stress on cost-cutting, efficiency and cutback management"	Campbell – "Getting costs under control [is] at the top of government's agenda"
	Dobell – "We need different skill sets: contract management skills, creation and enforcement of outcome-based regulations, even downsizing skills"
"A general preference for monetary incentives rather than non-monetary incentives"	"A 20% hold-back of your Ministerial stipend pending measurable results of your Ministry and the government"
"Devolution of management control" and "disaggregation of large bureaucratic structures into quasi-autonomous agencies"	Creation of BC Land Title and Survey Authority, Consumer Protection BC, and the BC Safety Authority as devolved special-purpose, quasi-autonomous agencies

Sources: Jonathan Boston et al., eds., *Reshaping the State: New Zealand's Bureaucratic Revolution* (Oxford: Oxford University Press, 1991), 9–11; Boston et al., *Public Management,* 26; BC Liberal Party, *New Era,* 8; Campbell to Abbott, 25 June 2001, 1, 2, 5, 7; Campbell to all ministers, 30 July 2001; Campbell quoted in cabinet minutes, 27 June 2001; Dobell quoted in Lindquist, Langford, and Vakil, "Government Restructuring," 227.

During the 1980s, David Lange's Labour government undertook a radical economic restructuring of New Zealand. Both that and its purported rescue of the country from the economic abyss were cited as object lessons on more than a few occasions in Liberal caucus meetings between 1996 and 2001.[37] The New Zealand example not only suggested vital ingredients for New Era reform, but it also indicated the pace at which it should proceed. Sir Roger Douglas, minister of finance in the Lange government, was (like Milton Friedman before him) a prominent exponent of speed as a weapon in public policy reform. He addressed the Alberta Progressive Conservative caucus in 1993.[38] Although his speech was in camera, Douglas probably emphasized a theme he frequently articulated elsewhere: "Speed is an essential part of any reform programme ... If action is not taken fast enough, support for the reform process can collapse before the results are evident while the reform programme is only partway through."[39] Douglas's ideas resonated in British Columbia, as well as Alberta.

He stressed boldness, persistence, and political courage. "Governments need the courage to implement sound policies," he said, "take the pain at the beginning, and be judged on the basis of the good results that follow later."[40] His ideas about speed were accepted as fact in the BC Liberal caucus and given shape via well-circulated maxims such as "when it comes to government restructuring, you get only one chance to do it right," or "never give your enemies the opportunity to mobilize," or "everyone who's been through this says 'If I had cuts to do again, I'd go bigger, faster, and deeper.'"

An excellent anecdote in this vein was provided by Ken Dobell, deputy to the premier, in a speech to public servants that was subsequently leaked to the media. Dobell referred to a "very senior" federal public servant who led the downsizing of his ministry by 25 percent: "He said: 'Going in, I thought it was impossible. In the process, I thought it was really difficult. Now that it is a few years behind me, we should have taken 35 percent.'"[41] Short-term discomfort was cast as a small price to pay for long-term economic recovery.

The New Zealand storyline followed the invariable arc of decline, aggressive restructuring, and miraculous economic turnarounds. It fostered a genuine belief among some BC Liberal politicians that "bigger, faster, and deeper" was the best (or only effective) model for change. Such beliefs contrasted powerfully with those expressed by the Deputy Ministers' Council on receipt of a draft "270-day plan" tendered by the Premier's Office in January 2002: "All Deputies agreed there are far too many initiatives going on and the system will not be able to sustain the workload ('system will implode')."[42] As discussed in Chapter 5, politicians who believed – on the basis of received wisdom from New Zealand, Ontario, and Alberta – that they had just one brief opportunity to remake government felt little sympathy or understanding for public servants who might drown in process along the way.

New Public Management exerted a profound influence on the unfolding of the New Era. However, civil servants were not asked to consider and implement it within a static environment. Part of the challenge in assessing the impact of NPM on the New Era is the complexity and intensity of political and administrative change between 2001 and 2005. Government policy agendas are invariably crowded. Even setting aside its NPM dimension, the New Era agenda was extensive and ambitious, predictably straining government's analytic capacity to plan and implement new policies and programs. Governments, to borrow Hugh Heclo's memorable phrase, "'puzzle' as well as 'power.'"[43] In the early days of the tax cuts, the Campbell government enjoyed the luxury of powering. As the cuts failed to generate the expected revenues, and as ministries faced demands for drastic budget cuts, the puzzling began.

Policy Transfer: Learning Lessons from the World

Before and during the New Era, British Columbia was an active importer of political ideas, policies, processes, strategies, administrative practices, and institutions. Premier Campbell set the tone in his mandate letters of 25 June 2001, stating that ministries "need to examine the approach being taken in other jurisdictions to ensure we maximize the benefit of others' experience."[44] As ministries puzzled to meet ambitious New Era goals, they drew on lessons and expertise from around the world. In the twenty-first century, a potential solution to an intractable problem may be just a computer key stroke away in New Brunswick, New Zealand, or Norway.

British Columbia offered abundant evidence of David Dolowitz and David Marsh's suggestion that "almost anything can be transferred from one political system to another."[45] The case studies of three social ministries presented in Chapters 6, 7, and 8 provide numerous examples of policy transfer that was aimed at solving domestic problems. "Governments copy other governments," Christopher Pollitt and Geert Bouckaert note.[46] They face a host of complex challenges, and understanding what works elsewhere helps define policy options. "Policy tourism via the Internet is now in easy reach of most policy-makers," Mark Evans writes, "as the majority of public organizations provide detailed information of their activities on their web sites."[47] The fact that a policy or program has succeeded elsewhere confers legitimacy on a transfer that might otherwise be dismissed as risky or unproven. "In policy-making circles, experience has a unique status as a justification of effectiveness; it shows that a proposal is not just based upon 'head in the clouds' speculation," states Richard Rose, a leading scholar on public policy lesson drawing.[48]

An early and excellent instance of policy transfer is chronicled in the BC cabinet minutes of 29 August 2001, where the minister of management services "was encouraged to look more broadly for examples of shared services in the UK, and in the US (Orange County, California) prior to finalizing his strategic plan."[49] MCFD Minister Gordon Hogg provided another compelling example. In response to a question posed in legislative debate about the delivery of school-based support programs, he explained that "over 20 models were looked at ... in terms of ways of providing those services" based on "research from around the world."[50]

British Columbia's interest in exogenous experience was not at all unusual. Evans, for example, notes the extensive two-way policy transfer in a broad range of areas between the Tony Blair and Bill Clinton administrations in the late 1990s and early 2000s.[51] Jurisdictions with strong ideological alignment or with comparable demographic profiles, political cultures, and government institutions will be of particular interest (as was the case of New Zealand and British Columbia).[52]

The impetus for policy transfer is entirely unsurprising, as jurisdictions "import innovatory policy from elsewhere in the belief that it will be similarly successful in a different context."[53] All modern governments – municipal, provincial, and national – learn from the experience of others, a potential "dynamic against insularity and incremental change," as politicians and officials devise "new approaches to old dilemmas."[54] Just as policies and program details are shared across jurisdictions, so too are ideas and normative beliefs, such as the faith that tax cuts ultimately pay for themselves. Dolowitz and Marsh describe policy transfer as "the process by which knowledge about policies, administrative arrangements, institutions and ideas in one political system (past or present) is used in the development of policies, administrative arrangements, institutions and ideas in another political system."[55]

The New Era offers abundant evidence of transfer in all areas: policies (for example, curtailing welfare payments to able-bodied recipients), administrative arrangements (restructuring service delivery), institutions (Government Caucus Committees), and ideas (fixed election dates), ideologies (smaller government is better), and attitudes (cut bigger, deeper, and faster). Policy transfer in the New Era was largely a process of emulation, where, as Colin Bennett notes, "state officials copy action taken elsewhere," rather than a negotiated or direct coercive transfer driven by the federal government or other outside organization.[56] Transfers were not coercive, but many were driven by what Dolowitz and Marsh describe as "perceived necessity," typically in response to core review or budget pressures.[57]

Policy transfer that is incomplete or inappropriate can have unforeseen negative consequences. In the former, the jurisdiction fails to carry over all the elements of a policy; in the latter, the transfer is not consistent with the political values, norms, and culture of the recipient jurisdiction. As Pollitt argues, "contexts matter. What is conceptually supposed to be the same technique or model ... may turn out very differently in different contexts." What is successful in one jurisdiction may fail completely "in another sector or country or at another time."[58]

The New Era encompassed more than a few instances of failed policy transfer. The Ministry of Community, Aboriginal and Women's Services (MCAWS) cast its net widely (and unsuccessfully) for exogenous approaches to social housing that might meet the expectations of Premier Campbell and the core review committee, including a look at the United Kingdom's Right to Buy program, where council housing was sold off to low-income occupants as part of Margaret Thatcher's policy agenda.[59] As discussed in Chapter 7, the Ministry of Human Resources imported an American approach to social assistance, under which employable individuals and couples were prohibited from receiving welfare for more than two years out of five. The "two-years-in-five" rule was highly controversial but was ultimately rendered far less consequential by the addition of numerous exemptions as five-year deadlines neared.

As Pollitt suggests, policy transfer may also fail if it occurs at the wrong time. An obvious case in point is the tax cuts. Basing their conclusions on the 1990s experiences of Ontario, Alberta, and other jurisdictions, the BC Liberals – most notably their premier and finance minister – presumed that a decrease in taxes would generate economic growth, even though the world economy was faltering. Nor were they the last to embrace that presumption. In 2012, for example, Kansas introduced major tax cuts for individuals and businesses, which its governor, Sam Brownback, claimed would act as "a shot of adrenaline into the heart of the Kansas economy."[60]

Like British Columbia, Kansas enjoyed "confident assurances" that slashing taxes would "'pay for itself' with economic growth."[61] Contrary to expectations, "overall growth and job creation in Kansas underperformed both the national economy and neighbouring states."[62] As in British Columbia, the Kansas cuts increased the deficit and resulted in major spending reductions for public services.

In 2001, Gordon Campbell did not just *think* that the cuts would work – he knew they would work.[63] His brassy confidence (obviously in tandem with his ideological beliefs) led him to conclude that his scheme would succeed irrespective of the economic environment into which it was introduced. Ontario, Alberta, and other jurisdictions had shown him that cutting taxes worked and that the bigger the cut, the bigger the return. With bold leadership, British Columbia would show the world that an enlightened jurisdiction really could have it all. Campbell urged his ministers to look at other jurisdictions and learn from their experiences. In fact, ministers and ministries did comply with this directive but often in hopes of solving intractable puzzles created by the tax cuts and the subsequent demands for deep budget reductions and a balanced budget in 2004. They simply did not have the time for strategic, comparative assessment of programs and jurisdictions.

Chapter 4 addresses key questions regarding the New Era tax policy: Did Campbell and Finance Minister Gary Collins believe that diminishing taxes would pay for itself in whole or in part? Or was it designed to create a burning platform that would reinforce demands for smaller government? In other words, was it just one more tool in getting to a bigger, faster, and deeper remaking of government?

PART 2

A DRAMATIC TAX SHIFT
AND A PROCESS BARRAGE

4

The Tax Cut: Leap of
Faith or Recipe for Austerity?

"Oh, I didn't see that big black cloud hanging over me."
– Traveling Wilburys, "Heading for the Light"

GORDON CAMPBELL LIKED BOLDNESS. He told a BC Liberal convention in October 2001: "Whatever you do or dream you can do, begin it. Boldness has genius, power, and magic in it."[1] As the premier-in-waiting and his soon-to-be finance minister Gary Collins eagerly awaited inauguration after the 2001 election, a decision on taxes was at the top of their agenda. Both believed in the efficacy of tax cuts; the question was whether to go bold or to go cautious. They chose bold, at 25 percent. When Campbell opted for this course, he also defined – inadvertently or otherwise – the face of his government for the next four years.

Campbell and Collins also chose to move swiftly. The new premier was far from apologetic about the speed of the announcement. *New Era* had promised to cut taxes "within 90 days," and as Campbell pointed out, during "the first day on the job we provided every British Columbian with a dramatic personal tax cut."[2] He had indeed promised to greatly diminish taxes during the campaign, but the only specific commitment was to "cut the base personal income tax rate to the lowest rate of any province in Canada for the bottom two tax brackets, on the first $60,000 of income, within our first term." *New Era* also promised to conduct "a comprehensive audit of the Province's finances within 90 days and make the results public," presumably so that informed decisions might be made on the magnitude and timing of any cuts.[3]

Why did Campbell and Collins proceed so rapidly? They could easily have waited until the Fiscal Review Panel offered its advice, as it did on 23 July 2001.[4] Or they could have delayed until Collins released his Economic and Fiscal Update on 30 July 2001, hence giving themselves the benefit of more time and experience in office. They obviously wanted to go bold and may have suspected that the Fiscal Review Panel, largely composed of accountants, might counsel caution given the prevailing economic conditions (as indeed it did). Campbell and Collins believed that a compelling signal was needed straight out of the gate. As Collins explained, "today's announcement puts the rest of the country and the rest of the world on notice that British Columbia is competitive again – we are open for business."[5]

During the election campaign, Campbell consistently argued that "it would be irresponsible for me to suggest what the tax cut will be until I know what the status of the books are [sic]."[6] As is customary, Campbell and Collins received confidential briefings from the Ministry of Finance during the interregnum. Public opinion polling universally pointed to a Liberal victory in the 2001 election, so unsurprisingly the ministry took a close look at the tax cut promise. "Before the election," Respondent J noted, "the Ministry of Finance did a lot of work on whether tax cuts pay for themselves and there was virtually no credible evidence that they do."[7] Consultations with experts and other jurisdictions did nothing to lessen this skepticism, particularly given the sharp economic decline since 15 March 2001.

The general content of Finance briefings can be discerned in reports generated by the Fiscal Review Panel (July 2001) and by the BC auditor general (January 2002). Both pegged the outgoing NDP government's year-end balance on 31 March 2001 as a surplus of approximately $1.5 billion, which was built on "a legitimate but one-time gain of $1.4 billion due to the change of public sector pension plans to a joint trusteeship basis."[8] Both reports also expressed concern that 2000–01 revenues relied on "high energy prices," which were "not expected to last."[9]

Collins's Economic and Fiscal Update of 30 July 2001 confirmed the economic malaise. He stated that the "economic outlook for the United States, Europe and Asia has weakened, and that has had a negative effect on British Columbia's exports including energy and electricity. *Since March 15* we have seen our revenues decline by $1.85 billion."[10] Notably, revenues had been in decline for at least three months prior to the 6 June 2001 tax cut announcement. In short, the decision to decrease taxes was made at a time when the books were very close to balanced (setting aside the one-time transfer of $1.4 billion), but key economic indicators were unfavourable.

For a measure that held such potentially sweeping consequences, the decision-making circle was exceedingly narrow. Martyn Brown, Campbell's chief-of-staff throughout the New Era, recalled in a 2013 interview that he was "quite astounded" to learn that the 25 percent cut would apply across all income brackets, well beyond the campaign pledge to instigate the lowest tax rate for the bottom two brackets by 2005. "I was a most nervous Nelly," said Brown, "because of what it obviously inferred for spending cuts that I knew would invite much more long-term political pain than any short-term gain those cuts might offer."[11]

Brown was not alone in his astonishment. Among the critics was columnist Les Leyne, who argued that the Liberals "came into office, had a cursory review of the books based on some quick briefings by Finance Ministry officials, and then slammed into place a tax cut that dwarfs anything ever attempted before in this country, even before the independent review of the books is done."[12] Did Campbell and Collins believe that their strategy would succeed, regardless of the economic and fiscal situation?

Reporter Chad Skelton framed the critical question well: "It's the billion dollar question: Can tax cuts stimulate the economy so much they pay for themselves?"[13] The *Vancouver Sun* reported "provincial treasury officials" as saying "their financial models show the tax cuts would punch about a $1 billion hole in the

budget delivered in late March."[14] Confronted with that suggestion, Campbell shot back: "Without exception, audited financial
statements have shown these tax cuts have produced significantly
higher tax revenues over time as the economy grows." After citing
positive examples from various corners of the globe, he declared,
"there is no reason to expect in British Columbia and only in British Columbia, when you cut personal income tax somehow or
other you're not going to generate the revenue."

Jason Clemens, director of fiscal studies at the Fraser Institute, supported Campbell's claim: "My hypothesis would be the
decrease in marginal rates will spur entrepreneurship and innovation. If you decrease tax rates, you increase revenues."[15] Helmut
Pastrick, chief economist for the BC Central 1 Credit Union, was
more cautious. He anticipated that the cuts would boost the economy by 0.3 and 0.7 percent in the following two years, but with
caveats around evident recessionary pressures internationally. He
predicted that the cuts would not pay for themselves until five years
had elapsed.[16] When a reporter asked Campbell what a longer-term
payback might mean for budgets, public service employment, and
debt, he responded, "we'll cross that bridge when we come to it,"
and went on to repeat his assertion about the efficacy of tax cuts
in Canada and abroad.[17]

The tax cut was also notable for its distribution: the top three
brackets would drop by 25.9, 25.2, and 24.9 percent respectively,
and the bottom two by 28.0 percent each.[18] Vaughn Palmer challenged Campbell on the seemingly sudden inclusion of the top
three brackets within the package, given that he had persistently
dismissed NDP pre-election claims that he was secretly planning
tax cuts for the rich. Campbell denied the suggestion, but as
Palmer stated, he "was unable to cite any new information that
has come his way since the election that would justify the sudden
expansion in his tax-cutting intentions."[19]

The new cabinet was briefed on tax changes during its inaugu-
ral meeting of 6 June 2001, in advance of the "announcement to
be made that afternoon."[20] The news was tendered to cabinet for
information, not debate; the scope and even the finer details of the

tax initiative had clearly been determined before cabinet received them.[21] Collins was within legal and constitutional bounds here – finance ministers carefully preserve their unique right to deliver taxation measures. However, the decision offered neither consultation nor transparency; nor, in the days that followed, were there extensive demands for same. The 25 percent break was popular with the public and with cabinet.[22] Had ministers (or the public for that matter) known that it would quickly translate into cuts of up to 45 percent in ministry budgets, enthusiasm may have been greatly tempered.

Any ministerial euphoria was short-lived. According to the cabinet minutes of 27 June 2001, just three weeks after the tax announcement, Campbell declared "that getting costs under control was at the top of government's agenda. If Ministers were going to come with a new program, they should come with the plan to find the dollars to pay for the program."[23] Collins reiterated this point: "Don't even think of coming to treasury board with any new programs unless you figure out how you are going to pay for it within your own budget."[24] The cheery tone and boundless horizons that characterized *New Era* and the tax cut quickly surrendered to preoccupation with the fiscal bottom line.

Tax Cuts: Let the Debate Begin!

Economic historian Bruce Bartlett traces the debate around tax cuts as an economic stimulus back to *The Muqaddimah,* written in 1377 by Muslim philosopher Ibn Khaldun. Khaldun argued that "at the beginning of a dynasty, taxation yields a large revenue from small assessments. At the end of the dynasty, taxation yields a small revenue from large assessments." As Khaldun explained, overtaxation inhibits initiative and investment, but when "tax assessments and imposts upon the subjects are low, the latter have the energy and desire to do things."[25] Over six hundred years later, Khaldun found expression in the New Era, when Campbell was confronted by questions about the unexpected extension of tax cuts to the more affluent. The step was necessary, he argued, to "keep skilled British Columbians from fleeing to lower-taxed jurisdictions."[26] His comment was consistent with the *New Era* narrative that "high taxes, over-regulation and hostile business policies have driven workers and employers out of our province."[27]

Debate about the optimal level of taxation has continued since the early twentieth century, when income taxes were introduced. As Bartlett notes, much of that debate in recent decades has revolved around the Laffer curve, a graph designed by American economist Arthur Laffer in the late 1970s to track the relationship between taxation rates and resulting levels of government revenue. "Long before Laffer drew his famous curve," Bartlett writes, "it was well established, historically and theoretically, that tax rates may be so high as to diminish revenue and that a rate reduction could raise revenue. The real question has always been where we are on the curve."[28] The BC Liberal plot line, developed over a decade in Opposition, was that NDP overtaxation inhibited investment. As Campbell declared in his introduction to *New Era*, "we can cut personal income taxes and unleash the power of a thriving free enterprise economy." Lower taxes meant "more jobs, more taxpayers and ultimately more revenue to improve the public services you want and need."[29] To paraphrase Bartlett, the real question was where on the conceptual curve between overtaxation and undertaxation did British Columbia sit? And what would that positioning mean in the context of a declining economy?

Tax cuts were the subject of vigorous debate in the months and years leading up to the 2001 election. On 31 March 1998, the NDP government introduced its own cuts for individuals and businesses, valued at $415 million over three years. Opposition leader Gordon Campbell stated that "drastic, bold action" was needed and that "he would have introduced a 10 or 15 percent tax break."[30] The NDP claimed that a drop of such magnitude would severely undermine social services, but Campbell maintained that it "will spark economic growth, creating billions in revenues."[31] The New Democrats clearly believed that the Liberal commitment to deep cuts was a potential vulnerability. Their 2001 Throne Speech asks: "What comes first – public health care and education or dramatic tax cuts?" The NDP answer was unequivocal: "We can't have more public health care, better education and balanced budgets and also have dramatic tax cuts. My government believes that the public services that families rely on must come first, not tax cuts."[32]

As Opposition finance critic, Gary Collins was an ardent advocate of lowering taxes. When public-sector unions raised concerns regarding tax cuts with the legislature's Finance Committee in 2000, Collins claimed that he had canvassed every Canadian jurisdiction over the past five years and had discovered that "in no place where provincial income tax was reduced, has there been a drop-off in revenues."[33] Collins and his colleagues were far from alone in their confidence.

In the campaign preceding the federal election of 27 November 2000, the governing Liberals and the dominant Opposition party, Canadian Alliance, offered duelling tax cut promises of $100 billion and $134 billion respectively, both over five years.[34] Further, those promises came on the heels of the government's "getting government right" program review of 1994–97 (in many ways a model for Campbell's core review of 2001–04, as detailed in Chapter 5).[35] Getting government right involved harsh retrenchment for some federal ministries and programs, but that dissuaded neither Jean Chrétien's Liberals nor their opposition from calling for tax cuts.

A few months before the 2001 election, David Bond, former chief economist of HSBC Bank Canada and no fan of the NDP, provoked Collins's ire by publicly questioning the efficacy of potential tax cuts. The New Democrats, Bond argued, "took nine years to destroy the provincial economy. You can't turn a supertanker on a dime." Bond supported tax cuts in theory but not in the context of a weak economy. Their probable consequence, he believed, was at least a short-run deficit. The Harris government's cuts had succeeded because "the American economy was booming," but such was not the case in 2001: "I said if you cut taxes and expect the same kind of hit as Harris got, you're nuts. I said don't expect a miracle."[36] In turn, Collins challenged Bond to "prove" that tax cuts "would precipitate a drop in government revenues."[37]

As in 2000, Collins argued that in "every jurisdiction in Canada which has reduced personal income tax rates in the last five to six years there has been no significant drop-off [in revenues] and the ones that have cut the most, like Alberta and Ontario, have seen the biggest increases in revenues."[38]

David Bond was not the only skeptic. The problem, as Les Leyne noted, was that "all the examples they [the Campbell Liberals] point to are jurisdictions where tax cuts coincided with an economic boom. There's no perfect experiment to measure the impact in the absence of other factors."[39] Leyne proved remarkably prescient in his assessment, six months before the 2001 election: "If they [the Liberals] cut taxes and there is no corresponding economic boom, then they'll be left with a giant hole in their revenue picture, one that by law they'll have to fill in, as a balanced budget will be mandatory."[40]

No such gloom populates the *New Era* document; it prominently features a graph that summarizes the Ontario tax and revenue results from 1996 to 2001, suggesting that tax cuts are anything but fiscally reckless. The graph shows that the basic income tax rate declined from 58.0 percent in 1996 to 38.5 percent in 2001 (based on percentage of federal tax), whereas provincial income tax revenue grew from $15.6 to $18.9 billion throughout the same period. Just as importantly, it charts year-over-year growth in revenues, with only one modest decline of $100 million in 1998. The Ontario experience appeared to confirm (or at least conform to) the central premise of the Laffer curve, that high levels of taxation stifle economic growth, thereby reducing revenues to government; conversely, tax cuts trigger growth that produces new revenues, more than offsetting initial losses. Or, as *New Era* claimed: "Provinces like Ontario have proven that lower personal income taxes lead to *higher* revenue – not less."[41]

Prior to the 2001 election, Campbell was entirely dismissive of the possibility that tax cuts could prompt a deficit and concomitant fiscal restraint: "If I thought we were going to reduce a billion and a half in revenue because we were giving people back a tax cut, then that would be a real issue. I don't believe that happens."[42]

Alas, David Bond proved correct in disparaging the prospects of a quick economic turnaround; the cuts would not be paying for themselves any time soon. He was less than reluctant to take a last shot in his battle with Collins: "I could be tempted to say, 'I told you so,' but I shouldn't. After all, Mr. Collins, who was saying there wouldn't be any deficit, is a certified flight instructor and all I've got is a PhD in economics."[43] And contrary to Campbell's expectations, deep tax cuts did equate to deep budget cuts. So, were the expenditure reductions a product of misreading British Columbia's tax competitiveness in the global economy, or were they a pretext for starving government through a burning platform created for that express purpose?

Faith in Tax Cuts Did Not Die Quickly or Easily

The finance minister's Economic and Fiscal Update of 30 July 2001 was his first formal "state of the province" address to the legislature since the election. As with an annual budget speech, words in a fiscal update are chosen carefully. Collins reconfirmed what he and the premier had announced on their first day in office, a 25 percent drop in personal income taxes. He also announced a series of tax changes that were "designed to increase investment," including elimination of the corporate capital tax on non-financial institutions, a decrease in the corporate income tax rate, and a reduction in sales tax on production machinery and equipment. Together, these measures comprised a "made-in-BC" tax stimulus package that, for government, represented approximately $2 billion per year in relinquished revenues, absent a Laffer curve revenue rebound through new economic growth. Collins also reported that the economic outlook for the United States, Europe, and Asia had deteriorated, resulting in weaker BC exports and declining revenues to government.[44]

Campbell and Collins were not victims of a sudden economic shift that occurred after their tax cut announcement of 6 June 2001. Since 15 March and perhaps earlier, economic indices pointed downward to minimal or even negative growth and diminishing revenues.[45] Regardless of whether it decreased taxes, the incoming government would be facing substantial deficits during its first year or two in office. Given that environment, Ministry of Finance modelling predicted only a 10 percent return on tax cuts in the first year.[46] However, Collins believed that the Finance model underestimated the beneficial impact of cutting taxes: "I expect we will see better [results] than that."[47] Colleagues such as Deputy Premier Christy Clark also remained true believers (at least as of 2 August 2001). She claimed: "In every jurisdiction where personal income tax cuts have been tried, they've worked. It's meant more revenue to government from personal income taxes."[48]

Despite the impact of foreign markets on provincial exports, Collins was convinced that the appropriate remedy for fiscal woes would be developed domestically: "Number one, we need to make our tax system competitive, as our first step to revitalizing economic growth. Number two, we have to bring some discipline to spending."[49] To light the path for discipline, his Update brought immediate spending reductions of $50 million, much of it from social programs administered by the Ministry of Community, Aboriginal and Women's Services.[50]

The Update offered some residual optimism around the efficacy of tax cuts as a stimulus to job creation and investment: "Already people are seeing our province in a new light. Business confidence is up dramatically and so is consumer confidence ... We believe this confidence will translate into growth of 3.8 percent in our economy next year." The 3.8 percent growth figure was sharply at odds with projections from the Ministry of Finance but was not drawn from thin air. Senior private-sector financial advisers to Campbell and Collins remained far more optimistic on the efficacy of tax cuts than did David Bond. Not surprisingly, none have since come forward to claim credit for the 3.8 percent growth projection.

Notwithstanding the bleak international picture, Collins believed that British Columbia would buck the trend as a direct response to the tax cut's "message here at home and around the world that

BC is back."[51] The Premier's Office shared his optimism. In a 23 July 2001 letter to all deputies, Deputy to the Premier Ken Dobell noted that the "scale of the deficit" identified by the Fiscal Review Panel ($3 billion) was apt to "cause some anxiety within the public service" and would "require very tight management of expenditures, and likely program reductions." Nevertheless, he added, "government anticipates that its program of tax cuts will result in significant economic improvement, and thus higher revenues."[52]

On 30 July 2001, Collins and Campbell remained confident in the wisdom of applying the 25 percent tax cut; indeed, they doubled down (to employ an appropriate gambling metaphor) with comparable reductions in corporate taxes, as noted above. Like the *New Era* narrative, they believed that NDP overtaxation had British Columbia poised for a Laffer curve rebound.

Cutting Taxes Worked Everywhere Else: Why Not Here?

Gordon Campbell's British Columbia offered a somewhat different test of the Laffer curve than Mike Harris's Ontario. Harris promised a 30 percent income tax reduction, but it was to be spread over three years, providing some opportunity to adjust in response to emerging conditions.[53] In contrast, the $2 billion BC tax cut package – personal and corporate – kicked in during the 2001–02 fiscal year.[54] Collins argued that if this step was not taken, British Columbia would "wither away and end up being a have-not province without the economic strength to support the quality of social programs that everybody wants to provide."[55] But if there were no prompt and dramatic revenue returns, as anticipated by the Laffer curve, what would be the fate of those same social programs?

Ontario's tax cuts were well timed, coincident with strong economic growth across much of the world. The province enjoyed average annual real GDP growth of 4.7 percent from 1996 through 2000. Its finance minister, Jim Flaherty, boasted in 2001 that its "growth was much stronger than that of any G-7 nation," producing "the fastest-growing economy in Canada," a stark contrast to the faltering BC economy of 2001.[56]

Just five weeks after the 30 July Economic and Fiscal Update, confidence in the magic of tax cuts was beginning to fade. "We don't have an exact number," Collins told reporters on 4 September, "but I wouldn't be surprised to see it [economic growth] come down a full point, perhaps more, depending on what we see develop over the next number of months."[57] In his quarterly budget update ten days later, Collins temporized even further. Now, the cuts would put British Columbia "in a position to benefit when the global economy turns the corner."[58] In 2001, the Ministry of Finance estimated that each point of economic growth yielded about $250 million in revenue.[59] As the anticipated 3.8 percent growth was supplanted by the harsh reality of 0.6 percent growth, the implications were not lost on Vaughn Palmer, who noted that "the Liberals will have to rely, more than ever, on their review of government spending."[60]

British Columbia did not enjoy the immediate revenue rebound as suggested by the *New Era* graph for Ontario. In fact, its revenues declined precipitously, partially as a consequence of lost revenues from the tax cuts. The cuts did not coincide with strong growth in provincial, national, and world economies. Nor would they induce sufficient domestic initiative and investment to produce a made-in-BC recovery. Collins may have seen the cuts as delivering a powerful global signal, but world financial markets appeared not to be getting the message. Growth of 0.6 percent fell far short of expectations, provoking subsequent social and financial consequences.

Tax cuts in combination with revenue losses and new spending produced a yawning chasm of $4.4 billion. In the absence of Laffer curve rebound revenues, that gulf could be filled only by cuts to the 30 percent of government that was not Health, Education, or Advanced Education. "Not for five years," Palmer notes, "did the income tax proceeds climb back to the earlier level and the cuts, thereby, as the Liberal rhetoric had it, 'pay for themselves.'"[61]

The giant hole in the budget would indeed be filled but by dramatic reductions in expenditures.

Were Tax Cuts Part of a Prescription for Austerity?

The historical record suggests that Campbell and Collins expected a stronger positive economic response to tax cuts and a made-in-BC recovery. After all, Collins stuck his neck out when he predicted that the BC economy would grow by 3.8 percent in just one year. Had he not believed this to be possible, he is unlikely to have made such a claim. In Question Period on 9 August 2001, NDP MLA Jenny Kwan accused him of "playing a high-stakes poker game" with a growth forecast "that no one believes is actually achievable." Collins replied that even "in the terrible economic and investment climate that the members opposite created last year our economy grew by 3.8 percent. I think we can manage that."[62] The prospect that a BC Liberal government might somehow underperform the NDP in the economic arena was unimaginable to Collins, hence his bold prediction.

Similarly, if Campbell had harboured even the slightest doubt about the efficacy of a drop in taxes, his public statements betrayed no hint of it. Could tax cuts fail in a faltering economy? They had worked everywhere in the world, he said, and there was "no reason to expect" that only in British Columbia "you're not going to generate the revenue." Could the cuts blow a billion-dollar hole in the budget? "I don't believe that happens," he said.[63] Campbell was every bit the tax cut "slicer-dicer pitchman" that Frances Bula met during her 2001 dinner interview with him, but the record also suggests that he may have expected some lag before the cuts paid for themselves and may also have seen some advantage in that prospect.

In Premier's Estimates of 5 March 2002, MacPhail asked if there was a causal link between budget cuts and core review outcomes. Campbell steered clear of a direct answer but importantly noted, "I really think that in times where there is economic constraint ... and when we are facing the deficit that we are facing, that's *exactly the time* when you should be looking at what the critical services are that government provides. You make sure that you're providing the critical services *within the affordability framework* that you have."[64] This comment appears to suggest that a $4.4 billion deficit was precisely the burning platform he had envisioned. Or, alternatively, is it just an example of the "public Campbell" that Bula described as someone "who seems utterly incapable of admitting a fault," in this case misjudging the efficacy of tax cuts amid straitened economic circumstances?

During a closed-door (but subsequently leaked) breakfast speech to public servants, Ken Dobell, deputy minister to the premier, reinforced Campbell's theme of cutbacks as a virtuous necessity: "We have this marvellous budget crunch. I'm sure folks would argue – well, this government would argue, at least – we're 10 years behind everybody else. We have the misfortune to be doing it [budget reduction] now, but nevertheless we have to do it."[65] Dobell articulated the belief that underlined core review: British Columbia must undertake a thorough cleansing of wasteful and unnecessary programs and services, just as New Zealand, Ontario, and Alberta had already achieved. The responses of Campbell and Dobell, together with the early inclusion of core review in mandate letters of 25 June 2001, reveal that the push for downsizing government was obviously coming *regardless* of the fiscal situation.

Christopher Pollitt argues that "austerity eases reform, because it can be used by astute policy makers to create an atmosphere of crisis in which it becomes possible to consider a wider range of more radical reforms than would usually be admissible in 'normal times.'"[66] So, were tax cuts designed to create a resource-deprived environment that would drive smaller government through core review? Was Campbell the latest exponent of never wasting a perfectly good prefabricated crisis? In short, as one former public servant suggested, were the cuts designed to create a burning platform that demanded action?[67]

My first conclusion – based on Campbell and Dobell's comments regarding cutbacks as virtuous necessity – is that induced austerity, via deep tax cuts, aimed to underline the imperative of smaller government through core review. My second conclusion – based on the fact that Campbell and Collins appeared to nurse optimism about the 3.8 percent growth until September – is that their burning platform was a greater conflagration than they had anticipated.[68] Tax cuts proved no elixir for an ailing economy.

The terrorist attack in New York on 11 September 2001 threatened to escalate world and local economic problems (and perhaps provide some indirect and inadvertent cover for the failure of tax cuts to deliver as expected). Collins's first quarterly report for 2001–02, released two days after 9/11, finally acknowledged the reality of profound spending cuts, conceding that government had "some difficult and possibly unpopular decisions to make over the next few months."[69] Nonetheless, he contemplated no course change on tax cuts. In an 18 September 2001 "message sheet" entitled "Message for Use by Ministries," Collins admitted that the "global economy is slowing and this has impacted BC," but the essential remedy was "act now to bring the deficit down and get spending across government under control." Curbing the deficit would require "difficult and unpopular decisions," as well as "short-term discomfort," but a brief bout of pain was the price of long-term gain through "a stronger economy and affordable, healthy social programs."[70]

Collins offered a further update on provincial finances in early October at an Open Cabinet meeting in Penticton. Reiterating the bleak forecast of declining revenues and growing deficits, he then introduced ministers to another dark subject: the budget target review. Budgets for all ministries, with the exception of Health, Education, and Advanced Education, would be reduced by an average of 35 percent. The premier had earlier directed ministries to prepare scenarios involving 20, 35, and 50 percent reductions, though not in anticipation of better or poorer times. As Vaughn Palmer wrote of the Open Cabinet meeting, Collins "made clear that the cuts would have to average out at 35 percent. If one ministry gets away with 20 percent, another will face a bigger cut to make up the difference."[71] Thus, the table was set for "a far more ambitious program of fiscal restraint than was undertaken by the

Bill Bennett Socreds in 1982–85."[72] Public confirmation of pending deep cuts came in the Throne Speech of 12 February 2002.

The 2002 Throne Speech: More Harsh Medicine

The Throne Speech of 2002 was an early opportunity for the new government to lay out its vision in a comprehensive way. Throne speeches are heavily and predictably scrutinized by the media and the public for hints regarding the future. They express a government's long-term vision, but they also outline its political agenda for the year ahead and its prescription for achieving that agenda. They often foreshadow the dominant messages – good or ill – that are apt to appear a week later in the budget speech. The 2002 Throne Speech was no exception to this rule.

The Throne Speech had a huge gap to bridge. Only eight months earlier, the Liberals had inaugurated a rescue plan to move from the ostensibly dark days of NDP waste and incompetence to sunnier times under new leadership. The message that Lieutenant Governor Iona Campagnolo delivered on 12 February was anything but sunny. She noted at the outset that the imminent provincial budget would cover "the fiscal challenges at hand and the tough decisions that must be made ... Fundamental change is required in the size and scope of government and to the role it serves in people's lives and in our economy."[73]

The agenda for the foreseeable future was an amalgam of "tough decisions" and "difficult choices" driven by "scarce resources" and "the enormity of a $4.4 billion deficit problem." Despite those decisions and choices, Campagnolo stated, "my government's vision remains the same: to usher in a new era of hope, prosperity and public service in British Columbia ... Over time, they will lead our province to new fields of hope and opportunity."[74] In short, a dose of unpleasant medicine and short-term pain would be required if the tantalizing possibility of long-term gain was to become a reality.

Like the *New Era* document, the Throne Speech spoke only of a dramatic tax cut, not one of 25 percent. Perhaps its authors hoped to avoid the inevitable parallels between the latter and the disheartening revelation that "over the next three years all ministries, not including Health and Education, will experience an average reduction of 25 percent in their budgets."[75] Health and Education were by far the largest ministries.[76] Extracting sufficient savings from the remaining 30 percent of government to achieve a balanced budget in 2004–05 proved extraordinarily challenging.

An average 25 percent cut across the nine smallest ministries (whose budgets collectively totalled $565 million) would yield only $141 million in savings.[77] A 25 percent cut to somewhat larger ministries, such as Forests (which had a $538 million budget), Public Safety and Solicitor General ($498 million), and Attorney General ($564 million), would yield $400 million, though in the latter case only so many courthouses could realistically be closed. The government had saddled itself with what one former official described as "a fundamental math problem ... It left itself with very few places to go."[78]

If the $4.4 billion deficit problem were to be significantly addressed, extensive cuts would have to be made in large and socially sensitive ministries, such as Children and Family Development (MCFD), Human Resources (MHR), and Community, Aboriginal and Women's Services (MCAWS), whose budgets collectively amounted to about $4.05 billion. The decision to exempt 70 percent of the budget and then exacerbate a looming deficit with a drastic tax cut guaranteed a disproportionate hit on the ministries that comprised 30 percent of the budget. Further, as the large social ministries offered programs aimed at economically and socially disadvantaged populations, all these factors guaranteed an inequitable distribution of pain in the BC Liberal New Era.

Perhaps in anticipation of political vulnerability on this front, the Throne Speech made multiple references to protecting services for women and children, among them "my government will put children and families first" and "my government also remains committed to long-term improvements in services for women, children and families."[79] This sentiment was plainly at odds with the budget cuts aimed at social ministries. Putting children and families first was tough to reconcile with the Throne Speech's grim statement that the "government must eliminate or scale back a number of services that many British Columbians would like to see maintained or increased."

The speech promised that government would "seek to moderate the impact on people by phasing out several less vital programs and services over the next three years," a reference to the ongoing core services review. Significantly, the stated aim was only to moderate, not eliminate, impacts on "vital" programs by removing the "less vital." Even vital programs would suffer from the collective weight of tax cuts, expenditure reductions, and sundry economic challenges. Conversely, the combined benefit of tax-related economic growth, savings from the termination of non-vital services, and the purging of purported NDP waste and duplication could only moderate – not offset – the impact on vital services. Achievement of budget targets demanded the rationing of vital services along with the elimination of those deemed not vital through core review. As discussed in later chapters, vital programs were eroded, whereas political priorities were protected.

The Throne Speech claimed that government was responding to "an overwhelming mandate for change" from the electorate: "By voting for my government's pledge to dramatically cut income taxes within its first 90 days, British Columbians also made it clear what they meant by their ability to pay. They wanted the lowest base personal income tax rates in Canada."[80] In other words, the government was simply following the course that British Columbians had so overwhelmingly approved in May 2001 when they voted Liberal. Consequent diminution or elimination of public services, though unfortunate, was necessary to meet their demands for lower taxes and the government's need to get its fiscal house in order.

This narrative employed heaping portions of revisionist history. The *New Era* document contained more than two hundred promises, most of which were entirely unrelated to tax cuts. Many undertook to maintain or expand public services. Voters may have been attracted to any number of these commitments, but nothing in the document suggested a need for the harsh measures prescribed in the Throne Speech. Nor should one assume that the Liberal election sweep of 2001 somehow offered a mandate for government to proceed with tax cuts regardless of the consequences. The 25 percent figure was not made public until almost three weeks after the election. Given this, how could British Columbians have known that the "dramatic" cuts mentioned in *New Era* would translate to 25 percent rather than to the 15 percent promised in the 1996 campaign or perhaps the 10 percent that Campbell mentioned in 1998?

Because *New Era* made such a strong commitment to tax reduction, Campbell was obliged (politically at least) to honour its promise. Given the prospect of a pending deficit, with or without this step, did the choice of 25 percent versus 10 or 15 percent really matter? Indeed it did. The size of the cut determined the size of the hole that must be filled if the 2004 budget were to be balanced, particularly since it would be filled by ministries that comprised only 30 percent of the overall provincial budget. As detailed in Chapters 6, 7, and 8, the magnitude of the cut obliged ministries to ration "vital" programs and to eliminate "non-vital" ones.[81] To echo Pollitt's warning about prescription before diagnosis, engaging in a more thorough diagnosis before prescribing the tax cut may have produced better program outcomes.

Such debates were of little interest or consequence in the New Era, which was a time for remaking government, not revisiting bold decisions or retreating from self-imposed austerity. As the 2002 Throne Speech promised, "my government's priorities will not waver, and its mission will not be altered."[82] Government would not countenance retreat, even to keep crucial public services whole. "It is simply not possible to pay for everything that government used to do and also balance the budget," the speech declared. "It is simply irresponsible to put off the tough changes that must be made to bring spending into line with revenues. My government will not break its trust with the people."[83] Given the looming deep cuts to social ministries that delivered programs to

the socially and economically disadvantaged, one might appropriately ask, "trust with what people?"

The *New Era* platform promised $2 billion in new public spend-
ing, which, in combination with the siren song of incremental revenues driven by tax cuts, would have encouraged voters to dream
of doing more with more rather than less with less. Very few would
be eagerly anticipating profound cuts to social ministries. The
Throne Speech asserted that when "our economy suffers, people
pay the price," to which NDP leader Joy MacPhail responded,
"you bet they pay the price, and some people suffer more than
others."[84]

One week later, in his Budget Speech of 19 February 2002, Gary
Collins made no mention of his 3.8 percent growth prediction
from eight months earlier, but he did acknowledge current projections of 0.6 percent economic growth and a $4.4 billion deficit.[85]
He attributed this decline to "a long list of economic challenges,"
most notably "not just a national but a global economic slow-
down," the impact of 9/11, and declining energy and commodity
prices and sales. He did not acknowledge that the efficacy of tax
cuts was largely if not entirely lost under such circumstances.

But MacPhail had no intention of letting him wriggle off the
hook. The 2002 budget featured two controversial changes: a sales
tax increase from 7.0 to 7.5 percent and a 50 percent increase in
Medical Services premiums, ostensibly in response to escalating
health care costs. To MacPhail, those measures were further confirmation that the premier's "right-wing, supply-side experiment"
had failed badly, along with his promise that "tax cuts pay for
themselves."[86]

Campbell assumed that investors would react quickly to the
bold signal of the tax cuts. As Opposition leader, he had tirelessly
bemoaned NDP overtaxation and particularly the fact that British
Columbia had the highest personal income tax (PIT) top marginal rate in Canada. At 48.7 percent (of the prevailing federal
rate), the province did have the highest rate, but seven other provinces had rates of greater than 46.0 percent.[87] With the tax cut of
6 June 2001, British Columbia moved to 43.7 percent, higher than

Alberta at 39.0 percent but slightly lower than Saskatchewan at 44.5 percent. The Liberals could now boast (and frequently did) of having the second-lowest rate in the nation. But would it spur investment?

Tax cuts gave little indication of working through 2002. Despite higher than expected housing starts, British Columbia finished second-last among all provinces on investment, at -4.7 percent compared to Nova Scotia (12.7 percent) and Quebec (8.2 percent).[88] Notably, the latter provinces had PIT top marginal rates of 47.3 and 48.2 percent respectively, well above the new BC rate of 43.7 percent. Further, private-sector forecasters were predicting that British Columbia would be among the poorest-performing economies in 2003 before moving to the middle of the pack in 2004. In July 2003, a bleak confidential update informed cabinet "that we have no fiscal room in 2004/05 and very little in 2005/06." The update noted that "the main issue is whether North America will return to the high growth rates seen in the late 1990s."[89] In short, the fortunes of British Columbia would largely be determined by shifts in the US economy, not its own tax environment.

The Business Council of British Columbia released "A Decade by Decade Review of British Columbia's Economic Performance" on 5 November 2012. As it pointed out, British Columbia "is a very small market, representing less than 1% of total North American gross domestic product." As a consequence, "cause-and-effect assertions" – such as the claim that tax cuts pay for themselves – "can be difficult to prove." In the short term at least, the economic impact of the cuts was heavily outweighed by factors such as energy and commodity prices, the value of the Canadian dollar relative to other currencies, the strength of the US and Asian economies, interest rates, and economic conditions elsewhere in the country.

The Business Council review reported mixed results in its comparison of the 1990s and the 2000s. Average GDP growth, for example, was greater in the 1990s under the NDP than in the 2000s under the Liberals. The same held true for new investment in machinery and equipment, notwithstanding tax cuts on those items announced on 30 July 2001.[90] For a small jurisdiction such as British Columbia, the timing and magnitude of returns from tax cuts would hinge on factors other than the hopes or expectations of the premier and finance minister who authored them.

Which Came First: Core Review or the Resource-Deprived Environment?

The core review was launched in the premier's mandate letters of 25 June 2001. It was about "doing government right," but as the deficit grew, the line between core and budget target reviews became blurred. Unlike the Chrétien government's 1990s "program review," discussed in Chapter 5, the Campbell government attempted to maintain a distinction between core and budget target reviews. Though that distinction may have been clear to the premier, it was not to all members of caucus and cabinet. One minister of state described core review as a process "that the government as a whole underwent to develop our budgets."[91] The confusion was understandable, as Vaughn Palmer observed, "especially amid expectations that the whole purpose of both exercises is to prepare for budget cuts."[92]

More often than not, attempts to explain the difference between core review and the contemporaneous budget target review succeeded only in further muddling it. As Ken Dobell wrote in a letter to all deputies, core review was "not directed *specifically* toward reduction of expenditures ... However, it will provide ... an information base for a service planning model that deals with both 'doing government right' and fiscal requirements."[93] During a closed-door meeting with public servants, Dobell was more candid: "Core services [review] may or may not be sufficient to address the budget issue, in which event we will still be dealing with the question of how to balance the budget over three years."[94]

Gary Collins also took the opportunity to remind his colleagues that "core review is about DEFINING the business of government and setting priorities around what we SHOULD AND SHOULD NOT be doing. The budget target process is about WHAT WE

CAN AFFORD to do in government." His subsequent words suggested that the relationship between the processes might be subtler than his use of capitalization. The processes, he said, "have to walk hand in hand. Let's be clear. They are about different things – but as each progresses and decisions are made, we are working carefully to ensure that these processes inform one another."[95]

The finance minister's metaphorical walk had one unalterable destination: a balanced budget. Although Collins recognized that budget targets presented "significant challenges to all of us," he was abundantly clear that "it is critical that we manage within these targets in order to ultimately balance the budget by 2004/05." Ministries were obliged to fund all "costs associated with base pressures, including wage pressures, debt service and amortization costs associated with capital projects, and continued implementation of New Era commitments" in their current base budgets.[96] In a legislature where virtually every corner of the province was represented by a Liberal MLA, most cuts aroused some measure of local sensitivity. Nevertheless, meeting the budget targets was mandatory, not optional; reductions had to be found, no matter how difficult they were. Relief in one program simply meant a deeper cut in another.

Core review provided officials with an opportunity to address some of their budget pressures. "I welcomed core review," one former deputy noted, "*because* of the aggressive budget targets we had been given. We needed to challenge decision-makers about the 'appropriate role of government' then push our programs through the lens that came back."[97] Another former official believed that core review was "a chance to cull out failing programs and a rare opportunity to rethink government." This individual also found the preparation of strategic shifts within core review an "early and important opportunity to identify values and priorities of the incoming government."[98] A third respondent felt that core review was a legitimate and potentially valuable exercise: "Programs are initiated across time in response to the crisis of the day, then linger long after the crisis has passed." Given the immediate imperative of delivering budget cuts, core review provided a chance to shed "non-essential programs that had accumulated over time." Regrettably, the official added, decreases of up to 45 percent "forced ministries to not just cut to the core, but go well into the core."[99] But would the burning platform induce sufficient programmatic sacrifices to meet the government's fiscal goals?

The premier was not about to countenance any cabinet resistance or dissent around his New Era political bookends: the 25 percent tax cut and a balanced budget in February 2004. The ethic of sticking to the plan despite short-term pressures and adversity was central to the New Era and consistent with restructuring in Alberta, Ontario, and New Zealand: take the pain early and be judged on the good results that follow. If politics was uncomfortable, the plan must be working – at least with a huge majority and more than three years until the next election. As government waited for tax cuts to pay for themselves, massive savings would have to be found within ministerial budgets.

As Collins was finalizing his Economic and Fiscal Update for 30 July 2001, Campbell was advising cabinet of his expectations for ministerial service plans. Henceforth, he noted, "there will be a 20% hold-back of your Ministerial stipend pending measurable results of your Ministry and the government."[100] Recovery of the holdback was tied to completion of ministerial service plans that reflected achievement of *New Era* commitments, as well as core review and budget target goals. The first set of three-year service plans would be made public, Campbell said, along with the provincial budget on 19 February 2002. Failure to comply portended loss of income, as well as an unstated but obvious loss of the premier's confidence. The holdback aimed to ensure that ministers would meet their expenditure reduction goals. The same rule applied to the ministers of health, education, and advanced education. Despite budgets that were "protected" (in Liberal language) or "frozen" (in NDP terminology), they faced formidable challenges wedding lofty New Era goals with scarce resources.

The holdback was consistent with the experience of New Zealand and with New Public Management.[101] It joined the impressive numbers of New Era elements that came from the NPM playbook and were enshrined in the premier's mandate letters of 25 June 2001: tax cuts, deregulation, smaller government, private-sector-style management, competitive outsourcing, devolution, and public-private partnerships. Every element entailed its own processes, ensuring that there would be no idle hands in the New Era. Boldness may be imbued with genius, magic, and power, but for at least some cabinet ministers, it brought little more than endless process, perplexing dilemmas, and agonizing choices.

5

Process Makes Perfect and
the Drive to Survive

"I'm so tired, I haven't slept a wink.
I'm so tired, my mind is on the blink."
— Beatles, "I'm So Tired"

THE NEW ERA was a time of action, not of reflection. Premier Gordon Campbell set its blistering pace on day one, with his 25 percent tax cut. He followed up two weeks later with an extensive process road map, detailed in his nine-page mandate letters to new ministers, encompassing – among other components – ministerial reorganization and service plans, core review, and deregulation. Like tax cuts, New Era processes were all components in the New Public Management (NPM) prescription for an ailing economy.[1] The term "smaller government" may have vanished from the Liberal electoral lexicon in 2001, but it was still evident in Campbell's thinking.

In stark contrast to expansive *New Era* commitments, New Era processes aimed to reduce the size and scope of government. The premier then underscored the importance of those processes with an NPM-style 20 percent holdback on ministerial stipends. As noted in Chapter 4, freeing up the holdback was tied to completion of ministerial service plans reflecting achievement of *New Era* promises as well as core review and budget target goals. Best efforts were no substitute for success.

Multi-tasking was the key to success – and to survival – in the New Era. Campbell was never reluctant to flag his priorities with ministers and deputies; his mandate letters of 25 June 2001 offered a small glimpse into his wide-ranging expectations: "I want all members of Cabinet to be continuously focused on the issues that will drive our economic recovery and performance"; "I would ask you to *immediately identify* good opportunities to eliminate unnecessary and costly regulation ... Turn your immediate attention to this topic and be prepared to provide suggestions within 30 days"; "We will expect Cabinet and Caucus to devote intense energy to the Core Review"; and "I would ask that you focus attention on our New Era commitments associated with your Ministry."

As processes wound through the Agenda and Priorities Committee, Government Caucus Committees, Treasury Board, Legislative Review Committee, Open Cabinet, and cabinet itself, Campbell warned that there "will be *no* tolerance for deviations from the accepted process protocols unless they have regard to circumstances that can *truly* be described as pressing and dire emergencies."[2]

Columnist Les Leyne remarked that the letters were "a telling example of how deeply immersed he [Campbell] is in detail. They hint at how much control he'll retain, however much he talks about teamwork."[3] The premier cautioned ministers to resist "the temptation to be diverted by the agenda of others" and not to succumb to "strong pressures to take different directions [other] than those we have agreed to implement" even though "your mettle will be severely tested." When such occasions arose, he wrote, "please remember that my confirmation of your appointment as a member of my Cabinet stands as a testament to my confidence and respect for your abilities as an essential member of my team."[4] Despite the reassuring tone, an astute minister might have noticed that "Cabinet" and "team" were prefaced with "my," not "our." The premier liked to keep a tight leash on people and processes, a trait that he quickly demonstrated around core review.

Core Review Gets New Leadership Early

Campbell described core review as an "exercise in rethinking government," which was consistent with his broader goal to "remake government."[5] The purpose of core review, he declared, was "to critically examine all aspects of government and its agencies." In apparent anticipation of ministers' pride of ownership regarding programs within their portfolios, Campbell emphasized "it is very important to the success of our review process that we see these examinations as being on behalf of our government and not just within the purview of individual Ministers."[6] Ministers should entertain no doubts that core review was near and dear to the premier: "To ensure a thorough and timely review, I have appointed a Special Task Force to lead this project," and "Cabinet and Caucus will devote significant energy and resources to ensure that the review takes place within the bounds set by our fiscal framework."[7]

Initially, the core review committee was chaired by MLA Val Roddick (Delta South). She faithfully reported to cabinet on committee discussions until 22 August 2001. In what proved to be her final report, she stated that the committee had "learned" from the Ministry of Children and Family Development (MCFD) "that a high-level vision of the Ministry's purpose was necessary before individual programs were discussed." That report may have strained the premier's often finite patience, since the cabinet minutes of the following week note that "as Val Roddick will chair and be travelling extensively with the Special Standing Committee on Health, the Premier will now chair the Task Force."[8] Vaughn Palmer suggested that Roddick "had neither enough authority nor sufficient experience in the ways of government, and the process bogged down."[9] The process would not lack for authority under the premier's leadership, and the rethinking of government commenced in earnest.

Ministries were provided with an "overview" of core review on 5 July 2001. This offered a guiding vision extracted from ten elements in the *New Era* document and "stated government principles" from the premier's mandate letters of 25 June 2001. The bar was set very high for program retention. If a given program met the *New Era* vision and the premier's stated principles and priorities, did it fulfill "a compelling public policy objective?" If it did, was it a "critically necessary program? What would happen if the program was eliminated? Suspended for five years?"

If elimination was not possible, were there "other methods of service provision?" The overview offered a "spectrum of service provision options" from devolution to co-sourcing, outsourcing, franchising, and privatization. And if an agency, board, or commission could not be eliminated, could its scope, membership, or meeting frequency be reduced?[10]

The premier offered further detailed advice on core review in a letter of 31 July 2001. He laid out the framework for assessment, including tests of public interest, affordability, effectiveness and role of government, efficiency, and accountability. The tests again set a very high bar for retention. The "public interest test" required demonstration that the agency, board, or commission (ABC) served "a compelling public policy purpose." The "effectiveness and role of government" test required ministries to show "that there are absolutely no alternatives to the current structure." Further, under the "affordability" test, the activity of the ABC "must be affordable within the current fiscal environment."[11] If the public interest, effectiveness, and affordability tests were met, ministries must pass the efficiency test – proving that the ABC was the most efficient way to manage and deliver the activity.

As Table 6 suggests, the core review "doing government right" process appeared to be modelled closely on the federal Liberal

TABLE 6
Comparative federal program review and BC core review questions

Canada program review	Is the program still in the public interest?	Is it affordable, given fiscal constraints?	How can it be redesigned for efficiency?	Is this program a legitimate and necessary role for government?
British Columbia core review	Does the program continue to serve a compelling public interest?	Is it affordable within the current fiscal environment?	Is the current model the most efficient way to manage and deliver the activity?	Is this program a legitimate role for the province?

Sources: Massé, "Getting Government Right"; "Appendix 2: Core Review Questions," in Office of the Premier, "Overview of Streamlining."

government's "getting government right" program review of 1994–97, although no attribution was offered.

Some differences of approach also existed. As detailed in Chapter 4, the Campbell government attempted without great success to keep core and budget target reviews separate, at least in concept. Conversely, the federal program review explicitly incorporated a simultaneous evaluation of programs *and* budgets. Unlike the Campbell government, the Jean Chrétien administration made no pretense that the review was not about the money.[12]

The Chrétien Government's Program Review, 1994–97

The Chrétien Liberal government was elected on 4 November 1993, but program review had its roots in the Brian Mulroney and Kim Campbell Progressive Conservative administrations that preceded it. The Mulroney review borrowed from earlier Australian models. A ministerial task force led by Mulroney's secretary of state, Robert de Cotret, "concluded that the structure of the Canadian government had to change, and set out a plan to reorganize the federal government on a portfolio basis." As a consequence, the number of ministers and departments dropped "from 32 to 23, with ministerial portfolios encompassing broader policy domains, where coordination and trade-offs could be made."

When they came to power, the Chrétien Liberals "took most of the de Cotret plans and made them their own."[13] Budget targets ranged from 17 to 40 percent cuts, with the exception of Indigenous programs, exempted on Chrétien's initiative. Evert Lindquist suggests that the "changes were difficult; they were departures from previous ineffectual across-the-board interventions. A key ingredient was that the government staked its reputation on securing results out of the process; this was not just a bureaucratic exercise or external commission."[14]

The Chrétien Liberals, Donald Savoie notes, "had become quite concerned about Canada 'hitting the wall,' as New Zealand had done." Program review engaged two streams, one of senior ministers, including Finance Minister Paul Martin, the other of top-ranked public servants from the Privy Council Office, Finance, and Treasury Board. The Liberal *Red Book* campaign platform had committed to limiting the federal deficit to 3 percent of GDP, and Chrétien left "no doubt whatsoever that he was four square behind Martin" and the deficit reduction imperative.

Not surprisingly, the program review encountered ministerial resistance at multiple points. However, it succeeded through a combination of resolute support from Chrétien and, just as importantly, propitious timing. The latter included "the Mexican currency crisis and the jump in interest rates in December 1994–January 1995 [that] shot the review into crisis management mode."[15] According to Savoie, the review ultimately produced $29 billion in cuts, including the elimination of forty-five thousand public service and military positions.

Notably, the Chrétien review was undertaken at a time when the government was widely and severely criticized for its failure to repeal the "hated" Goods and Services Tax, as promised in its 1993 election platform. Would the review have been "a political success" had the government's focus been fragmented by GST and other reforms?[16] Unlike the Campbell government's core and budget target reviews, the federal review did not attempt to combine administrative reorganization, service delivery reform, and steep budget reductions in a broad remaking of government. Like the Ministry of Health Planning's regionalization mission (discussed in Chapter 3), the federal review was not shackled by tax-cut-driven budget reductions and competing process imperatives. In short, it did not attempt to do everything at the same time, and its focused character appeared central to its political success.

Core Review: Early Results and the Rise of the External Panel

On 31 July 2001, Premier Campbell advised his ministers that core review extended to "all of your ministry's programs, activities, business units, Agencies, Boards and Commissions [ABCs]." Ministerial review and identification of "service delivery alternatives will be completed this fall." On a more sympathetic note, he added, "I know this will not be easy. However, the wishful thinking of the status quo must be replaced by critical analysis, an orientation to results, and measurable accountability." The Core Review and Deregulation Task Force was created, he said, to "ensure that this project takes a high priority within our government."[17]

Additional reinforcement was supplied by a PowerPoint presentation entitled "Core Services Review: Themes and Issues," which clarified the thematic direction. Among the "emerging" themes were "Think Boldly" and "Greatly reduced direct delivery: local delivery, outsourcing, shared services, and private sector sponsorship." Bullet points under the heading of "Issues, Questions, Things Missing" re-emphasized those themes: "Think Bold, Think Small, Think Focussed," "Regional Delivery Models – a Panacea," and "Self-supporting = user fees."[18] The presentation was a distillation of recurrent NPM elements, whose purpose was to inspire the drive toward smaller government.

By the Premier's Office count, 730 independent agencies, boards, and commissions were operating as of 5 June 2001. Of these, some were either adjudicative bodies (such as boards of variance) or boards of independent not-for-profit agencies to which the province made appointments. In these cases, "elimination" was simply a matter of leaving the appointments to local authorities and organizations. In the case of the 191 boards of variance, the task force recommended to cabinet that the Ministry of Community, Aboriginal and Women's Services (MCAWS) "discontinue provincial appointees and delegate all appointments to municipalities."[19] A similar resolution was found for university senate and foundations boards (17) and continuing care facility boards (47). Had the original 730 ABCs suddenly, and seemingly painlessly, been reduced by 243, or 33 percent? No. For the purposes of core review, the 191 boards of variance were treated as one entity of the 33 within MCAWS. The balance of the process proved much more challenging.

A few weeks after the core review announcement, ministries began reporting in with what they thought the premier was demanding. Portions of ministerial presentations that won early approval, such as "strategic shifts," were relayed through Open Cabinet. The process ground on through the winter but obviously did not meet Campbell's expectations, as he indicated in a letter of 17 May 2002: "Some Ministries completed a core services review of their ABCs, but many did not, and a majority of those Ministries that did complete reviews came back with a recommendation for the status quo."[20] His message was explicit: far too many ministers and deputies had failed to capture the spirit of smaller government the first time around; consequently, "all of the remaining 124 ABCs should be eliminated unless it can be clearly shown that the entity passes all of the Core Services tests."

The premier's letter was intended to catch the attention of even the most tone-deaf ministers and deputies: "The measure of success in this endeavour is to eliminate all ABCs which do not clearly and compellingly meet the criteria outlined above, as well as to ensure there are no duplications of authority and effort. It is my hope that Ministries will be extremely creative and diligent in completion of this task." The status quo was neither bold nor creative: "It has therefore been determined that a more rigorous process will be required to finalize the Ministries' ABC reviews in a comprehensive and timely fashion."[21]

The new and "more rigorous" process made removing ABCs the easiest as well as the preferred course. An elimination recommendation required "only a brief document ... not longer than one page," whereas a "non-elimination" recommendation necessitated three pages of supporting paperwork, including "rationale on each of the core review tests" and "reference to relevant New Era Commitments." A retention recommendation also required sign-off by both minister and deputy, hence establishing joint accountability before not only the core services task force but also a new adjudicative entity, the External Panel.

The panel consisted of "individuals with senior business experience, high level financial and/or board governance experience, senior level experience in restructuring organizations, and strong analytical skills." The premier's letter again offered a blunt warning to the recalcitrant or the insufficiently cowed: "The Panel has been instructed to apply an extremely critical eye to status quo or scope adjustment recommendations."[22]

Much of the debate before the External Panel centred on the fate of ten ABCs. Nine of them resided in MCAWS, and one, the Law Courts Education Society of BC, was in the Ministry of the Attorney General. MCAWS argued that some of its ABCs (such as the Advisory Council on Multiculturalism and the First Peoples' Heritage, Language and Culture Council) were vital to the fulfillment of *New Era* commitments. In other cases (such as the Provincial Child Care Council and the Building Safety Advisory Council), MCAWS was in the midst of strategic reviews that would be disrupted or derailed by elimination. Further, it asserted that decreases in budget and staffing had "significantly reduced the ministry's capacity to deal with current and emerging regulatory and policy issues," particularly given concurrent demands for regulatory reductions.[23] Members of the Building Safety Advisory Council's five committees provided "their expertise free of charge," whereas consultants would cost $125 per hour (at an estimated $300,000 per annum), no small consideration for a ministry in straitened circumstances.[24] None of those arguments persuaded the panel.

As a result of the External Panel's deliberations, cabinet was asked to approve the elimination of seventy-four ABCs (including the ten in dispute) and the retention of fifty-three others. The ten disputed cases were subsequently placed in a "yellow" category to "be directed to the relevant Government Caucus Committee for review and recommendation," then on to cabinet for the final decision.[25] After one turbulent year into the New Era, MLAs on the Government Caucus Committees were not, by and large, looking for more reasons to be beaten up by their constituents and chose to support the ministers. Cabinet's final decision in September 2002 called for the retention of all ten contested ABCs, a small victory for the status quo amid the wholesale remaking of government.[26]

Reducing the Regulatory Checklist by One-Third?

Like many other New Era processes, deregulation was firmly rooted in NPM. It found early expression as a *New Era* commitment, specifically to reduce the regulatory burden by one-third in three years. The initiative came complete with a minister of state for deregulation (Kevin Falcon), a Regulatory Reform Office, and a Red Tape Reduction Task Force. Ministries were asked to provide Falcon with "30-day" ideas and three-year proposals. The former identified regulations "that could be eliminated without raising significant policy issues," whereas the latter pinpointed those that "require further analysis or consultation." The second group would be included in three-year deregulation plans that were due on 31 January 2002.[27] In the interim, any new legislation, regulation, or legislative amendment was obliged to demonstrate compatibility with the "Regulatory Criteria Checklist," which consisted of "ten criteria including competitiveness, cost-benefit, timeliness, plain language."[28]

As a first step, ministers were to "count all requirements in the statutes, regulations and interpretive or administrative policy under their areas of responsibility" by 1 October 2001. Early counts prompted heated debate over how to calculate what constituted a regulation: "Is subsection 3 (f) one reg or .5 of a reg? Is the handbook one reg or 468?"[29] Further, all regulations were not created equal. For example, the goal of securing a one-third reduction in regulations pertaining to the construction/housing industry, without compromising safety, proved very complex. For MCAWS, home of the Safety Engineering Services Branch, the challenge was multi-dimensional, engaging safety standards, economic considerations, competition, the intersection with local and federal regulations, insurance coverage and cost, and liability. Dozens of industry organizations, municipalities, and regulators rightly expected to be consulted.[30]

There were more than a few pointed reminders that deregulation was a Campbell priority, not just a Falcon priority. Campbell's mandate letters, as noted above, asked ministers "to *immediately identify* good opportunities to eliminate unnecessary and costly regulation."[31] Twenty months later, his deregulatory passion had not cooled: "We are now just six weeks away from year end, I would ask you to consider how you will meet our deregulation target in your ministry, so that the Honourable Kevin Falcon is able to achieve his goal of a 12% reduction of regulatory burden across government by March 31, 2003."[32]

To satisfy this demand, ministries unleashed an intensive search for regulations that had long been inoperative, ignored, or forgotten. Some of the early candidates for repeal included the Drainage, Ditch and Dike Act of 1907 and the University Endowment Land Park Act, both long "spent" or "obsolete." The Ministry of Water, Land and Air Protection delighted pundits by unearthing the Weather Modification Act, which was decades into desuetude.[33] And MCAWS must have prompted cross-government envy when it axed the *Heritage Orientation Handbook,* banishing four thousand regulations with a single stroke of the pen.[34]

One official saw deregulation as an example of "management by slogans," in this case "what gets measured gets managed." He complained that the ministerial "policy shop was consumed with going through statutes going back a hundred years to find outmoded regs to shed" while critical policy challenges waited for attention. Further, the relentless demand to "hit the number" forced the ministry "to take away regs that still made sense in meeting government demands for policy solutions to emerging problems."[35] Another respondent suggested that demands to "just get to the number" translated to "counting regs instead of doing meaningful deregulation."[36] A third official stated, "at a time when the burning platform was forcing critical decisions without policy analysis, ministries were consumed with finding and eliminating outdated regulations."[37] Deregulation was deployed within an intense New Era change environment replete with contemporaneous processes such as core and budget target reviews. In a government that had so many irons in the fire, as prescribed in the premier's mandate letters, priorities were sometimes lost in the fog.

The Regulatory Reform Office did not underestimate the challenge ahead: the "move toward regulations that are innovative, results-based and improve competitiveness requires a culture shift and capacity building within the BC public service."[38] Despite this challenge, Gary Collins could proudly report in his 2003 Budget Speech, "we've eliminated 233 agencies, boards and commissions; over 1,000 unnecessary fees and licences; and almost 38,000 needless regulations."[39] And the battle had only begun!

One year later, Kevin Falcon reported that the deregulation initiative had actually exceeded its target by eliminating 143,000 regulations, a net reduction of 37 percent. He offered more news: a 0 percent increase in regulatory requirements over the next three years. In short, any ministry that wished to introduce legislation requiring regulations would have to find a corresponding number of regulations to discard elsewhere. If a brilliant new idea were to advance, an existing but deficient or ineffectual measure would have to be expunged (no small feat, given that most of these had already been extirpated). The government quickly offered up a compelling candidate for extirpation: the Waste Buster website was a vaunted *New Era* commitment that proved a complete bust in the course of its short life.

The Waste Buster Website: A Bust and a Waste

New Era promised (twice) to "establish a 'Waste Buster' website for taxpayers to help identify, report and stamp out government waste."[40] Waste was a major theme in the document, under provocative headlines such as "Where Has Your Money Gone?" and "It's Your Money That's Been Wasted." *New Era* provided a compendium of over $2 billion in purported "NDP waste and mismanagement," highlighted by the "fast ferries fiasco." Like claims of high taxes and over-regulation, this narrative was constructed "to lead an audience ineluctably to a course of action" where "labels of policy discourse" are strategically employed to "evoke different stories and prescriptions."[41] In *New Era* language, NDP waste and mismanagement were the maladies afflicting the province, thereby setting the stage for the NPM prescription of tax cuts and (via core review) smaller, more efficient government.

As the narrative suggested, this prescription would work at two levels: elimination of the NDP's profligate spending would remove the need for unsustainable levels of taxation; in turn, the reduced taxation would grow the economy and generate higher revenues, thereby averting risk to public services. The storyline, alas, worked far better in theory than in practice. Most examples of NDP waste involved past capital rather than current operational expenditures, so targeting them did little to offset the immediate budgetary hole created by tax cuts.

The Campbell government clearly harboured unrealistic expectations that the Waste Buster website and related measures would produce budgetary savings. In his Economic and Fiscal Update of 30 July 2001, Collins reiterated the theme: "We are implementing an all-out attack on red tape, business subsidies and waste. Thanks to our new waste-buster website, we'll have four million sets of eyes looking for and reporting on government waste across the province."[42] Despite hopes that the website would be a "populist triumph," it was not a boon to taxpayers.[43] Among early suggestions posted on the site were "create one central government library," "eliminate school boards," "amalgamate private mobile radio systems across government," and "eliminate open cabinet meetings."[44] Four million sets of eyes may have been watching, but the volume of suggestions quickly declined, and the site was quietly dismantled two years after its creation.

The Business Subsidies Review Unearths Little Gold

The business subsidies review commenced with a Ministry of Competition, Science and Enterprise (MCSE) Open Cabinet presentation on 15 August 2001 and ended with another on 24 July 2002. The premier kicked off the review by advising cabinet that there "will be no further loans issued under the Industrial Development Incentive Act," a program dating back to the Bill Bennett government in 1985.[45] The review was contemplated by a *New Era* commitment (twice repeated) to "eliminate government subsidies to business that give some companies an unfair advantage over competitors."[46] The document offered substantial expectations for savings based on claims of NDP waste, including "$1 billion in business subsidies," "$340 million for the Skeena Cellulose bailout," and "$463 million wasted on the 'fast' ferries."[47] According to MCSE minister Rick Thorpe, "getting rid of business subsidies sends a clear signal to all investors that British Columbia is open for business."[48] As a signal to investors, review results proved muted at best.

Twenty-three programs were recommended for termination. Of these, three involved hiring incentives for students or welfare recipients, four targeted fisheries enhancement, and several supported green energy and technology research and development. The search for corporate welfare bums produced scant results: modest subsidies from the Ministry of Transportation for operation of the Shuswap Lake ferry service and road maintenance for the Mt. Timothy ski hill were terminated, along with prospectors' assistance grants. Hardly the prototypical free-riding bloated capitalists one envisaged!

The business subsidies review – even in combination with the Waste Buster website and the deregulation initiative – may have helped complete the *New Era* narrative but did little to fill the $2 billion hole created directly by the tax cuts. Curiously, or perhaps ironically, by 2005 the government was extolling its multi-million-dollar investments in (among others) Fuel Cells Canada, an oil and gas training centre, and a Selkirk College aviation program – none of which would have survived either the business subsidies or core reviews.

Devolution: If You Love Something, Set It Free

Devolution was an important element in the remaking of government. As suggested by the Osborne and Gaebler mantra, ministries should "steer not row." In other words, they would retain policy levers but would put responsibility for day-to-day service delivery into the hands of special agencies that were financially and operationally free from government.[49] British Columbia was far from a pioneer in the devolution process. The Next Steps program in the United Kingdom, launched in 1988, led to the creation of more than 140 specialized executive agencies.[50] In 1995, Sandford Borins noted that the British government, "following Sweden, has concluded that over 60 percent of its activities can be given over to executive agencies while a much more hesitant Canadian federal government has given over to special operating agencies less than 5 percent of its activities."[51]

Specialization through devolution, as Peter Aucoin suggests, "has been a corrective to the tendency, especially in Canadian government, to force integrated departmental structures onto distinct, if related, organizations that fall within a minister's portfolio, which, in many instances, would have been better structured as separate organizations but managed within a portfolio framework."[52] To Aucoin's point, the Safety Engineering Services Branch was a distinct, if related, organization within MCAWS. As such, it faced budget and workforce cuts, as well as the reality of doing less with less, a poor prescription for safety in the built environment.

In their drive to separate policy from operational responsibilities, as Aucoin notes, "either enthusiastically as the means to greater performance or simply as a means to greater economy in a context of budget restraint, governments have pushed many services and operations out from under the management of departmental public servants to government agencies of various kinds, some more independent than others."[53] As with many initiatives in the New Era, MCAWS drew on exogenous experience. Both Alberta and Ontario had created special-purpose, not-for-profit safety authorities in the 1990s, which provided practical examples for emulation by British Columbia.[54] After extensive consultations with industry, business, labour, institutions, and associations, the Safety Authority Act of spring 2003 set the stage for a comparable entity, the BC Safety Authority.

In the New Era, devolution was largely driven by budget imperatives, but most shifts proved successful. As Aucoin argues, "the separation of policy and operational responsibilities does not have to result in organizational designs that conflict with the principles of good public management."[55] For the BC Safety Authority, devolution provided an exceptional opportunity to embrace good public management; it brought liberation from arbitrary budget and workforce cuts, and from political determination of fees.[56] The Land Titles Branch in the Ministry of Sustainable Resource Management faced a similar situation, including the closure of multiple offices and rapidly growing delays in completion of property transfers, making it another strong candidate for devolution.[57] In 2004, it became a special operating authority as the Land Title and Survey Authority.

The BC Safety Authority and the Land Title and Survey Authority have thrived as special operating agencies after struggling as ministerial functions, particularly given post-2001 resource constraints. BC Ferries followed a comparable (and largely successful) model, but because of its public reach and impact, it remains of policy interest to governments of all stripes. Conversely, the product of the Ministry of Children and Family Development's (MCFD) devolutionary efforts, Community Living BC, continues to struggle due, at least in some measure, to the difficulties of its birth (discussed in Chapter 8). Devolution has proven most challenging when the devolved organization lacks the opportunity to build sustaining funding outside of government.

Devolution, where it was possible, was perhaps the least painful way to achieve budget-driven workforce reductions. For example, MCAWS had to diminish its employees from about 1,200 to 532 FTEs (full-time equivalents). The devolution of the Safety Engineering Services Branch saw "about 210" staff move to the BC Safety Authority.[58] The transition of the Royal BC Museum (including BC Archives) from ministerial function to Crown corporation resulted in a further staff transfer of 133 away from MCAWS.[59] Sadly, devolutionary initiatives could only very marginally affect the number of layoffs demanded in the "workforce adjustment" process.

Black Thursday Signals Workforce Adjustment

On 17 January 2002, Premier Campbell officially announced the reduction of as many as 11,700 public service employees, one-third of the entire civil service. The announcement, subsequently labelled Black Thursday, was not foreshadowed by the cheery contents of *New Era* nor by Campbell's pre-election comments. "We're not planning massive layoffs in the civil service," he said. On election eve, his deputy leader, Christy Clark, was even more positive: "What you'll see is probably the same number of employees just doing a heck of lot more productive things."[60]

The Campbell narrative on public service layoffs shifted as the reality of a $4.4 billion deficit began to hit home and was reflected in a speech of 27 September 2001. In it, "Mr. Lean-and-Mean" (columnist Michael Smyth's depiction of Campbell) revived his recurrent theme of doing more with less in an anecdote that raised more than a few eyebrows: "I had one public-service deputy minister come to me and say, 'Currently we are providing a service with 280 people. I believe we can provide an equivalent or better service with 70.'"[61]

On 21 November, Campbell suggested that as many as one-third of government jobs could face elimination. Asked why *New Era* made "not the slightest mention" of service cuts, Campbell replied: "Well, because we didn't believe we were going to have massive cuts."[62] His response employed a hearty measure of calculated ambivalence. He may not have expected major job cuts, but core review was clearly designed to downsize government by shedding programs, expenditures, and employees. If layoffs were massive rather than of lesser impact, the difference lay in the magnitude of tax cuts that failed to pay for themselves in a timely way.

Campbell's mandate letters of 25 June 2001 offered well-articulated goals for smaller government via core review, regardless of how well his tax cut measures worked. Workforce adjustment was not a spontaneous budget-shedding exercise; it was part of the wholehearted subscription to New Public Management strategies, as succinctly laid out by Ken Dobell in 2002: "Many services previously delivered within government will now be delivered by the private sector through contract arrangements and public-private partnerships. We need different skill sets: contract management skills, creation and enforcement of outcome-based regulations, even downsizing skills."[63]

In the cold light of Black Thursday, Campbell described the job cuts as "thoughtful and innovative" and "the right thing to do."[64] Vince Collins, deputy minister at the Public Service Employee Relations Commission, had seen four waves of downsizing during his thirty years in government but declared that "the magnitude of this one [2002] is larger than any one previously."[65] The huge scale of workforce adjustment prompted widespread anger and disbelief. "The self-inflicted deficit," Vaughn Palmer wrote, "has forced the Liberals into spending cuts and staff reductions beyond anything attempted previously in this province."[66] Thirteen human resource companies were contracted to provide grief counselling to laid-off employees, some of whom, in the finance minister's words, would "not deal with the news well."[67] Not all public servants may have immediately grasped how their termination was a "thoughtful and innovative" step toward the goal of smaller government.

Workforce adjustment was an issue in small-town British Columbia, as well as in Victoria and the Lower Mainland. Ministry documents detailing dozens of office closures were laden with repetitive phrases such as "office to close," "service with a 1-800 number," "small office maintained but no public access," "services by appointment only," and "functions move to regional centre." With consolidation in larger towns such as Kamloops and Kelowna, apprehension was high in smaller communities. As one service provider noted, "we currently have 2.5 social workers assisting people in Salmon Arm ... Our question is, when there is a crisis, or when a placement breaks down who will assist the people?"[68]

Resource ministries such as Agriculture and Forests were among the hardest hit in both staff reductions and community office closures. For instance, staff at Forests dropped from 4,183 in 2001–02 to 2,628 in 2004–05.[69] Job cuts came through a combination of not filling vacancies, early retirements, eliminating auxiliary workers, "buy-outs," and other "voluntary" departures. Eleven of forty-two Forest District offices were converted from full-service operations to minimally staffed field offices. Additionally, three regional offices were closed.[70] Among the worst-hit positions were compliance and enforcement staff. "Professional reliance" and industry self-regulation were not only political choices, but were also imperatives driven by budget and workforce reductions. The pattern was replicated across resource ministries.

The justice system was not spared. To meet budget targets, the attorney general was obliged to close twenty-four fully staffed courthouses even where closures were not justified by their use rates, such as Burnaby (126 percent of capacity), Maple Ridge (138 percent), and Squamish (106 percent).[71] On the other side of the system, the Corrections Branch in the Ministry of the Solicitor General faced a 30.5 percent cut at a time when all twenty correctional centres had full occupancy. The primary remedy was consolidation of twenty centres into nine, the layoff of 500 of 1,800 staff, and unprecedented double bunking in the consolidated facilities.[72] The ministry was fortunate to be operating in a target-rich environment, where far more public sympathy accrued to patients and children than to inmates.

One former deputy recounted the staff reduction challenge: "Budget cuts were huge and couldn't be done by trimming at the edges. Whole programs were wiped out with very little forethought, other than the urgent need to meet targets, or else." The demise of a program and subsequent layoff notices meant that a "person from the cut program would bump someone else. That person would bump someone else and so on. The process dragged on for months ... In the meantime, the programs that weren't being cut had New Era commitments to meet, and were expected to do more than before with less resources than before." That difficulty was exacerbated by bumping provisions, as "people who had never done a job were expected to do it faster and better than the person they had bumped, plus take on new priorities."[73]

Another former official flagged a "fundamental flaw" in the voluntary departure program: often, those who were most inclined to take a government buyout were also most able to quickly secure employment in the private sector. As a consequence, the official noted, "government often lost their best and brightest at a time when their skills were needed most." In more than a few cases, government needed to reacquire those skills through consulting contracts.[74]

Office closures and employee layoffs made Liberal MLA constituency meetings invariably unpleasant or downright miserable in 2002. Chris Tenove describes a town hall meeting held by MLA Dave Chutter (Yale—Lillooet): "Nearly 400 people had come to vent their confusion, frustration and anger ... More than 50 public service jobs would be cut. The local office of the Ministry of Forests would be closed, along with the courthouse, the Legal Aid Office, an elementary school, and the Human Resources office." Decisions on the fate of the hospital were pending.

The local newspaper described the sudden loss of fifty jobs in Lillooet as "like axing 43,750 of the best-paid and best-educated people in the Lower Mainland, or 5,230 in Victoria."[75] The experience of hard-hit communities such as Lillooet provided a jarring reminder that, as Evert Lindquist warns, "behind the rhetoric and themes of the new public sector management is the reality of fiscal restraint and dramatic restructuring of public services."[76] Workforce adjustment frequently entailed community adjustment.

Cumulative Impacts Prompt a Social Policy Review

As social ministries struggled to cope with severe budget cuts, they were also cognizant of risks inherent in fundamental restructuring: that service reductions in one ministry might lead to caseload pressures in another. The minister of state for women's equality told the legislature,

> One of the things we did [in preparing budgets] was look at an overview of all the ministries and whether there would be groups that may be disadvantaged or disproportionately affected by the decisions government made. When we did this, it was clear that women and children were going to be bearing the brunt of a lot of these decisions.[77]

MCFD, MCAWS, and the Ministry of Human Resources (MHR) met regularly to deal with overlaps, issues, and concerns. For example, when MHR advised that it was discontinuing the "children in the home of a relative" program, MCFD was rightly concerned that such a cut would have "a dramatic impact" on it. MCFD Minister Gordon Hogg explained how the situation was resolved: "After pointing that out and working out some strategies with them, they were able to keep that program intact. We have to keep being aware of the issues as they occur."[78] Unfortunately, no amount of collaboration could mask the broad challenges produced by deep budget cuts.

The diminution of social programs through the combination of budget cuts and core review provoked consternation among the media and social service providers. The severity of cuts also perplexed and dismayed some backbench Liberal members. A proposal from MCAWS to remove tens of millions from its $560 million budget prompted intense debate in a Government Caucus Committee between "MLAs with a larger social conscience against those whose prime objective is smaller government – the Liberal Liberals versus the Alliance Liberals, as one insider put it."[79] In one memorable exchange, a distressed MLA asked the MCAWS minister: "So what happened to the two billion dollars in waste and duplication from the *New Era* document?" No satisfactory answer could be provided.[80]

Social ministries – along with the premier and his deputy, Ken Dobell – met in Victoria on 15 July 2002 to assess cumulative impacts and the potential for a co-ordinated response. A background paper entitled "Towards a Coherent Social Policy Strategy for British Columbia" was circulated prior to the meeting. It attempted to strike a balance between the relentless retrenchment of the New Era and the ongoing service challenges faced by social ministries. "As a result of the current fiscal situation," it noted, "government policy development is constrained by budget limitations. When a ministry amends its policy (often in isolation) to restrict eligibility for potential clients to meet financial limitations, the result can have a negative impact on client groups that are also served by other ministries." A "coherent" strategy, it suggested, would enable a "shift towards self-reliance ... and reduce long term dependency on government" while recognizing that some challenges could exceed "family and community capacity" and may require government intervention.[81]

Some ministerial officials framed the situation differently. Asked to identify the cumulative sources of gaps in violence-against-women programming, some MCAWS officials revealed an impatience with the core review canon:

As of 2004/05, resulting from core review, MCAWS will no longer fund Women's Centres, which provide referral and support for women victims of violence ...

– As of 2003/04, resulting from core review, MCAWS will no longer fund the Bridges Employment Training Program, a program for women on Income Assistance who have experienced violence that prepares women for entering the workforce ...

– As of 2002/03, resulting from core review, MCAWS will no longer provide funding for core training of Transition House workers, and counsellors in Stopping the Violence and Children Who Witness Abuse programs.

They argued that gaps were exacerbated by the loss of funding for Indigenous family violence initiatives, the reductions to victim services, courthouse closures, cuts to legal aid, decreased MHR supports to women fleeing abusive relationships, and diminished access to safe and affordable social housing, thereby prompting a return to abusive relationships.[82]

Similarly, in connection with a new requirement that parents must seek employment when their children reached age three, MHR noted that it "may result in poor outcomes for young children. Research from other jurisdictions shows increased incidence of abuse and neglect with similar policies." Further, income assistance clients with young children could potentially lose supports under "two-years-in-five" time limits.[83]

Ministries offered up thirty pages of concerns, such as elimination of at-cost hearing aids for children and seniors, reduction of dental care for children of income assistance recipients, new user fees for geriatric residential care at Riverview Hospital, elimination of funding to the Regional Aboriginal Health Council and the Aboriginal Health Association (both of which offered early intervention on family violence), and MHR policy changes that affected clients aged sixty to sixty-four, including time limits and reduced support rates. The thirty pages were a compendium of cuts that ministries found grievous or objectionable but that budget targets nevertheless obliged them to undertake.

Typically, proposals to mitigate social impacts were greeted with a splash of cold fiscal water. Gary Collins pointed out that "ministries are expected to identify any risks to their budgets and develop mitigation plans to ensure that their budgets and the government's bottom line are not compromised. Any policy proposals with financial implications must be reviewed by Treasury Board prior to proceeding to [Government Caucus Committees]." Any new initiatives would have to be funded internally by "reprioritized spending."[84] As one official noted, "in a social ministry, every dollar has somebody's name on it; reprioritizing spending is redistributing heartburn."[85]

The social ministries raised real-world issues that could not be resolved without supplemental funding from broader government. But government simply responded with suggestions of how to do more with less, typically invoking New Public Management staples such as "streamlined service delivery" or "enhanced strategic planning and management." Unfortunately, even the best management advice was not an effective substitute for the massive loss of fiscal resources.

The Drive to Survive: Points of Resistance in the New Era

Only eight months into the New Era, the senior public service was worn down by the unending stream of core review, budget target review, deregulation, service plans, *New Era* commitments, ministerial reorganization, budget cuts, staff reductions, service delivery reform, and the ninety-day agenda. In January 2002, the draft 270-day plan was unveiled. This amalgam of ministerial initiatives, generated at the premier's request to meet *New Era* and other commitments, was greeted with scant enthusiasm. As noted in Chapter 3, the Deputy Ministers' Council warned that "there are far too many initiatives going on and the system will not be able to sustain the workload ('system will implode')."[86]

Senior officials in the Premier's Office appeared to understand and sympathize with comments such as "too much on the front burner to do it all, much less do it well" and "we need to pace for 2002."[87] The "assumptions" that prefaced the draft 270-day work plan also conveyed some understanding of the pressures facing ministries: "Virtually all Ministries will be undergoing restructuring and downsizing as an outcome of the Core Services Review initiative and the Treasury Board process; for many Ministries this will require a great deal of time spent planning and implementing in this 270 day period."[88]

None of that sympathy and understanding resulted in an easing of the process and product workload. For example, the 270-day plan encompassed the following priorities for MCFD:

- develop plan for greater local service delivery
- deregulation: *Child, Family and Community Service Act*
- implement deregulation plans
- build service delivery capacity in Aboriginal communities/ review opportunities for federal funding

- redesign funding model
- child prostitution (new legislation, *Safe Care Act*)
- streamline youth correctional facilities, amend *Corrections Act*
- review and amend *Adoption Act*
- long term autism strategy
- develop and implement plan to improve child and youth mental health services.[89]

These priorities would be extraordinarily daunting even with a full and stable staffing complement and even if core review, deregulation, regionalization, and devolution were not also underway. Remaking the world required attention to many moving parts, as demonstrated in the case studies offered in Chapters 6, 7, and 8.

The Heartlands Strategy and the Coquihalla Highway

The Campbell government ranks, particularly the rural and Interior MLAs, were feeling bruised and beaten by the unrelenting bad news through 2002, prompting the premier to deliver a televised "state of the province address" on 12 February 2003. The address was multi-purpose. First, it reminded viewers of the positives, claiming that tax cuts, new jobs, and a drop of fifty-five thousand in people on premium assistance put "almost a billion dollars in the pockets of British Columbians." It also attempted to give government a more human face by converting some pain to gain, notably by bumping up the income exemption (on employment earnings) for people with disabilities. "We have made progress," Campbell said, after "some pretty difficult decisions. We understand that. And some of them have been pretty tough on you and your communities." Now was the time for reinvestment in those communities (christened the "Hurtlands" by some cynics) through the Heartlands Economic Strategy.

Headlining the strategy was $609 million for rural, remote, and resource roads, which would be funded by a 3.5 cents per litre addition to the gas tax. "I want you to know this," Campbell added. "Every single cent will be spent on transportation improvements."[90] The new tax triggered short-term protests, but it raised revenues to bankroll a continuous flurry of good-news construction announcements across the province. It also indirectly supported the government's retreat on its controversial attempt to institute tolls on inland ferries, a particularly unpopular initiative in areas where dams and flooded valleys had created the need for ferries.

Campbell used the transportation theme in attempting to reframe the *New Era* commitment not to "sell or privatize BC Rail."[91] In the opening salvo of what became another long and painful saga, he declared, "some people have suggested we should sell BC Rail. We simply won't do that."[92] However, he left the door open to "innovative solutions," including, as was subsequently approved, a 999-year lease of the railbed to the Canadian National Railway. As cabinet considered future direction for BC Rail in the spring of 2003, the government's leading privatization initiative – sale of the Coquihalla toll concession to a private operator – was quickly falling apart.

Much like the governments of David Lange in New Zealand and Margaret Thatcher in Great Britain, and consistent with BC Social Credit's contracting out of highways maintenance in the 1980s, the Campbell government laid considerable emphasis on competitive tendering and privatization, ostensibly with the goals of smaller government and better value for taxpayers (all core staples of NPM). Among many other functions, the maintenance of parks, recreation, and heritage sites, and the catering and cleaning of hospitals, were offered up for competitive tenders.[93] Partnerships BC was created as the instrument of public-private partnership in the construction of major infrastructure such as hospitals, bridges, and highways.

The Campbell government's flagship for privatization was sale of the toll concession on the Coquihalla highway. Two years into the New Era, tensions were running high in portions of the southern Interior adjacent to the Coquihalla. Sale of the concession was neither a *New Era* platform nor a campaign commitment, and as the process moved forward and became public knowledge, regional opposition took hold and grew. Initially, it was strongest in Kamloops, but it soon became intense, visceral, and emotional throughout much of the southern Interior. Residents contended that they had already paid for the Coquihalla through tolls and suspected that they would pay even more to a private operator.

Growing grassroots opposition to "privatizing the Coq" was reflected in the proliferation of "The Coquihalla is *not* for sale" signs in shop windows, places where BC Liberal MLAs might normally expect to find support. Those same MLAs enjoyed strong attendance at their constituency annual general meetings, but as one noted, "virtually every question revolved around the Coquihalla ... Sentiment is strong enough that several current or prospective Executive members refused to stand for the new Executive. A number of those who did stand told me they did so to support me, notwithstanding their anger."[94] That reaction was common in at least a dozen constituencies.

In a confidential note to the premier, one southern Interior MLA argued that the Coquihalla debate had "become a lightning rod for a range of regional discontents," from hospital, school, and forestry office closures to the tolling of Interior ferries: "While some of the criticisms are from predictable sources, we should be very concerned with the alienation of those who have stuck with us through the rough patches: our own party members, business-people, many seniors and many in local government. I am not at all confident that this situation can be contained if uncertainty persists for long."[95]

Campbell remained at least officially unpersuaded on 19 June 2003, when an opinion poll came in very heavily against the sale of the Coquihalla concession. "I understand some of the concerns," he stated. "But I also understand all over BC people are asking for additional transportation improvements."[96]

The very real threat of a resurgence in provincial Reform and/or Conservative Parties was undoubtedly part of the political calculus in dropping the initiative. "We had a good business plan that made a poor public case," Campbell said in a press release of 23 July 2003. "It's time to put that plan behind us and move on."[97]

The failed privatization of the Coquihalla concession was confirmation that "supply of a technically proficient solution to a policy problem is not a sufficient condition to produce a politically effective demand."[98] Despite the loss of revenue "the partnership would have provided," the $300 million in infrastructure improvements announced since February would still proceed. The government could not afford any more political hurt in the Heartlands.[99]

Although "smaller government" was never explicitly mentioned in the *New Era* document, it was obviously front-and-centre in Gordon Campbell's mind as he assembled the multiple processes launched in his mandate letters. These processes unfolded in tandem, not sequentially, and proved enormously difficult for ministers and public servants. Many of the process demands and dilemmas discussed above were reflected in the experience of MCAWS. As an amalgam of seven former free-standing NDP ministries, MCAWS frequently found itself on the wrong side of the firing line in the battle against big government.

PART 3

THE IMPACT OF TAX CUTS: REAPING THE WHIRLWIND

6

Community, Aboriginal and Women's Services: Ministry of Lost Causes?

"But nothing worth having comes without some kind
of fight."
                    – Bruce Cockburn, "Lovers in a Dangerous Time"

As NEW MINISTERS were being sworn in on 6 June 2001, the BC
government released a ministerial "summary of responsibilities"
as a handy guide to the largest-ever cabinet in the province's history.[1] One new ministry – Community, Aboriginal and Women's
Services (MCAWS) – was notable not only for its capacious title,
but also for its extensive list of responsibilities. The new ministry encompassed thirty-one "general responsibilities" drawn from,
in whole or in part, seven former NDP ministries. Among those
responsibilities were a host of socially sensitive policy areas: multiculturalism, immigration, Indigenous services, child care, arts
and culture, museums and heritage sites, social housing and leaky
condominiums, violence against women, library services, and others. The unique character of the new ministry inspired Opposition
leader Joy MacPhail to rechristen it "the ministry of lost causes."
The nickname was neither the last nor the least appropriate sobri-
quet that MCAWS enjoyed.

Early reductions in MCAWS funding, announced in Finance
Minister Gary Collins's Economic and Fiscal Update of 30 July
2001, prompted its rebranding as "the incredible shrinking ministry" (in the black humour of the day).[2] Some programs of the
former NDP government did not survive long enough to be

considered in core review. For MCAWS, this first wave of down-sizing saw the virtual elimination of what had, under the NDP, been the Ministry of Community Development, Cooperatives and Volunteers. It was stripped of its entire $7 million budget, a discordant note in 2001, the United Nations International Year of Volunteers.[3]

MCAWS learned of the changes through a confidential communication note of 29 July 2001, which advised of program reductions and eliminations to be announced the following day in the Economic and Fiscal Update. This advance notice was not an invitation to debate, but rather a warning to quickly prepare ministerial responses to the awkward questions that were sure to follow.

MCAWS constituted an attractive target for a government that was intent on proving it was "serious about cutting costs and spending."[4] In addition to the $7 million hit, the Update cut $16 million from child care and $6 million from social housing.[5] This was just a small taste of the incredible shrinking that would occur through the budget target review in the months ahead. The unstated expectation of the premier was that MCAWS would be a flagship for smaller government via devolution, deregulation, attrition, and elimination. Unfortunately, that expectation was combined with wide-ranging *New Era* promises.

MCAWS was home for twenty-four *New Era* commitments, all reconfirmed in the premier's mandate letters of 25 June 2001.[6] Many were of a complex and challenging character. MCAWS was to "pass a Community Charter that will increase autonomy for local government," "implement a flexible, innovative program to increase the supply of affordable housing," "aggressively support and champion BC's bid to host the 2010 Winter Olympics," "increase efforts to protect and promote aboriginal languages," and many more. The premier also asked MCAWS to "focus attention" not only on *New Era* commitments but also on what he described as "key projects for which you will be accountable":

- examine all service agreements with aboriginal communities (health, education, etc.) and develop a strategy ...

- recommend mechanisms to improve the delivery of services to all aboriginal communities
- review Homeowner Protection Office, work with Minister of State for Intergovernmental Relations on federal/provincial funding issues
- review Housing, Homeowner and Code issues and rationalise regulation of the construction/housing industry, and develop a plan to deal with the immediate "leaky condominium" problem
- review the *BC Heritage Trust Act* and disclosure provisions
- examine the feasibility of a strategic plan for library services throughout British Columbia.

In addition, MCAWS subsequently became the delivery agent for the *New Era*'s "additional 5,000 new intermediate and long term care beds by 2006."[7]

All of these formidable challenges became exponentially more difficult with the grim news that MCAWS would be subject to a 30 percent budget reduction and an over 50 percent staff reduction (from a June 2001 base of about 1,200 full-time equivalents). As a new ministry with an expansive mandate and contradictory instructions to get dramatically smaller, MCAWS provided a compelling example of what Christopher Pollitt and Geert Bouckaert warned against: "Different kinds of objectives will sometimes trade off against each other ... Decision-makers are obliged to decide what they think is most important – they can seldom hope to have everything at the same time."[8] Broader government clearly wanted everything at the same time and was not reluctant to demand it; the MCAWS story is one of survival and resilience amidst sustained adversity.

The 270-day plan priorities for MCAWS ensured that those who had survived the staffing reduction would have plenty to do:

- *Community Charter*
- develop new *Safety Standards Act*
- develop Childcare Plan

- develop plan to deal with Aboriginal urban issues and build capacity
- review and make recommendations on inventory of transition houses and emergency shelters
- establish First Citizens Forum
- leaky Condo Plan
- review service agreements with Aboriginal communities
- Community Transition Assistance: Tahsis, Skeena communities, central coast
- 30 Day Deregulation Submissions
- rationalization of housing, homeowner, code, and regulations
- streamline *Local Government Act*
- legal protections for local government
- 2010 Olympics
- streamline *GVSWDD Act*.[9]

A brief deferral was offered for an Indigenous languages preservation plan, but as a *New Era* commitment, it could not realistically be set aside. Burnout? No time for that!

Core Review: MCAWS Embraces New Public Management

With its thirty-one general responsibilities and thirty-three agencies, boards, and commissions (ABCs), MCAWS was destined to receive a great deal of attention in the core review process. Its first visit to the core review committee, now chaired by Campbell, was on 20 September 2001. Its presentation attempted to emulate the language and spirit of New Public Management (NPM) by offering nine "fundamental shifts" to its business model:

1 From Direct Delivery ... to Third Party Supplier
2 From Victoria leadership ... to Community Leadership
3 From Charity ... to Investment
4 From Subsidies ... to Capacity-building

5 From Silos ... to Integrated Service Delivery
6 From Over-regulation ... to Self-regulation, minimal regulation
7 From Unfocussed funding ... to Performance-based outcomes
8 From Duplicate Services ... to Shared Service Delivery
9 From Boutique ministries ... to an Accountable, professional, integrated organization.[10]

MCAWS completed its NPM cornucopia with the promise, as a next step, to undertake an "analytical review of specific programs and activities to identify: elimination, reduction, consolidation, transfer to private sector, transfer to other units within government, and build local government capacity."[11]

The MCAWS presentation even espoused the premier's 25 June 2001 mandate letter direction "to examine the approach being taken in other jurisdictions." It offered an example of potential (and ultimately successful) policy transfer with references to Australia's Centrelink, Ontario's Government Information Offices, and Service New Brunswick, which subsequently became the model for Service BC.

MCAWS was home for Government Agents offices across the province. Initially, it feared that at least some of these offices might fall victim to core and budget target reviews. That concern proved unfounded as the offices took on enhanced importance with the extensive closure of provincial offices, including human resources, children and families, forestry, conservation, and land titles. Government Agents offices (subsequently transformed into Service BC) became the effective storefront for a host of services that no longer had independent offices.

As MCAWS minister, I believed that our core review presentation was comprehensive and inspired. The committee was less than impressed. It asked: "How would all of those words make government smaller and more effective?" And: "What, exactly, was the Ministry going to stop doing tomorrow that it was doing today?" And: "Why was the Ministry continuing ineffective programs that the NDP had created?"[12] Such questions were indicative of the very considerable difficulty that the ministry experienced in attempting to hit the right notes in rethinking, remaking, and reinventing government.

MCAWS was back to core services review on 5 November 2001. In response to the committee's "vision for the future" questions, it promised a ministry that would be "much smaller" and "committed to innovative service delivery through e-government and third-party service providers."[13] The biggest change from September was its addition of a section entitled "Non-Core Functions – Eliminated," which was clearly the gold (or more bluntly, the blood on the floor) the committee was waiting to see. Ten program areas were proposed for removal. Some – such as Cooperatives and Volunteers – had already been effectively ended by the budget cuts of 30 July 2001. The termination of others – such as audiobooks for the blind, multicultural programs, the BC Festival of the Arts, and funding for women's centres – proved highly controversial and politically painful.

By November, the twin pressures of the core and budget target reviews to make government smaller and more affordable were intense, visceral, and personal for both ministers and public servants. Ticking yet another box in the elimination category was the equivalent of taking one more bullet for the team. No entity or program was too small or too politically sensitive to escape scrutiny. Failure to act was viewed as failure to show courage and commitment to the Campbell team. Axing a program or service, as discussed in Chapter 5, was the premier's preferred outcome and the easiest route of escape from core review.

The drive for smaller government became a noble mission inspired by legends drawn from Sir Roger Douglas and the restructuring experience of New Zealand – show courage, be decisive, take the pain, and then be judged on the longer-term benefits. As one official put it, the drive for government downsizing through bigger, faster, and deeper cuts entailed the constant danger of moving from "out-of-the-box thinking to out-of-your-mind thinking." The ongoing demand to produce more with less brought frequent invocation of Green's Law of

Debate: "Anything is possible if you don't know what you're talking about."[14]

MCAWS was, as noted, home to thirty-three of the agencies, boards, and commissions (ABCs) identified in the Premier's Office count.[15] As a result of the November core review meeting, three were eliminated or winding down, five were referred to the Administrative Justice core review stream, and four to Crown Agencies Secretariat review. The remainder were sent back to the ministry for further review. Those processes ground on until 17 May 2002, when the premier advised that far too many ministers and deputies had remained mired in the status quo, hence failing to capture the spirit of smaller government. The premier's missive provided one more opportunity for ministers and ministries to be "extremely creative and diligent" in their consideration of ABC elimination.[16] Should they fail, they would be scheduled for a visit with the recently convened External Panel, where the sufficiency of their analytical rigour would again be tested.

The External Panel provided a compelling example of how, in the rush to remake government, various processes inspired by New Public Management could move from mutually supportive to mutually contradictory (to borrow Pollitt and Summa's words). As noted in Chapter 5, devolution of the Safety Engineering Services Branch (SESB) out of MCAWS and into an independent special-purpose authority easily won approval from the core review committee. In the midst of extensive consultations on devolution, MCAWS was obliged to defend the continued existence of the Building Safety Advisory Council – a key support to the SESB – before the External Panel.

The MCAWS deputy minister and I argued that eliminating the council might disrupt or derail consultations leading to devolution of the SESB and, by extension, the council itself. We also stated that budget and staffing reductions had "significantly reduced the ministry's capacity to deal with current and emerging regulatory and policy issues," particularly given concurrent demands for regulatory reductions. MCAWS was under pressure to diminish regulations by one-third, a daunting task in the area of technical safety. Regulated technologies – such as gas, electrical, boilers, and elevators – could not be deregulated without extensive consultation and professional review, both aimed at the broader goal of protecting public safety. Unswayed, the External Panel summarily recommended that the council be terminated. The process tools of core review and deregulation (and the great haste to show results from both) thus threatened to undo SESB devolution and the wider goal of smaller government.

The juxtaposition of ambitious *New Era* commitments with core and budget target review objectives sometimes produced results that were awkward if not overtly contradictory. For example, the sport and physical activity branch was slated to lose one-quarter of its budget just as MCAWS was leading the government's drive to win the right to host the 2010 Olympics. MCAWS underlined the obvious disjunction between hosting one of the world's highest-profile sporting events while simultaneously jettisoning supports to the BC Seniors Games and other amateur sports activities, successfully retaining its budget for the branch.[17]

At times, MCAWS was literally pulled in two directions at once: double to $44 million the Physical Fitness and Sport Fund but terminate monetary contributions to the Athlete Assistance Program and to the National Coaching Institute; create an Olympic Arts Fund while simultaneously eliminating funding to the BC Festival of the Arts; protect and promote Indigenous languages but discontinue the First Peoples' Heritage, Language and Culture Council (created by the NDP government in 1996). In the early years of the New Era, smaller government and reduced expenditure invariably trumped programmatic coherence.

Heritage Preservation in the Hurtlands

The management of public lands and their heritage resources provided one more opportunity for MCAWS to be pulled in different directions. The *New Era* document promised creation of a BC Trust for Public Lands "to encourage and facilitate the expansion of public lands through private land donations."[18] As part of core review, the BC Heritage Trust – a government entity – was shut down and its assets (along with a $5 million initial endowment from government) were rolled into the new BC Trust for Public Lands, which was officially decreed "an entity outside of government." With the elimination of the old trust and its replacement by the new trust, government was (in theory at least) ever-so-slightly smaller, and just as importantly, another *New Era* promise was fulfilled.[19]

The *New Era* platform was silent on heritage resources, but core review direction was definitive: get out of the heritage business. A MCAWS communications note of 27 May 2002 was less than subtle: "Running heritage attractions is not a core service of government – providing policy, direction and standards for the preservation of provincial heritage values is." Heritage sites were "attractions," not, in a different telling, irreplaceable touchstones of our history. Here too, government should confine itself to steering (providing policy, direction, and standards), not rowing (running the attractions itself). "The provincial government recognizes the value of heritage sites," the note continued, "as well as the need to responsibly manage public dollars." The note promised savings of $1.5 million starting in 2004, making the dream of smaller government one step closer.[20]

Confronted by the stark reality of dramatic budget and staff reductions, MCAWS was always receptive to solutions that did not entail wholesale eradication of programs and positions. The sale of heritage sites, the privatization of the Royal BC Museum, or a formulaic reduction in safety services generated no enthusiasm at MCAWS. Devolution embraced "steering not rowing," without the pain of privatization and layoffs. In the heritage portfolio, thirty sites were identified as candidates for devolution, typically involving transfer of ownership and operational responsibility to a non-profit or local authority. Most were designated national historic sites but without funding from the federal government.

In some cases, properties were transferred free of charge to First Nations, the Land Conservancy, or the Royal BC Museum. Some sites, such as Fort Steele, Barkerville, and Hat Creek Ranch, also enjoyed the legal status of Class A provincial parks. They had "province-wide not just local heritage significance," and many artifacts had been donated "with the expectation that they would be preserved and maintained by the Province for the enjoyment and education of all British Columbians."[21] The ministry's objective in such cases was to identify local or non-government management entities and to move operations out of government.

Heritage devolution was fiercely resisted in small communities, as in Wells, which directly and indirectly derived almost all of its employment from nearby Barkerville. Resistance even gave rise to caustic humour, such as a brochure entitled *Visit the New Ghost Towns of British Columbia*. Author Murray Bush exhorted readers to see "abandoned schools, hospitals, courthouses, forestry offices, entire towns! Even ghost towns are becoming ghost towns!"[22] Critics rightly disparaged the notion that heritage could be preserved, protected, and presented to the public without ongoing support from government. Where heritage was concerned, government could not hope to have everything at the same time without more hurt in the Heartlands.

The Community Charter: High Principle
Meets Raw Politics

Premier Campbell offered some good news to the Union of BC Municipalities (UBCM) convention in September 2001 by committing to cut no local government grants. His promise was consistent with the *New Era* pledge to create a Community Charter, which would "outlaw provincial government 'offloading' of costs onto municipal governments."[23] Like the exemption of Health and Education, this step also diminished the pool from which savings could be extracted. Provincial grants to local governments would surely not have met the core review tests, but Campbell was loath to scuff the gloss off the long-promised Community Charter before it was even completed.[24]

The charter was well connected with New Public Management principles. NPM espouses the principle of "subsidiarity," which suggests that services and the decision-making entities that support them should reside closest to the people who receive them. In the political vernacular, senior governments should "strengthen local autonomy" or "empower local government and get out of its way." A less intrusive hand from the province implied, in theory at least, a smaller provincial bureaucracy necessary to manage municipal affairs. The charter would offer, in NPM terms, a "rationalization of jurisdiction" that would maximize public benefit by minimizing intergovernmental interference.[25]

The charter was also well connected with Gordon Campbell as a political leader in local and provincial government. In 1991, a draft version was first endorsed by UBCM (and its president of the day, Gordon Campbell); in 1995, it was reintroduced as a private member's bill by Opposition leader Campbell.[26] The charter's import was emphasized in *New Era,* with promises (twice repeated) to outlaw offloading from provincial to local governments and to increase autonomy for the latter.[27] In his introduction of the Community Charter, Minister of State Ted Nebbeling argued that it "goes further than any other legislation of its kind in Canada in treating local government as an order of government based on principles of municipal-provincial relations."[28]

The charter was a ninety-day agenda item that became subject to a two-year consultative process "after municipal leaders raised a host of concerns – financial, jurisdictional and otherwise."[29] Giving practical statutory expression to the platitudinous rhetoric of early versions of the charter proved challenging, and UBCM was in "show me" mode, demanding substance to back up the rhetoric. The eventual legislative introduction in March 2003 came with the expansive claim of "most empowering local government legislation in Canada."[30]

The charter had its roots in a 1980s Federation of Canadian Municipalities campaign to recognize municipalities as an order of government within the Meech Lake Accord.[31] When that campaign failed, debate shifted to the "broad powers" model, providing municipalities with more authority to create their own services without the requirement of provincial approvals, assuming such services did not offend existing constitutional powers. The first application of the broad powers model was in Alberta during the late 1980s and early 1990s.[32]

In British Columbia, the Glen Clark NDP government attempted to mend some fences with UBCM by agreeing to develop a broad powers model. This process engaged substantial policy transfer from Alberta and, to a lesser extent, Ontario (which had its own fences to mend after controversial amalgamations in Toronto and other cities). The Community Charter was the product of extensive consultation and negotiation with UBCM and other players, but as one key official noted, "the Charter project essentially needed to repackage and rebrand what had already been done into something the Campbell government could claim as its own."[33]

However, one essential component in the Campbell support base – "the BC business community" – was not enamoured with an expansion of local government powers.[34] For Campbell, the Community Charter was a win-win on the road to a smaller provincial government. For business, local governments that were freed from provincial constraints represented a greater threat than the status quo. "We see it as fraught with potential dangers," said John Winter of the BC Chamber of Commerce. For its part, the Business Council of British Columbia believed that the charter "could add to the existing thicket of taxes and regulation." Business demanded "checks and balances" that would, in Minister Nebbeling's view, "fundamentally change the nature of the charter." A retreat to meet business objections would severely alter the government's "legislative intentions."[35]

Business found a more sympathetic ear at the Ministry of Competition, Science and Enterprise (MCSE), home of the government deregulation initiative. The competing interests and perspectives of UBCM and business organizations proved irreconcilable despite the efforts of MCAWS and MCSE. The result was a pitched battle between powerful adversaries, both with robust connections to the Campbell government. In presenting their case, both effectively employed the government's own language. UBCM extolled the enhancement of local autonomy, whereas the business interests cautioned against densifying the thicket of taxes and regulation.

As MCAWS was attempting in the spring session of 2003 to finalize provisions within the charter, MCSE was pressing forward with a body of countervailing measures, which was introduced as Bill 75, the Significant Projects Streamlining Act (SPSA), in the fall session of 2003. The SPSA provided Victoria with the statutory authority to override local zoning and land-use controls in circumstances where they conflicted with the deemed provincial interest. In the words of its sponsor, Minister of State for Deregulation Kevin Falcon, it would reduce "red tape and the regulatory burden" and slash "inefficient review and approval processes."[36] The charter promised to end provincial paternalism; the SPSA was the statutory embodiment of the idea that the province knew better than short-sighted local governments, at least on "significant" projects.

Bill 75 encountered strong opposition from the UBCM and even a few Liberal MLAs. For example, MLA Blair Lekstrom (Peace River South) argued, "we're stepping into jurisdictions that I believe wholeheartedly should remain within the realm of local government and those bodies to act upon."[37] Falcon contended that provincial power to override local bylaws already existed via section 874 of the Local Government Act. In response, UBCM pointed out that section 874 had been enacted in 1977 and never once been used. The charter "promised us recognition as an independent, accountable and responsible order of government," wrote UBCM. "Bill 75 has a minister assuming all the powers of a duly elected council or board and substituting his/her decisions for those of local councils and boards."[38]

Unable to reconcile competing interests within the bounds of a single statute, and not wishing to alienate either proponent, the government sacrificed statutory coherence for political expediency. Both bills received final approval of the legislature and royal assent; the SPSA remains in the statute books but has never been invoked. The Liberals had fallen short of the lofty expectations cultivated in the *New Era* document. "At the end of Gordon

Campbell's first term," Paddy Smith suggests, "the provincial-municipal relationship was still more top-down than locally led."[39] High principle was sacrificed on the altar of political expediency.

Women's Services: Ambiguity and Uncertainty Prompt Fear and Loathing

The simultaneous demands for both smaller government (via core review) and reduced expenditures (via budget target review) acted in tandem to drive cuts that often appeared petty and mean-spirited. Among them was a $47,000 annual grant to each of thirty-seven women's centres around the province. Under questioning in Estimates, Minister of State for Women's Equality Lynn Stephens noted that the centres were focused primarily on the areas of resources, referrals, and advocacy. In funding them, the government would concentrate instead on protecting "direct crisis intervention services for women." She committed to "working with them to find the replacement for the $47,000 or to find partners in their communities."[40]

Why, for a maximum saving of $1.7 million, would a ministry suffer the political grief of defunding a service to vulnerable women and children? Part of the answer lay in Stephens's reference to advocacy: some caucus and cabinet members believed that women's centres were a locus of anti-government sentiment and that funding them was effectively funding political opposition (echoes of the Milton Friedman argument noted in Chapter 2). Another part of the answer lay in the relentless demands for every ministry to do its part in shrinking government's budgetary deficit, regardless of short-term political optics.

By 2003, support to women's centres came in the form of a $3,000 grant "to each of them to explore ways in which they can partner with other organizations in the community ... to find ways that those services they currently provide will be able to be accessed by women in communities."[41] Those services were worthy of support from others but not from government – an extraordinarily awkward and discordant message when juxtaposed against *New Era* commitments on domestic violence.[42]

The fiscal imperative sometimes pushed decisions forward prematurely to match up with timelines for budget and core reviews. In 2002, Minister Lynn Stephens acknowledged that the Bridges Employment Training Program – which provided support specifically to women emerging from abusive relationships – was being terminated. As she recognized, "there is a need there, and we are committed to making sure we meet those needs." However, through core review the ministry had determined that funding would be focused on "direct essential priority services" and that the Bridges program "is one that can be maintained in another ministry."

Stephens stated that she was "in discussions" with the minister of human resources to determine if the program could "be incorporated into his plans in some form." She wanted to ensure that "women who are leaving abusive situations and trying to get back into the workforce have the opportunity to do that" – but, given that her discussions were still under way, her good intentions came with no guarantees.[43] For the Bridges program, the twin imperatives of downsizing and shrinking expenditures trumped programmatic certainty. Thus, Bridges joined the ranks of vital programs that were endangered by cumulative impacts across social ministries.

Expansion of Child-Care Spaces Confronts Contraction of Funding

The outgoing NDP government had created some high expectations for new child-care programming in the weeks and months prior to the 2001 election. The Child Care BC Act that had received royal assent on 29 March 2001 envisioned $14 per day, per child full-daycare subsidized at an estimated $400 million annually through the Financial Assistance Program (FAP) to licensed daycare centres. The FAP was an early candidate for Treasury Board scrutiny. MCAWS prepared an extensive communications package for ministers in anticipation of cuts to daycare that soon followed in the 30 July 2001 Economic and Fiscal Update.[44]

New Era included two child-care funding commitments, one to target funding "to help parents who need it most," the other to "increase child care choices for parents by encouraging the expansion of safe, affordable child care spaces."[45] In the early New Era, helping parents who needed it most translated to removing subsidy from those who were seen as needing it less: targeted funding simply meant that fewer dollars were being distributed, via a reduced income threshold, to fewer clients. The commitment regarding safe and affordable child-care spaces was also cast into doubt by early cuts. By August of 2001, BC Liberal MLAs sensed a growing and disconcerting gap between the reassuring words of *New Era* and the harsh reality of self-induced austerity. On child care, MLA Ida Chong (Oak Bay—Gordon Head) pointed to "a lot of confusion out there in the public. There is some confusion ... as to what parents are going to be able to access in the fall and what is going to happen in January."[46]

Lynn Stephens responded that "we were very clear about our new-era commitment to ... provide targeted funding for those families who need it most and to expand child care spaces in the province." Although she accurately portrayed her *New Era* obligations, she was less than convincing. According to her, the "previous administration's child care program was not sustainable ... We have made the commitment that we will, within our limited financial resources, do the best we can with the most money that we have available."[47] In short, the reduction in child-care funding drove the reduced income threshold, not broader principle.

In early 2002, the income threshold for child-care subsidy was reduced: recipients who previously qualified for subsidy at $1,500 per month could now earn a maximum of only $1,215. Stephens reported that as a result of this change, up to nine thousand families (of a total base of thirty-nine to forty-two thousand) lost their subsidy. The shift reduced the number of families qualifying for subsidy and forced some of them to abandon child-care spaces.

Child, Youth and Family Advocate Paul Pallan was deeply troubled by the threshold shift. Even before pending reductions, he said, fewer than 10 percent of children under twelve had access to a licensed child-care space, as the cost "puts quality child care out of reach for many families." The threshold shift at MCAWS, along with policy changes at MHR that pushed single parents with young children back into the workforce, raised Pallan's concerns that "cross-ministerial impacts have the potential to undermine MCFD's [Ministry of Children and Family Development's] intentions to strengthen community capacity."[48]

Pallan was among the first to raise the question of cumulative impacts across social ministries. He reiterated a crucial point: "65 percent of children who are taken into care come from single parents on income assistance – a pattern that has remained unchanged for the last decade." The loss of child-care supports to nine thousand families, Pallan argued, stood "in direct contradiction with MCFD's intention to increase capacity of families to care for their children."[49] He concluded that cascading cuts throughout social ministries would simply exacerbate the risk of children being taken into care.

Multiple cuts hit many not-for-profit service providers hard. MLA Richard Lee (Burnaby North) raised the case of the Burnaby Association for Community Inclusion, which saw its year-over-year funding reduced from $575,585 to $154,788 due to a combination of cuts, among them termination of "Munroe payments" and the "out-of-school-care" funding program.[50] Stephens acknowledged that 880 child-care providers were receiving less operational funding as a consequence of budgetary reductions, including 150 "childminding centres" that had lost all their government funding.[51] The problem, in her view, lay with employers who had negotiated unsustainable wage agreements with their staff: "We have no relationship with the employees. The employers are those who are responsible for reaching those kinds of agreements."[52] Cuts were unfortunate, she argued, but blame lay beyond the walls of government.

In 2003, Stephens was pleased to report at least modest relief. She noted that the threshold had been increased by one hundred dollars, thus returning the subsidy to three thousand of the nine thousand families who had lost it the previous year: "Frankly, we look forward to the day when we can restore it to the full amount and perhaps increase it beyond that."[53] Stephens implicitly confirmed that, in child care at least, funding cuts were a product of the self-imposed austerity (or rationing of a vital service) that flowed from the magnitude of 2001 tax cuts rather than a "strategic shift" toward ostensible sustainability.

Child-care funding was just one example of the disjunction between what was appropriate, desirable, or needed within service provision and what was possible or workable within the bounds of budget target constraints. Such disjunction proved a persistent theme in the social ministries. Severe budget constraints demanded that "vital" programs would be rationed and that programs deemed not vital would be cast off. As the following chapter reveals, the New Era experience of the Ministry of Human Resources reconfirmed this reality.

7

Human Resources:
A Bad Time to Be Poor?

"Nice work if you can get it,
And you can get it, if you try."
– George Gershwin, "Nice Work If You Can Get It"

WHEN THEY COMBED the *New Era* document for clues regarding
post-election priorities, public servants at the Ministry of Human
Resources (MHR) would find nothing that hinted at welfare
reform.[1] In fact, it never mentions the subject. By contrast, the
1996 BC Liberal platform, *The Courage to Change,* devoted a full
page to the topic. The Liberals lost the 1996 election, and as
detailed in Chapter 2, welfare reform was one of several areas
deemed too controversial for inclusion in the 2001 platform.
Unstated certainly did not mean forgotten, particularly in the
budget target review: MHR emerged with a staggering cut of $581
million, tumbling from $1.937 billion in 2001–02 to $1.356 billion
in 2004–05 – a 30 percent decrease.[2]

MHR's jaw-dropping budget reduction would be allayed, at
least in theory, by "strategic shifts" that heavily reflected the tenets
of New Public Management (NPM). MHR would be shifting, said
Minister Murray Coell, from "a culture of dependence and entitlement into one of personal responsibility and self-sufficiency," and
from "income assistance into employment with long-term checks
and balances there to keep them [former clients] in employment."[3]
As the ministry explained, it aimed to "redefine the BC income

assistance system" with "a new approach" backstopped by a novel set of guiding principles:

- *personal responsibility* for maximizing potential
- *active participation* by clients
- *innovative partnerships* between the ministry and the private sector and communities
- *citizen confidence* in the income assistance system
- *fairness and transparency,* with less red tape
- *clear outcomes,* whereby the ministry measures success by the success of the people being served
- *accountability for results* achieved.[4]

As with MCAWS, the new guiding principles that drove MHR borrowed heavily from the NPM playbook of "performance-based" programs and contracts, reduced regulation, innovative partnerships with the private and not-for-profit sectors, a new alternative service delivery model, and enhanced accountability. And as at MCAWS, the NPM lexicon was no substitute for the hard work of diagnosing and addressing the endless and intractable puzzles facing MHR.[5]

MHR had a massive budgetary goal to reach and only a short time in which to reach it. For its executive, attaining that goal required extraordinarily long days "scouring every expenditure line right down to the finest detail." Fortuitously, the outgoing NDP government had been active in caseload reduction, "providing a very strong data base critical to understanding the client base."[6] Given its fiscal and temporal imperatives, the executive also moved quickly to learn from other jurisdictions on welfare reform and to determine what might be incorporated into domestic programs. "A lesson is seen as a short cut," Richard Rose suggests, "utilizing available experience elsewhere to devise a programme that is new to the agency adopting it and attractive because of evidence that it has been effective elsewhere."[7]

The drive for exogenous learning was reflected in Minister Coell's promise to build on "the successes that Alberta, Ontario

and some of the American states have seen with income assistance redefinition or reform."[8] One former senior public servant recalled that California welfare reforms were particularly
useful examples, but the scale of the BC cuts "meant applica-
ble experience would be welcome from *anywhere!*"[9] Decades of
exogenous welfare reform experience, as well as that of British
Columbia itself, were promptly put to use. Employable recipients were required to file an employment plan and to participate,
as required, in job placement and training programs. The ministry promised to spend $300 million on such programs over three
years while reducing its budget by at least $581 million by 2004.[10]
The format of training for employment programs was well established under the NDP, but it was renewed and expanded under
the Liberals.[11]

The ministry's strategy was largely successful, at least from a
budget reduction perspective. Unfortunately, like other social
ministries, MHR was driven to harsh and unsustainable objectives by unprecedented budget reductions, necessitated, in turn,
by tax cuts that failed to deliver as expected. With MHR, as with
MCAWS, the Campbell government again hoped to have everything at the same time. The effectiveness of key initiatives was consequently undermined by hasty implementation – spurred on by
the balanced budget imperative.

MHR's Mission in Context

Like the Ministry of Children and Family Development (MCFD),
MHR served a very large clientele. The major difference between
the two ministries lay in the nature of their clienteles. Many of
MCFD's adult clients had little or no prospect of entering the
workforce and fully exiting from government supports; for many
MHR clients, in contrast, support was transitional rather than
permanent.[12] Both ministries cast their nets widely to capture
exogenous experience that might guide their strategies for budget
reduction; both linked their strategies, in turn, to anticipated caseload reduction. For reasons fully explored in Chapter 8, MCFD

enjoyed less success on this front, due largely, but not entirely, to the nature of its clientele.

Coell noted in 2002 ministerial Estimates that MHR served about 251,000 people each month, or nearly 6 percent of the BC population.[13] The magnitude of the MHR caseload was one of several "immediate concerns" identified in core review, including the following:

- Almost 40 percent of all single parents in the province receive income assistance.
- People are cycling on and off the caseload. The majority of income assistance clients leave the caseload within six months; however, two-thirds of those who leave return within two years.
- People are dependent on income assistance over the long-term. More than 70 percent of income assistance clients older than age 35 have an income assistance history longer than 10 years.
- Persons with disabilities who want to and are able to work are not getting the supports they need to get and maintain employment.
- Current training programs do not always lead directly to jobs.[14]

In short, MHR faced a challenging mandate as well as a daunting budget plan.

As caseload reduction initiatives got under way, MHR served two major streams of clientele: about 45,000 people with chronic disabilities and about 206,000 people who were capable of working but who had been unemployed for long enough to qualify for benefits. Early efforts focused on the latter stream. MHR pursued caseload reduction strategies that had been utilized nationally and internationally. Many other jurisdictions had wrestled with welfare reform, providing numerous lessons to be learned.

The BC Liberals were far from pioneers in welfare reform, which had been ongoing internationally since at least 1980. As

Guy Peters, Jon Pierre, and Desmond King note, "workfare (under various guises of welfare-to-work or community participation programs) has been introduced in Denmark, Australia, New Zealand, and Ireland, but in greatest measure in the United States and Britain."[15] Katherine Teghtsoonian argues that even the NDP governments of Mike Harcourt and Glen Clark were not immune to this trend, as "the provincial government's approach to social assistance policy began to reflect a less generous and more coercive tone well before 1996." NDP governments highlighted "welfare fraud and abuse" as an issue "needing urgent attention. New policies and procedures were adopted that the government argued were necessary to address this issue, many of which increased the level of surveillance and monitoring directed toward benefit recipients."[16]

The Canadian Centre for Policy Alternatives (CCPA) certainly noticed the shift in NDP welfare policies in 1995–96, characterizing it as "harmful, mean-spirited and unjustified."[17] In 2002, Opposition NDP MLA Jenny Kwan implicitly acknowledged the NDP's harder line on welfare during an exchange with Coell. She vigorously denied that "a culture of welfare entitlement" existed in British Columbia and disparaged the notion that an American-style remedy was required. She noted that "BC's welfare caseload declined 32.6 percent between December 1995 and August 2001, when there were 120,700 fewer people on BC Benefits. If ever there was a 'culture of entitlement,' it ended a long time ago."[18] In fact, as noted above, Coell and MHR leadership made good use of job-training research initiated in the latter years of the NDP government; given its challenges, MHR welcomed insights from every corner.

The ministry was able to get out of the gate early on cost-saving initiatives. Employable welfare recipients received letters in October of 2001, advising them to look for work or risk loss of benefits.[19] MHR pursued its core strategy of transforming "dependence to employment" through expansion of job-training programs in combination with the stated threat – imported from America – of time limits on support.

Policy Transfer and Lesson Learning
Inform Caseload Reduction

Like MCFD Minister Gordon Hogg, Murray Coell was a frequent target for the small but tenacious NDP Opposition. Fortunately, both Coell and Hogg brought professional knowledge and experience in social work to their new roles. Both were well aware of international trends in welfare reform, and neither was reluctant to recognize the role of exogenous learning in the development of BC programs.

As MHR attempted to convert what it saw as a culture of dependence and entitlement into one of self-sufficiency, it drew lessons from several jurisdictions. For example, Manitoba and Ontario used liens on homes in which welfare recipients had an equity stake. MHR moved quickly to emulate this example, although in British Columbia liens would "not be put on until the seventh month of being on income assistance."[20] Similarly, when Opposition leader Joy MacPhail accused Coell of following Ontario's workfare program, he readily acknowledged the program as one of the influences on BC initiatives.

Much of the Opposition's attack focused on the purported Americanization of BC welfare programs. American influence was most frequently associated with a controversial provision that barred employable individuals and couples from collecting welfare for more than two years out of five. The "two-in-five" rule was the object of much Opposition and media criticism, particularly its application to parents or families with children as young as three years old.

When Jenny Kwan asked Coell about the research the ministry had undertaken before concluding that time limits should be part of the new BC Benefits model, he responded, "The ministry has thoroughly examined the cross-jurisdictional analysis that's available in the United States and has monitored US research." Asked if MHR decision making had been based solely on that information, Coell replied that it was "one of the considerations. We looked at a

BC approach, where it would be two years out of five years rather than the American approach, which is a five-year lifetime maximum. So, if a person [in British Columbia] lived 50 years as an adult, they could be on income assistance for 20 years."[21] Recipients who were on continuous assistance (typically those with persistent physical or mental disabilities) might be exempted from the two-in-five limit, but the new rules would "leave no doubt" that "most people getting temporary assistance will be required to look for work."[22]

Kwan noted that after two years of income assistance, single-parent or two-parent families would see their support reduced first by 11 percent and then escalating up (unlike able-bodied recipients without children, who, subject to relevant exemptions, could lose benefits immediately on hitting the two-year benchmark). "What," she asked, "have been the outcomes of time restrictions on income assistance [elsewhere]?" Coell responded that "many of the states are just coming off their five-year limit at this point. It was introduced by the Clinton administration, so there are a number of states getting close to that five-year limit." MHR was monitoring the American experience, but "early indications ... show that the time limits are a motivating factor. That's the essence of what we are trying to produce: a program that helps to motivate individuals into employment programs."[23]

The two-in-five rule was new to British Columbia, and MHR leadership privately expressed anxiety about some of its aspects, notably the potential impact on single parents with children as young as three. They were not alone in their concern. Child, Youth and Family Advocate Paul Pallan, for example, flagged the issue in his final report as an independent officer of the legislature.[24] The rule prompted extensive debate around the numbers of people who might be kicked off welfare when the timelines came into play. Some critics, according to Vaughn Palmer, feared that as many as 30,000 recipients could be affected. In the event, 37 clients lost their benefits in April 2003, as did another 172 during the next twelve months.

Ultimately, the two-in-five limit turned out to be less sweeping than its critics feared. The key difference between apprehension and reality, as Palmer pointed out, lay in the exemptions to the rule. Originally, there were six of these, but they eventually numbered twenty-five, including what Palmer described as an "all-purpose escape clause" – recipients who had "an employment plan, are complying with their plan, are actively looking for work, but have not been successful in finding employment" would not be deprived of their benefits.[25] The two-in-five rule may have served the immediate purpose of encouraging some welfare recipients to look for work, but as caseloads declined and budgetary savings were secured, MHR added more and more exemptions to the list.

Arguably, the sink-or-swim nature of the rule, in the absence of exemptions, was inconsistent with prevailing norms and values in British Columbia. Conversely, the tattered two-in-five rule may fit the Dolowitz and Marsh definition of a flawed transfer: the ministry "searches hurriedly for a solution to an urgent problem ... because the need for a 'solution' is imperative," but without a thorough search for alternatives, increases its odds of choosing a flawed model.[26] In either case, what appeared dramatic or radical in 2001 was rendered far less consequential by 2004.

The shared application of time limits (albeit of differing severity) suggested at least a superficial resemblance between British Columbian and American welfare reforms. In fact, the BC Benefits program, with its pronounced emphasis on education and employment training, was similar to the Danish model, where "participation, although compulsory, is closely linked with increasing educational skills for future reintegration into the labour market."[27]

British Columbia's pursuit of exogenous experience on welfare reform was unexceptional. Peters, Pierre, and King compare the Bill Clinton and Tony Blair administrations' shift to workfare in the 1990s. In 1996, building on the experience of Denmark, New Zealand, Australia, and others, Clinton "signed a welfare reform act mandating 'workfare' for welfare recipients and imposing a lifetime limit of five years for the receipt of benefits." Elected in

May 1997, the Blair Labour government "immediately enacted a massive New Deal workfare scheme for the 18-25-year age group ... [since] extended to cover older workers and now lone parents and the disabled."[28] Welfare reform ideas were widely disseminated in advance of the New Era.

MHR's drive for caseload reduction predictably had its share of critics. For example, in a CCPA essay, Bruce Wallace, Seth Klein, and Marge Reitsma-Street argued that the reductions were driven by the "3Ds" of discouragement, delay, and denial. In their view, the three-week job search that potential recipients were required to conduct before being granted an intake interview forced them to find alternatives, as did the two-year "independence test" (a minimum two years of living independently apart from the parental home) for young people potentially fleeing an abusive home. The CCPA was also critical of MHR's new electronic "alternative service delivery" systems, including a 1-800 line and "compulsory use of an online computer orientation." Both had the impact, in its view, of depersonalizing contact and discouraging potential recipients from initiating further inquiries.[29]

Not surprisingly, the CCPA's ideological nemesis the Fraser Institute had no time for the 3Ds. Instead, in a paper written for the institute, Chris Schafer and Jason Clemens advanced a "D" of their own – "diversion." In their opinion, diverting "potential welfare recipients to other types of assistance before they enter the welfare system" was the best approach, "since experience has shown that once someone enters the system, they are far more likely to use the system again." Schafer and Clemens praised the BC government for being the first in Canada to employ time limits and other "successful US welfare reforms," thereby earning an "A" grade for "ending the entitlement to welfare." The strategies that the CCPA disparaged earned British Columbia a "B+" for diversion. To raise that grade to an "A," Schafer and Clemens suggested adoption of Wisconsin's Job Access Loan program, "which would offer a cash payment to social assistance applicants who have an employment-related need that, when solved, would enable the applicant to either maintain or obtain employment, and as a result, avoid going on welfare."[30] For MHR, offers of Wisconsin-like cash payments were tough to reconcile with the demand that it quickly and drastically reduce its expenditures.

In an essay by Seth Klein and Andrea Long, the CCPA also suggested that New Era welfare reforms were flawed by an incomplete policy transfer. British Columbia had "chosen to import only policy 'sticks' not policy 'carrots.'" Klein and Long insisted that the carrots, such as enhanced child care, transportation support, increased minimum wage, and expanded earnings exemptions, were integral to the success of American welfare initiatives.[31]

The Fraser Institute and the CCPA enjoyed some surprising agreement on this point. The institute argued that other Canadian provinces "promote the incentive to work in welfare recipients in part by disregarding some of their earned income through an earnings exemption; they can keep a certain amount of what they earn without seeing any reduction in their welfare benefits." Unfortunately, British Columbia had not taken this path, choosing instead to eliminate virtually all earnings exemptions.[32] The institute's grade for "making work pay" was an emphatic "F." Of course, the Campbell government imperative was not making work pay but rather making welfare reform produce huge and prompt savings.

To that point, Klein and Long offered a vital and insightful observation: "In the US, welfare restructuring was not driven by a fiscal imperative to cut spending. In fact, notwithstanding its tough new rules, the US *increased* its spending on programs for low-income people during the post-1996 welfare reform period."[33] The BC reforms, in contrast, were driven by demands for at least $581 million in savings to be delivered within three years to produce a balanced budget in 2004–05. Savings lost through employment earnings exemptions or Wisconsin-like cash payments for welfare diversion were inimical to that goal.

MHR's tough-love combination of threats (such as time limits) and inducements (such as employment training) enjoyed considerable success in caseload reduction across time, particularly given the very weak economic growth of 2001–02. On 13

February 2003, Coell advised the legislature of his ministry's results to date: since June 2001, the MHR income assistance caseload had dropped by 22 percent, or sixty-six thousand clients. He attributed these reductions to enhanced employability through ministry-sponsored employment programs, to time limits on receipt of income assistance, and to the "two-year financial independence test" for young people. In November 2003, he reported that the number of welfare recipients had dropped by over 82,000, from 252,162 in June 2001 to 169,776. He also noted that twenty-six MHR offices had closed or been merged and that 859 staff had been laid off.[34]

The Campbell government obviously believed that welfare reform resonated with both its political base and "the silent majority" of British Columbians. The 2002 Throne Speech profiled welfare reform, including MHR's "strategic shift from a culture of welfare entitlement to a culture of employment and self-sufficiency ... In particular, the changes will insist on greater individual responsibility for those able to actively seek employment."[35] Unfortunately, the magnitude of budget cuts required from MHR demanded programmatic shifts that went far beyond pressing employment on able-bodied welfare recipients who were clinging to a sense of entitlement. A massive $581 million budget cut pushed MHR squarely into the realm of "bigger, faster, and deeper" and greater risk of political peril.

Retrenchment Blurs the Line between Motivational and Mean-Spirited

The imperative to meet expenditure reduction targets often blurred the line between motivational and mean-spirited policy, producing programmatic changes that undermined the moral authority of broader goals such as strengthening the culture of employment and self-sufficiency. As discussed in Chapter 6, demands for budget reduction, smaller government, and ever greater cuts drove MCAWS to eliminate support for multicultural programs, women's centres, and audiobook production.

Those same demands (often with similarly insignificant savings) produced some of the more controversial changes to MHR's assistance programs: discontinuing the bus pass subsidy to recipients of the federal government's old age security and guaranteed income support; phasing out the seniors supplement to the same group; eliminating hardship assistance grants to refugee claimants and individuals who were voluntarily leaving a job; and (in a move guaranteed to inspire Scrooge metaphors) abolishing the Christmas allowance for all but dependent children.

MHR was obliged to operate within a model that demanded severe reductions and brought every expenditure into question. Coell, who had once been a social worker, was frequently the target of caustic criticism from his former professional association.[36] He could take some satisfaction from enhanced employment programs, but he frequently carried the can for budget-driven punitive measures. In turn, those measures produced a steady stream of news stories detailing the impact on recipients.

Journalist Judith Lavoie offered a potent commentary on the state of the province one year into the New Era: "In April, single parents, employable couples and recipients aged 55 to 64 had their payments cut $50 to $100 a month, people can no longer keep up to $100 in child support or earnings and crisis grants are now capped at $20 a month."[37] Two billion dollars in ill-timed and overly aggressive tax cuts (or perhaps "well-timed" and "suitably aggressive" cuts if a manufactured crisis were the goal) had placed British Columbia in the position of meeting its fiscal targets through – among many other measures – clawbacks of child support payments to welfare recipients.

The 2002 Throne Speech buttressed its claim to "put children and families first" with a promise of legislation to streamline the process for obtaining and enforcing family maintenance orders. All well and good, said Joy MacPhail, but utterly hollow, given that the family maintenance exemption of a hundred dollars was being eliminated, as was the income assistance earning exemption of two hundred dollars.[38] Further, "shelter allowances for families with two children or more will be reduced ... This is how they are going to help you, the most vulnerable."[39]

Some measures strained caucus unity. In April 2002, Coell introduced a bill that required a potential recipient to hold a record of past employment prior to applying for income assistance. He argued that it would encourage people to undertake job training or return to school, but the bill met resistance within and beyond the legislature; notably, BC Liberal MLAs Val Anderson (Vancouver—Langara) and Tom Christensen (Okanagan—Vernon) joined MacPhail and Kwan in opposing it.[40]

MHR cost-cutting measures sometimes carried implications for other ministries as well as their clients. In July 2002, Judith Lavoie reported that welfare recipients, excluding children and the disabled, would no longer be covered for preventative dental care. Further, MHR would no longer fund general anesthetic dental surgery for children and the disabled except in hospitals, where wait-lists were often in excess of seven months. Advocates feared that the approximately two thousand ministry dental cases per year would only worsen hospital waiting times.[41]

The combined cuts across social ministries were particularly onerous to women in single-parent families. "Poverty advocates told of numerous women caught in a desperate [C]atch-22 as the result of the changes," Barbara McLintock writes. "Their human resources ministry workers told them they must get a job – but the changes to the daycare rules [via the MCAWS funding formula] meant that they would actually end up with less money from working than they received from welfare by the time they'd paid for daycare."[42] Stricter eligibility requirements forced single parents on welfare to seek work when their youngest child turned three instead of seven, prompting the ministry itself to privately question the potential impacts on a child in such a situation. MHR raised the issue in the 2002 "social policy review" (discussed in Chapter 5) but secured only modest relief. Single parents whose children were three or older would still be eligible for income assistance, notwithstanding the two-in-five rule, but their payments would be reduced by a hundred dollars a month.[43]

MHR returned to the issue at the 2003 summer cabinet planning session. It highlighted the hundred-dollar rate reduction for single parents and the two-hundred-dollar reduction for two-parent families on assistance on reaching two-in-five time limits for eligibility on 1 April 2004. The ministry recommended that reductions be alleviated or discontinued. As usual, the only barrier to such relief was finding the dollars elsewhere in its own pinched budget.

Demand for $581 Million in Cuts Prompts a Hasty Disability Review

The drive to find savings, and to find them quickly, prompted MHR to undertake a process commonly termed the "disability review." In April of 2002, Minister Coell introduced legislation entitled "the Employment and Assistance for Persons with Disabilities Act." Among other measures, it eliminated the lower level of disability benefit and toughened criteria for permanent disability benefits. The act took effect on 30 September 2002. In the interim, ministry staff carried out an internal review of all client files to ensure continuing eligibility. The files of 18,705 individuals were determined to be deficient in provision of necessary information. Shortly thereafter, in October 2002, MHR sent out a twenty-three-page form regarding benefit eligibility to those 18,705 people.

Coell spent much of his time in the legislature defending his ministry's disability review. For the Opposition MLAs, it epitomized the heartless, bottom-line approach of the BC Liberal government, and they were relentless in questioning Coell. The ensuing controversy predictably attracted significant media attention, and after reported suicide attempts by recipients suffering from mental illness, approximately five thousand clients in that category were automatically qualified for benefits.[44]

The issue also captured the attention of the BC auditor general, Wayne Strelioff, who released his report on 24 February 2004. It left no doubt that the overriding impetus for the review was money: "We believe that a key assumption of the ministry in arriving at this decision was that a large number of recipients would fail to qualify, therefore losing their disability status, and the result would be significant cost-savings to government and taxpayers." The ministry estimated that 6,200 or more of recipients might prove ineligible, but ultimately only 46 had their cases closed.[45]

Auditor General Strelioff recognized that the review was required under the new act, but he concluded that the ministry "moved too quickly" in its desire to find savings and that "the major cost savings the ministry expected the review to gain were not achieved. At the same time, the review created increased anxiety for many of the ministry's disabled clients."[46] Strelioff recommended that in future "an appropriate evaluation of risks is carried out before decisions are made about how and when the work should be done."[47] Such a recommendation, though undoubtedly sound, was entirely inconsistent with the imperative to find immediate savings to meet looming budget targets. The emphatic instruction was "find savings now," not "find savings, but do it in a careful and politically sensitive manner." A $581 million budget reduction over three years was incompatible with subtle or nuanced delivery of change.

MHR's anticipated savings formed such a large portion of the three-year balanced budget plan that submitting bi-weekly progress reports to Treasury Board became obligatory in 2002, even though the ministry routinely met its targets.[48] Broader government could not risk an MHR fiscal failure.

By February 2003, the very substantial progress made in reducing the caseload for the employable unemployed allowed a kinder, gentler approach to the disability stream. Notably, Coell framed some budget pressures in a positive manner. For example, MHR was adding $80 million to its budget for people with disabilities in response to a 7 percent growth in that caseload. He offered some signals that government's uniformly parsimonious approach to income assistance was beginning to shift, at least to some degree. Earning exemptions for persons with disabilities doubled, and the definition of disability was extended to include mental illness, bringing "our legislation more in line with other Canadian provinces."[49]

Government generosity expanded as the May 2005 provincial election neared. Persons with disabilities received a seventy-dollar monthly increase on 1 January 2005. The MHR minister noted that a smaller increase had been planned, but "because of the excellent strength in the economy and sound fiscal management, we were able to provide a much larger increase and provide it much sooner."[50] In short, persons with disabilities (like the mothers who fell short of thresholds for child care) were obliged to do with less while waiting for the tax cuts to pay for themselves.

In the aptly named publication "A Bad Time to Be Poor," the CCPA described BC Liberal welfare policies as "radical and unprecedented in Canada."[51] What was radical and unprecedented was less the policies than the magnitude of the demands for budget cuts. In fact, many of the policies had precedents in multiple corners of the world and had been adopted by British Columbia for its own use. MHR was required to deliver savings of at least $581 million within three years, a monumental task that compelled ministry leaders to look long and hard at *every* expenditure. Its combination of threats and inducements proved successful in meeting the budgetary goal but not without some blurring of the line between motivational and mean-spirited. MHR bore criticism for a hasty disability review when fault more appropriately resided with the ill-timed tax cuts.

MHR and other social ministries cast their nets widely in the search for policy lessons that might inform solutions to intractable problems. Like Murray Coell, MCFD Minister Gordon Hogg made frequent reference to national and international experience; sadly, no amount of exogenous experience could compensate for an unworkable budget and unrealistic expectations borne of prescription before diagnosis. As the next chapter shows, those realities came crashing home all too quickly at MCFD.

8

Children and Family Development:
Where Chickens Come Home to Roost

"Sorry seems to be the hardest word."
– Elton John, "Sorry Seems to Be the Hardest Word"

THOUGH THE *NEW ERA* document was silent on welfare reform, it offered a progressive and expansive vision for children and family development. The NDP government of the 1990s had been subject to intense public and media criticism in that area of policy, and the BC Liberals were among the loudest voices demanding better.[1] *New Era* highlighted "the human toll of the NDP's waste and mismanagement." Children, in particular, were deemed to "have suffered because front-line workers haven't had adequate resources to do their jobs." British Columbians deserved a better government committed to delivery of better services. "Government has an obligation," the document declared, "to properly protect and provide for those most vulnerable in our society – especially children at risk and those in foster care." The time had come "to build a future in every community that is ripe with opportunity for our children and families."[2]

Nothing in *New Era* hinted that the budget of the Ministry of Children and Family Development (MCFD) might be slated for drastic reduction. Indeed, *New Era* promised to "devote the resources to the job needed to put the interests of kids first": the government would "increase emphasis on early childhood intervention programs," "focus on early identification of at-risk children," "enhance preventative drug and alcohol efforts," and "enhance training, resources and authority for front-line social workers."[3] These costly and complex commitments were salutary, but they demanded additional fiscal resources. Without such resources, they added to the chronic challenges of a very large social ministry burdened by New Era processes. As MCFD Minister Gordon Hogg noted, his department served a very large number of clients – "some 400,000 people each year; that's one in ten citizens in this province." Its cases were complex as well, among them the province's ten thousand children in care, "many of whom are medically fragile and have special needs."[4]

Ambitious *New Era* commitments were starkly at odds with budget cuts. MCFD initially faced a cut of 30 percent, but this was reduced to 23 percent after Hogg resisted.[5] Les Foster, an assistant deputy minister and later the author of a first-hand account of New Era social policy, describes Hogg's "numerous trips to Treasury Board and individual meetings with the chair of Treasury Board [the finance minister]" and his "intense eleventh-hour lobbying for a smaller reduction," a point confirmed in Hogg's 2015 doctoral dissertation.[6] According to Foster, Hogg also took hope from the fact that "the reductions were heavily loaded toward the end of the three-year period." By that time, perhaps the "economy would improve, government revenues would increase, and the full reductions would not be necessary."[7]

The severity of the cut to MCFD was surprising from at least a few perspectives. Some officials believed that the ministry had been underfunded during the NDP years and that the Liberals had forcefully recognized such underfunding in the *New Era* platform (including a quote from the child, youth and family advocate disparaging NDP government efforts) and elsewhere.[8] A prescription of targeted supplemental funding was expected, not major budget cuts.

Reducing caseloads and rationing services are never easy in any context but are arguably much more difficult when the developmentally disabled rather than the employable unemployed are involved. Neither threats nor inducements can eradicate a disability. Nor does the family dysfunction at the root of child apprehensions magically disappear without human intervention, typically by social workers who are trained to deal with such sensitive interactions.[9] Children were a growing portion of the province's demographic composition, which would, officials believed, inevitably fuel caseload pressures. Further, at the other end of the client continuum, developmentally disabled adults were outliving their parents and belatedly coming into care of the state.[10]

Controversies surrounding the abuse, neglect, and deaths of children were recurrent not only in British Columbia, but also in other provinces and American states.[11] As Foster notes, "when something goes wrong, as it must – it is impossible to protect all of the children all of the time – there is a media furor and public outcry from whomever is the opposition political party at the time, focusing on problems with the system and demands for something new to be done or for someone's head to roll."[12] The BC Liberals led the furor and outcry when five-year-old Matthew Vaudreuil, an MCFD client, was killed by his mother in 1992 and the subsequent inquiry led by Judge Thomas Gove determined that the ministry had failed to protect him. Political memory was short. When the generous *New Era* vision for children and families proved incompatible with the twin imperatives of tax cuts in 2001 and a balanced budget by 2004, it did not survive.

In August of 2001, just weeks into his job as MCFD minister, Hogg was confronted by an unanticipated growth in demand for services. The "sombre reality," he noted, "is that after only three months of this fiscal year, the ministry is already facing an estimated $55 million in unfunded cost pressures" due to an unexpected surge in caseloads for children in care and adults with developmental disabilities.[13] Unfunded cost pressures, which proved a recurrent challenge throughout the New Era, demonstrated one point conclusively: demand for services may rise or fall for any number of economic, demographic, or social reasons, none of which will include concern for a finance minister's balanced budget.

The early budget challenges were not anomalous but rather underlined both the volatility of service demand and the precarious character of cuts in a ministry where every service was vital to its recipients. Among the first cost-containment initiatives in the fall of 2001 was "putting a lid on discretionary spending" for programs such as providing monthly bus passes to special-needs foster children so that they could visit counsellors or tutors. In the predictable media storm that followed, Hogg framed his dilemma well: "Anything that's a health and safety issue we must maintain, but ... in order to meet the deficit we have to make some decisions. Out of all the essential services we provide, some of them we cannot continue to provide."[14] His words foreshadowed those of the 2002 Throne Speech: tax and budget cuts meant that government could only "moderate the impact" on vital programs despite the elimination of those deemed less vital.[15]

Lacking a basket of non-essential or wasteful programs to delete, Hogg suggested that decreasing MCFD caseloads was the core element in his plan for budget reductions: "About 32 percent of children come into care as a result of neglect, as opposed to abuse, and we should be looking at ways to provide support for those children and their families rather than apprehending them."[16] Journalist Judith Lavoie put that proposition to Child, Youth and Family Advocate Paul Pallan, who responded, "let's move to have fewer kids in care, but let's make sure there are adequate supports to make sure that families function well."[17] In his estimation, decreasing the caseload was contingent on stable or enhanced provision of social supports.

Pallan's 2001 Annual Report (released after the 2002 provincial budget) was devoted almost entirely to his concerns regarding the 23 percent, or $360.0 million, cut to the MCFD operating budget. Among the cuts he highlighted were $185.7 million from child protection and family development, $34.5 million from youth justice, youth services, and child and youth mental health, and $15.6 million from early childhood development and special-needs services for children and youth. Existing resources, he argued, were failing to meet essential service needs of children and youth; diminishing them could only intensify the critical need for effective alcohol, drug, and mental health treatment. He urged the government to exempt MCFD from budget reductions.

Pallan supported the ministry's goal of lessening the number of children in care: "Ideally, a reduced child and youth in care caseload would be the outcome of enhanced family development services and supports. However, accomplishing this goal will take additional resources, not fewer ... Planned reductions in MCFD's primary service areas that support children, youth and families will decrease their capacity even further." In short, the goal was sound, but it was entirely incompatible with the budget imperative placed on MCFD, a challenge exacerbated by budget-driven changes in other social ministries. An inspired attempt to resolve a complex problem was doomed to failure by woefully inadequate fiscal resources.

Almost two-thirds of children taken into care, Pallan stated, were from single parents on income assistance, "a pattern that has remained unchanged for the last decade." Ministry of Human Resources assistance for vulnerable families (as detailed in Chapter 7) was being reduced through lower assistance rates to single parents and the compulsion to seek employment when the youngest child turned three. Even when employment was available, reductions in the child-care subsidy (via MCAWS, as discussed in Chapter 6) placed some single parents in perilous circumstances. Pallan's conclusion was blunt and prescient: "The program reductions now proposed by MHR put the most vulnerable children, youth and families at even greater risk and stand in direct contradiction with MCFD's intention to increase capacity of families to care for their children."[18]

Pallan pointedly noted that when Campbell was in Opposition, he "supported the recommendation in our 2000 Annual Report for a needs-based budgeting approach. However, we see no evidence that the pending cuts to MCFD's budget are based on an assessment of the actual needs of children, youth and families."[19] Reconciling past political rhetoric with current governmental action proved an arduous challenge in the New Era.

Ambitious System Reforms Undermined
by Severe Budget Cuts

MCFD enjoyed a very knowledgeable and passionate advocate in Gordon Hogg, who brought experience as a public servant in youth corrections and as a foster parent. He was philosophically "a strong supporter of increased community participation in human service delivery," influenced by "his own experiences and by his graduate studies, in which he looked at system-wide approaches to service delivery."[20] MCFD's core review direction emphasized community delivery and governance, a goal that Hogg emphatically embraced. In an MCFD presentation to Open Cabinet, the word "community" appeared several times in six bullet points identifying the ministry's core review strategic shifts.[21]

Hogg believed that community-based governance and service delivery were the right goals regardless of budgetary considerations. He had a vision for the ministry and no interest in presiding over the status quo, with or without cuts: "Even if we had twice the budget, or no budget at all, I fervently and firmly believe that we are going to the right service delivery and the right model for families."[22] He understood the daunting task of reconciling a new service delivery model with a deep budget cut: "It's a difficult time for all of us, given the political imperatives. I have had many a sleepless night as I struggle through this."[23]

Many in the disabilities sector appeared to share his passion. Intra-provincial ministerial consultations produced four hundred submissions and over 100,000 visits to the MCFD website. "The overwhelming majority of submissions," Hogg noted, "in some way stressed the need to move toward a community-based service-delivery model."[24] As discussed in Chapter 3, he anticipated the creation of five administrative regions that aligned with the recently established regional health authorities, along with a permanent pan-provincial authority to support "a coherent and corporate approach to delivering a broad range of services."[25] A parallel consultation on Indigenous governance also produced promising early results.[26]

The restructuring initiative appeared to fly in the face of the *New Era* promise to "stop the endless bureaucratic restructuring that has drained resources from children and family services."[27] Hogg was well aware of the apparent contradiction. In introducing MCFD's 2002 Estimates, he borrowed language from *New Era* itself: "We are committed to stopping the endless restructuring of the past. The ministry will make its choices, implement them quickly and stick with them." Permanent CEOs, he promised, would soon be selected. Kith and kin agreements and family court conferencing "as safe, humane alternatives to taking children directly into the ministry's care" would also be introduced in 2002.[28]

Following Hogg's plan, the Interim Authority for Community Living BC (mandated to provide support for people with developmental disabilities until a permanent authority was in place) was established in 2002, along with ten planning committees – five of them Indigenous – to guide regionalization. Completion of funding formulae, transfer agreements, and organizational plans were slated for 2003, with final transfers and full implementation of the new service delivery model in 2004. These remarkable transformation goals were on top of the extensive priorities in the 270-day plan for MCFD, as noted in Chapter 5. As one official argued, addressing such a wide-ranging and complex agenda required "the right people in place with the right skills and adequate resources. However, buy-outs driven by budget imperatives pushed some of the most experienced staff out the door when most needed."[29]

The transformation goals and priorities were accompanied by ongoing and time-consuming process imperatives. For example, MCFD was expected to identify its share of "unnecessary" regulations, despite the sensitivity and complexity of potential reforms. One former official suggested that the "crazy push for deregulation led to all kinds of nonsense about freeing people in the field to do their jobs and getting out of the way. That, in turn, led to a stripping of policy and oversight functions in the headquarters."[30] The extraordinary demands on the ministry executive produced frequent turnover in its ranks – both forced and unforced – exacerbating the process barrage of core review, budget target review, workforce reductions, office closures, regionalization, devolution, and much more.

The highly ambitious character of the MCFD change agenda was exceeded only by the daunting barriers that blocked its realization. One observer noted: "Another visionary minister, Gordon Hogg, found himself caught in the middle of a growing dilemma: how to do more with less."[31] His efforts to reform the system were undermined by the ongoing push for expenditure reduction. For some critics, "community" was code for a provincial government attempting to offload budget pressures and responsibilities.[32] As pressure mounted to find major savings, so too did suspicions that devolution and regionalization initiatives were (in the words of one former official) "a poisoned chalice."[33] The fact that community governance and service delivery stayed on the rails for as long as they did was a tribute to Hogg's persistence, tenacity, and collegial relationship with the disabilities sector.

Exogenous Experience Proves a Pale Substitute for Dollars

Hogg believed that MCFD's system reorganization should borrow from exogenous experience. Plans for reform, he said, followed extensive ministerial review of "a wide range of service delivery models and looked at the systems in place in other provinces and in other countries."[34] He was also candid about potential risks identified through exogenous experience: "One of my concerns has been that when Alberta looked at fundamental restructuring, there was about a 78 percent increase in the number of children that came into care." In Ontario, the figure was 50 percent.[35] By Hogg's reckoning, the solution was embedded in the problem. Many apprehensions involved single parents on income assistance, "often women who, with some support within the context of their family, would have the ability to support their children."[36] Reduction in the number of children in care was a laudable goal that, as a side benefit, would lessen his ministry's budget pressures.

MCFD examined various jurisdictions, national and international, in pursuit of policy and practice lessons. Hogg was particularly encouraged by community-level child protection initiatives, "albeit in very small pilot projects," in Ontario and Manitoba that were "very positive."[37] He noted that the number of BC children in care had grown by 60 percent during the previous seven years to more than ten thousand. Overall, the province had a high ratio of children in care – eleven per thousand – versus nine as the national average. Maintaining a child in care cost $40,000 annually, and if their numbers were reduced to 1996 levels, budget savings would follow.[38]

Hogg's plans to restructure services while simultaneously cutting budgets were greeted with skepticism from the NDP Opposition. For example, Joy MacPhail noted that Quebec's attempt to restructure while cutting budgets by 10 percent had produced "a serious crisis." How could Hogg manage a 23 percent budget cut in a comparable restructuring? Far from dismissive of her comment, Hogg replied that the experience of Quebec, Ontario, and Alberta – all considered by his ministry – suggested that "there are a number of issues we have to manage and mitigate." MacPhail was not persuaded: "The minister cites provincial examples where there have been cuts and restructuring that have led to devastating results for children and families, but there's one difference. Not one of the governments he mentioned has cut as deeply as this government – not one."[39]

Hogg and MCFD also aimed to learn from New Zealand's simultaneous restructuring and budget cuts of the 1980s, which, he observed, raised "concerns with respect to the impact it was having on the poorer, more vulnerable people in society, both families and children." Well aware of the New Zealand precedent, MacPhail cited the central conclusion drawn from it: "The importance of having effective mechanisms to monitor, protect and promote the interests of children, especially during times of major change, and how governments should carefully consider how their actions will impact on children, the most vulnerable and valuable members of any society."[40] That objective, she argued, could not possibly be reconciled with a 23 percent budget cut or with termination of "the persons who could possibly challenge them on that: the child, youth and family advocate and the children's commissioner."[41]

Hogg was as blunt as a minister could be without engineering his own exit from cabinet via resignation or dismissal: "Certainly, in the best of all possible worlds, I wouldn't want to be entering into restructuring at a time when we're also looking at some changes in budgets and reductions in budgets." He was compelled to cut his budget, with or without simultaneous restructuring. A stable, protected budget was not among his options, "but we do have the chance to put in place a much better service delivery model."[42] Outside the legislative chamber, Hogg was equally forthright in addressing the media: "Ideally, you wouldn't want to be doing this at a time when you have a reduced budget. Ideally, when you're building a new structure, you would want to have, at least, a budget you maintain. We don't have that luxury."[43]

Hogg remained convinced that the restructuring of service delivery was sound, despite budgetary pressures: "We've had some of the best experts in the world. We've had blue-ribbon committees with representatives from all over the world looking at this, ensuring that we are implementing the best practices, the best procedures and the best methods of getting to service delivery."[44] MacPhail saw Hogg's reforms as doomed to failure based on "the international experts' advice that the double whammy ... of governance change and deep budget cuts forms dark clouds on the horizon."[45]

On occasions when BC Liberal members held the floor in Estimates debate, hints of frustration sometimes emerged. When asked by MLA Lorne Mayencourt (Vancouver–Burrard) "what was driving the change" in supported child care, Hogg responded, "this ministry has a 23 percent budget target that we have to address in the future. There are no easy solutions as we go forward with that." The first principle in making those difficult decisions, he stated, was protecting the most vulnerable. Supported child care was "one of those programs as we went down that list that was right at the cut-off line in terms of doing it. We must meet those budget targets."

Hogg explained that the magnitude of the cuts forced gut-wrenching choices among vital programs:

> If the member is asking us to show supported child care up against what happens in terms of sexually abused children or up against child protection needs, there's a whole range of those things. We're really at a difficult challenge ... The ministry has such a wide range of programs dealing with so many vulnerable and fragile people in the province that cutting in any area becomes a challenge.[46]

The demand to do more with less surrendered to the reality of doing less with less.

In March 2003, Hogg was able to report some progress in caseload reduction: since June 2001, the number of children in care had fallen by over 1,000 (from 10,775 to 9,600, although more recently levelling out).[47] Les Foster attributes this trend to two key factors: children who had been taken into care during and after the Gove Inquiry were aging out of the system, and youth agreements, kith and kin agreements, and adoptions were diminishing the number of apprehensions. Despite this progress, Foster reports: "Treasury Board was concerned that the ministry might not meet its third-year budget target, given the backend loading of budget reductions and its focus on establishing regional authorities. The board ordered the ministry to undertake what became known as the 'mid-term review.'"[48] In less cordial language, the ministry was effectively "in receivership."[49] MacPhail's storm clouds were indeed massing on the horizon.

Dark Clouds and Treasury Board Close In

Many of the MCFD cuts were backloaded to the final year of the three-year plan. Treasury Board recognized that major budget savings were linked to caseload reduction, which would not be achieved overnight. Addressing the Certified General Accountants of BC, Treasury Board chair Gary Collins commented, "we needed time to build up that capacity [so] we pushed out a lot of those challenges to the third year of the fiscal plan."[50] From Treasury Board's perspective, backloading was aimed at a smooth transition to reduced caseload levels. This strategy had the unintended side effect of inducing increasingly vigorous debate as the months wore on.

The metaphorical chickens released with the 23 percent budget target of 2001 were coming home to roost in 2003. Through caseload and workforce reductions over two years, MCFD had managed to achieve a 7 percent decrease from its baseline 2001–02 budget. After early promising results, "the number of children in care levelled off," leaving the ministry with unrealized savings and only decidedly unsavoury options.[51] It would need to find savings of over $200 million in the year ahead to fill the budgetary gap. With year three of the balanced budget plan closing in, Hogg was forced to put program reductions on the table, arousing further concerns in the disability community.[52]

In May of 2003, Hogg found himself front-and-centre in Question Period, responding to leaked documents. MacPhail led the attack with a familiar theme: "It's impossible to implement a 23 percent budget cut as part of this restructuring scheme. The opposition has learned that the minister's own interim authorities are balking at the cuts, refusing to implement the orders." The most damning criticism came from the government-appointed executive of the Interim Authority for Community Living: "While we are satisfied that the 2003–04 financial plan can be met without risk to the safety and security of individuals and families, we have no such confidence that the same can be said of the 2004–05 budget targets."[53] The executive suggested that a substantial infusion of new funding might facilitate reconciliation: if "government can support a course correction of this magnitude ... while maintaining its commitment to the vision that has been put forth, we ... are prepared to publicly support the strategic direction of this government in our communities and in our sector."[54]

The fragile peace and partnership between Hogg and disabilities advocates and service providers appeared to be near a breaking point. Service organizations feared cuts of up to 40 percent. "The scope of the cuts is really catastrophic," one official declared after review of preliminary numbers.[55] MacPhail asserted that Collins had in fact put the restructuring project on hold because of financial concerns. Hogg denied her claim, but his normal optimism was clearly under strain as he acknowledged the "significant challenges in terms of the service delivery model and the 23 percent cut." He also said that his ministry was "looking at the service plan."[56]

The next week, MacPhail returned to the issue: "The opposition has come into possession of a risk register. According to the risk register, there is a high likelihood that as a result of budget cuts, none of the services required to implement his [Hogg's] new model will even exist."[57] Hogg was absent at the time, so MacPhail directed her questions to Deputy Premier Christy Clark, but Collins stepped in. Responding to the assertions of elevated risk to the vulnerable, he stated, "that is the exact reason why we are reviewing the plan and the service plan" of MCFD.[58]

MacPhail rose the following day with the revelation that consultants in data collection and management had been engaged to address the challenges at MCFD. In her view, this was an admission of waste and incompetence. In response, Hogg argued, "every international expert that has looked at us, including people who were here last week, has said this transformation is the right transformation."[59] Notably, Finance Minister Collins again intervened in the debate: "We have identified challenges in '04–05 to the financial plan for that ministry ... We're dealing with that now, eight months in advance."[60] Among the identified challenges was the glaring fact that making good on the backloaded program cuts would be a political disaster in the final year before the 2005 election. Behind the scenes, furious negotiations (in both intensity and temperament) were ongoing.

Treasury Board did not relent without a fight. Collins conveyed little sympathy for Hogg's predicament in noting, "what we've found is just giving people more money doesn't solve the problem, it just means they keep doing what they're doing."[61] Collins opened the door a crack, advising Judith Lavoie that the MCFD review was to "decide what can be done differently. That may mean reallocating money within the ministry budget or extending the transition timeline. Putting more money into the ministry is the last option, but, at the end of the day it could be considered."[62]

The end of the day came on 4 June 2003, with an announcement by Premier Campbell that $122 million "pulled from other areas of government, will be put back into the ministry's budget next year [2004–05]." The $122 million was almost exactly what the executive directors of the interim authority had demanded for their continued support. According to Campbell, "it was clear in December or January that that reduction in the number of children in care was not going to be realized, so we started the process of looking at the plan."[63] He told "startled reporters" (in Les Leyne's words) that the "purpose of establishing a plan is not to blindly follow it," a sharp departure from his "we shall not waver" rhetoric of 2001–02.[64]

Campbell's announcement followed on the heels of another leaked MCFD document that laid out the steps necessary to achieve its budget goals. Among them were elimination of behavioural support programs for children with autism, termination of taking at-risk children into care after the age of sixteen, curtailment of the fetal alcohol initiative, and closure of the Maples Adolescent Treatment Centre in Burnaby.

Hogg quickly moved to discount such suggestions. "These were never things we planned to do, it was just that Treasury Board wanted to know how serious the situation really was," he said. "They were not things we intended to do. They were just to demonstrate the gravity of the situation."[65] The document may have been designed to get Treasury Board's attention – functioning as MCFD's own burning platform – but any $200 million list of cuts would of necessity have included highly sensitive programs for the vulnerable. Less sensitive programs had long since fallen to the budgetary knife.

The ministry paid a steep price for the monetary infusion as, "for the second time in two years there was a major change at the executive level, with three assistant deputy ministers and an executive director being replaced."[66] In Open Cabinet, Hogg was obliged to state that his ministry's original assumptions were incorrect and that additional funding was required if MCFD clients were to be kept safe. As Les Foster remarks, "this 'humiliation' was the price Hogg would have to pay to get more money for his ministry."[67] For Hogg, a statement in Open Cabinet was a small price to keep his transformation agenda on the rails.[68]

The infusion of $122 million partially relieved the budget challenges at MCFD, though it by no means eradicated them; a gap of $70 million still needed to be filled. The termination of 525 positions, including 125 social workers, would save about $18 million, but a balance of $52 million remained to be found.[69] MCFD's plan as of 26 June 2003 – prepared for discussion with the service providers – was to re-tender contracts and "give agencies the chance to amalgamate or cooperate or reduce administrative overheads," leading to estimated savings of $35 million. The balance would be secured from further staff cuts and closure of some smaller group homes and youth custody centres, as well as from the budgets for foster care and children in care.[70]

A different controversy beset MCFD long before its 2004–05 budget was confirmed. Doug Walls, acting CEO of the Interim Authority for Community Living, resigned on 17 January 2004, following accusations of wrongdoing that produced internal and external audits, as well as the appointment of a special prosecutor. MCFD Deputy Minister Chris Haynes was fired five days afterward, and in the spirit of ministerial responsibility, Hogg resigned later the same day.[71]

After losing Gordon Hogg as its minister, disability agencies and advocates appeared to lose patience with cuts of any magnitude. MLA Jenny Kwan quoted extensively from leaked letters in the legislature's 2004 spring session. One letter, from the interim authority for Community Living BC, noted that it faced "a significant dilemma": "No one believes reduced budgets make any sense in an environment already characterized by wait-lists for those requesting support ... [but] the widely-held belief is that the budget reductions will be imposed regardless of community opposition." In the absence of agreement to meet the $70 million budget target, the ministry would "employ what was called 'mitigating strategies' to meet the budget objectives."[72] Those strategies had changed little from June 2003: termination and re-tendering of contracts, reducing supports for high-cost individuals and one-to-one day programs, closure of two-person homes, and across-the-board cuts. In the words of John Kehler, president of the BC Association for Community Living, "the only way to describe them [such cuts] is draconian."[73]

Service delivery reforms ground on slowly. Budget 2004 suggested that transfers to regional authorities would be implemented "incrementally, based on readiness."[74] The devolution of child and family services moved a step forward with the introduction of the Community Living Authority Act in October 2004. The sector welcomed the act but remained "concerned about the much-reduced budget for the services" that would be provided by the new authority, Community Living BC. It called, unsuccessfully, for restoration of $195 million in funding to the sector.[75]

New Era Budget Cuts Return to Haunt the Golden Decade

In the 2005 Throne and Budget Speeches, the government attempted to put the dark days of budget cuts and retrenchment behind it by unveiling "Five Great Goals for a Golden Decade." The Throne Speech promised that "financial prudence and new fiscal capacity will allow us to build the best system of support in Canada for persons with disabilities, special needs, children at risk and seniors." Additional funding would be allocated for those programs.[76] Despite these reassuring words, the transition to happier times proved less than smooth. The "constant pressure of managing the child protection mandate with reduced resources" was soon to be tragically exposed, with the death of Sherry Charlie.[77]

Nineteen-month-old Charlie was killed in 2002 by a relative while she was in government care under the kith and kin program. A heavily redacted report on her death was released after the 2005 election. Unsurprisingly, it incited media furor and Opposition outcry, precisely as predicted by Les Foster.[78] Among the issues raised around her murder was the "impact of deep cuts in budgets for children's services," which a reporter described as "one of the blackest marks on Gordon Campbell's Liberal government."[79]

The controversy took a new turn, as "concern about one death mushroomed into concerns about all children's deaths – particularly after the Solicitor General revealed that over seven hundred child deaths had not been reviewed during the transition period when responsibility for child death reviews moved from the Children's Commissioner to the Coroner's Office."[80] That move, as further discussed below, was impaired by the coroner's budget struggles, then exacerbated by insufficient funding for the transfer. Dislocation occasioned by New Era budget cuts now revisited the government as it moved tentatively into the Golden Decade.

The controversy prompted a 2005–06 review led by Ted Hughes, a highly respected former BC deputy attorney general and conflict of interest commissioner. Hughes noted that his "strongest impression" from his inquiry was that the child welfare system had been "buffeted by an unmanageable degree of change." The confluence of ministerial reorganization and service delivery reform, aggravated by deep budget cuts and a "revolving door" in senior leadership positions, created a "climate of instability and confusion that could only detract from the Ministry's work on behalf of children."

On the disjunction between demands for expenditure reduction and for concurrent organizational reform, Hughes reported, "it is commonly understood that organizational change costs money." The failure to recognize that fact stretched the ministry's "finite capacity for managing change ... far beyond its limits." Among the examples he cited was the fact that "new programs, intended to keep more children at home with their families, were introduced amidst budget cuts to the services that support families and youth in crisis; social workers received no training to help them implement these new programs."[81]

At the news conference following release of his report, Hughes told journalists, "I don't think there's any doubt that the core review of 2001 and 2002 took the knife too far." As a consequence, children "got caught in the cross-fire."[82] The MCFD experience provided a graphic, real-world example of Christopher Pollitt's broad warning that "cuts of 20% plus cannot be absorbed without real damage to the quality of services, and anyone who suggests otherwise, as some politicians have done, is, to put it charitably, mistaken."[83]

Hughes did not spare Premier Campbell in his report: "I cannot agree with the premier's earlier assessment that budget cuts did not contribute to the failure of the transition process [for child death reviews] ... The impact of budget constraints reverberated throughout the welfare system from 2002 until recently." Of the premier's assessment, Hughes bluntly told reporters, "he was wrong." Hughes noted that even before the botched transition, the Coroner's Office "was already struggling to carry out its statutory mandate to investigate unexpected and unexplained deaths." The transfer of $200,000 to support the expanded child death review function proved wholly inadequate: "Those responsible for the transition were under pressure to meet deep spending cuts across the board and as a result this small program got lost in the shuffle." By his accounting, "some 955 files of children who died were never properly reviewed," as the coroner's service attempted to cope with its own budget woes.[84]

Five years after *New Era* condemned the NDP for failing to provide front-line social workers with "adequate resources to do their jobs," the premier bore sharp criticism from a highly respected source for an appalling, budget-driven attenuation of services to the province's most vulnerable children. Campbell was reluctant to acknowledge the link between budget cuts and the failed transfer. On 16 November 2005, he stated, "yes, the government does take responsibility [for the failed transfer]."[85] However, pressed for an apology in the wake of the Hughes report a few months later,

Campbell first argued, "Mr. Hughes says that we perhaps took on too many initiatives at once. If we have any failings as a government, I would suggest that it was because we were trying to provide for the children of BC."

Confronted again, he stated, "I accept that we took on a big load. I accept that we took on many challenges. I accept that we may have demanded too much of the people that were at work trying to help us do that."[86] He did not acknowledge that the transfer was only one of the many MCFD services that had been impaired or lost due to the massive cuts to a ministry that, in Gordon Hogg's words, supported "so many vulnerable and fragile people."[87]

Alas, the pace and magnitude of expenditure reductions were driven, first, by the faulty belief that the tax breaks would pay for themselves regardless of the economic environment in which they were introduced and, second, by the self-imposed balanced budget imperative for 2004–05. Sustainability of vital programs finished, at best, a distant third in the pecking order of objectives. Tax cuts that failed to generate the expected revenue quickly extinguished the *New Era* promise to "devote the resources to the job needed to put the interests of kids first." The dramatic drop in taxes would indeed have dramatic consequences, particularly for the vulnerable and disadvantaged.

In his classic study of policy dynamics, John Kingdon suggests that politicians "need to ask themselves before unlatching [a policy window] whether they risk setting in motion an unmanageable chain of events that might produce a result not to their liking."[88] The New Era experience of MCFD was a painful and perplexing example of government's failure to appreciate the critical intersection of tax and social policy, thereby unleashing an unmanageable cascade of events.

9

Lessons Learned from the New Era

"It just reminds us of the cost, of everything we've lost,
Bad timing that's all."

– Blue Rodeo, "Bad Timing"

APHORISMS SOMETIMES PROVIDED vital links between inspiration and action in the New Era. Gordon Campbell despised indecision and was particularly impatient with long debates on matters on which he had already formed his conclusions. He preferred to act before doubters and naysayers could crowd his path. An aphorism from British mountaineer W.H. Murray captured this approach: "Until one is committed, there is hesitancy, the chance to draw back, always ineffectiveness."[1] Decisive leadership comes with heightened risks and rewards. Any initiative – such as a billion-dollar tax cut – that a new administration announces within hours of being inaugurated risks categorization as prescription before diagnosis, particularly if it affects every corner of government. If it succeeds beyond expectations, it may be judged politically courageous, perhaps even visionary, but if it fails or falls short, it may be disparaged as ill-timed and ill-conceived. The 25 percent tax cut proved to be the latter, a product of prescription before diagnosis. Why the rush to take such risk?

The tax decision flowed from the well-honed narrative of British Columbia as a jurisdiction that was overtaxed and consequently underperforming economically. *New Era*'s frequent promise of a dramatic drop in taxes certainly demanded its delivery, but government controlled its timing and magnitude. The premier and his finance minister chose quick and bold. Comments made by Campbell and his deputy Ken Dobell regarding cutbacks as virtuous necessity reveal that self-induced austerity, via deep tax cuts, underlined the imperative of downsizing government through core review. The mandate letters from Campbell to cabinet, laying out core review and related smaller government initiatives, came long before tax cut optimism began to wane, as did his direction to cabinet of 27 June 2001 "that getting costs under control was at the top of the government's agenda."[2] The hole in the budget was intended to focus ministerial minds as they entered core review.

However, given that into September 2001 Campbell and Finance Minister Gary Collins appeared to remain optimistic regarding the province's 3.8 percent economic growth indicates that their burning platform had become a far greater conflagration than they intended. They had not expected their tax strategy to fail. The *New Era* document bubbled with confidence that British Columbia under new and inspired leadership would rapidly return to economic health and wealth; hence, it offered up an ambitious social agenda, replete with extensive and expensive promises.

As faith in tax cut rebound revenues faded, the government protected two key imperatives throughout the New Era – the tax cuts in 2001 and a balanced budget in 2004. Balancing the budget was largely contingent on reducing the expenditures of ministries. In resource ministries such as Forests and Agriculture, government slashed budgets as deeply as it could without completely incapacitating operations. But it refused to abandon either the tax cuts or its commitment to a balanced budget, and it declined to break its hands-off promise regarding the budgets of Health and Education. Thus, it left itself no choice but to turn the knife on the social ministries.

Dramatic tax cuts were the mother of all policy transfers in the New Era; they also proved a failed transfer, the wrong tool employed at the wrong time. As David Bond pointed out in 2001, cutting taxes in Ontario during a record period of protracted growth will produce very different results than applying the same measure in British Columbia on the edge of recession. In one sense, the cuts were neither a hurried nor an uninformed policy transfer. The Liberals had studied and promoted them for years before making them the centrepiece of the *New Era* platform. In another sense, they were both hurried and uninformed; Campbell and Collins announced them on the day that they took power, ignoring strong evidence of economic decline, overriding the cautionary advice of the Ministry of Finance, and pre-empting a report due weeks later from their own Fiscal Review Panel.

Premier Campbell was convinced that cutting personal income tax would automatically generate revenues. Given that the strategy had succeeded elsewhere during the 1990s, why would it fail in British Columbia of 2001? Campbell assumed that investors would respond quickly to his bold signal. With his tax cut of 6 June 2001, he could boast of having the second-lowest top marginal tax rate in the nation. This may have been politically useful, but it was of little consequence from economic and investment perspectives.

More than a year later, British Columbia was languishing as the second-last Canadian province in investment, at -4.7 percent, despite moving to lower tax rates than some faster-growing provinces.[3] The New Era experience suggests that the efficacy of a tax cut may hinge, first and foremost, on the macroeconomic environment in which it is introduced. In 2001–02, the world was preoccupied with a bevy of economic and geopolitical problems. Tax signals from a jurisdiction that accounts for less than 1 percent of North American GDP may not broadly resonate, no matter how audacious. Local investors may have appreciated the message, but other factors – such as global and provincial economic conditions, interest rates, or energy prices – outweighed or obscured it.

Small jurisdictions such as British Columbia or Kansas can rarely hope to be the tail that wags the dog. Nor will domestic tax policy, no matter how skilfully employed, shield a small open trading economy from prevailing macro patterns and trends in global economies. Some may argue that tax cuts hastened the province's return to prosperity. Perhaps, but the Business Council of British

Columbia's comparison of the 1990s and the 2000s showed that average GDP growth, as well as new investment in machinery and equipment, was greater during the 1990s under the NDP than in the 2000s under the BC Liberals. As the council argued, cause-and-effect assertions are difficult to prove in a small open economy operating in a much larger world.[4]

Given that energy and commodity revenues had been steeply declining since 15 March 2001, British Columbia was headed for a deficit in 2001, its own naturally occurring burning platform, which would have ignited with or without the drop in taxes. When Campbell and Collins went all in (to employ an appropriate gambling metaphor) with their $2 billion cuts, the result was an overall $4.4 billion fiscal hole that had somehow to be filled. Government consequently sacrificed its *New Era* social agenda for the twin political imperatives of tax cuts and a balanced budget.

As Table 7 demonstrates, social ministries were subject to severe budget and staffing cuts, multiple process demands, and

TABLE 7
Social ministry comparative challenges

Challenges	MCAWS	MHR	MCFD
Percentage budget/staff cut or devolved	30% final/ 55% staffing	30% final/ 30% staffing	23% final/ 22% staffing overall/ 55% executive
New Era commitments	Extensive	Minimal	Extensive
General process engagement (e.g., core review/ deregulation)	Extensive	Substantial	Extensive
Ministerial process engagement (e.g., devolution)	Extensive: reorganization, devolution	Minimal	Extensive: regionalization, devolution
Caseload complexity: composition	Medium/low: child-care subsidy	High: employable unemployed, chronic disabilities	Very high: kids in care, developmentally disabled

obligatory *New Era* commitments. Such challenges were exacerbated by the complexity and sensitivity of their caseloads. For the Ministry of Children and Family Development (MCFD), these elements combined to generate a perfect storm symbolized by the death of Sherry Charlie and the flawed transfer of child death reviews.

MCFD may have enjoyed a slightly smaller budget cut than Human Resources (MHR) and Community, Aboriginal and Women's Services (MCAWS), but the complexity and sensitivity of its caseloads made *any* program reductions extraordinarily difficult. MCFD's simultaneous and extensive process barrage confounded both its service delivery reforms and its attempts to decrease its caseloads.

New Era budget cuts stood out for their depth and rapidity, forcing ministries to ration services that should not have been rationed. As a government contemplates the message that a tax cut might send, it should also consider what a worst-case scenario might look like if the measure fails to pay for itself. Budget and service cuts also send signals to investors about social stability, quality of health and education systems, and availability of child care to employees. In the twenty-first century, where a jurisdiction sits on a social justice continuum may be just as important as where it resides on a tax curve. During the New Era, the replacement of relinquished tax cut revenues with a combination of user fees and reduced public services translated to a disproportionate impact on the consumers of those services, often the vulnerable and disadvantaged. Tax and budget cuts were a poor prescription to achieve social peace and stability.

Seth Klein of the Canadian Centre for Policy Alternatives (CCPA) argues that the convergence of tax cuts and spending cuts simply negated any benefit that the poor might have acquired from the former: "In many respects we are witnessing a straight transfer of income from the poor (in program cuts) to the wealthy (who disproportionately benefit from the tax cuts)."[5] The social ministry case studies provided compelling examples of socially and economically disadvantaged individuals and groups struggling to live with less while government waited for tax cuts to deliver the expected results. For MCAWS, the *New Era* promise to direct child-care funding to "parents who need it most" meant reducing the income threshold from $1,500 to $1,215 and removing subsidy from nine thousand low-income (and often single-parent) families. After funding was partially restored a year later, Minister Lynn Stephens said that she looked forward to the time when the full amount could be reinstated, implicitly confirming that funding cuts reflected budget-driven austerity, not ostensible sustainability.[6]

In MHR, the drive to find $581 million in savings saw single mothers with children as young as three obliged to seek work. Ironically, changes to the daycare rules meant that once they had paid for daycare, their net salaries would typically be lower than their welfare payments had been. Further, single mothers on income assistance who were receiving spousal support through the Family Maintenance Enforcement Program would now have their welfare cheques cut by that amount, whereas they were previously permitted to retain an additional one hundred dollars. And if they and their children needed dental surgery, they must now secure it at a hospital rather than a dental clinic, meaning a delay of several months. Such punitive measures were not driven by a vision of smaller government but rather by deep budget cuts flowing directly from deep tax cuts.

The cumulative impacts across social ministries were felt most acutely in MCFD. Its budget targets relied on reducing the number of children who were taken into care. Minister Hogg noted that 65 percent of such cases involved single parents, typically women, who were on BC Benefits. He suggested that if they received "some support within the context of their family," they could continue to care for their children.[7] Alas, his worthy suggestion was entirely at odds with the reality of doing less with less amid staggering budget cuts. As demonstrated in all three case studies, ministries were forced to ration or eliminate supports for vulnerable children and families, not enhance them. Hogg exposed the core of the social dilemma. His ministry, he said, "has such a wide range of programs dealing with so many vulnerable and fragile people in the province that cutting in any area becomes a challenge."[8] Most cuts were painful for social ministries but no less mandatory.

Child, Youth and Family Advocate Paul Pallan made the point well: "Children and youth do not have to meet or achieve certain standards, measures or outcomes in order to exercise their rights. Rather, children and youth have an inherent right to the best quality of life that we can provide for them right now."[9] They should not be obliged – as they were in the New Era – to wait for critical services, as governments waited for tax cuts to pay for themselves. The push to find huge savings within short timelines also drove program reforms (and in many cases policy transfers) that were only policy "sticks," not policy "carrots."[10] Carrots are almost invariably expensive in either upfront cost or deferred savings; both were inimical to the realities of the New Era.

Does a Declaration of Victory Mean the War Is Really Over?

The Throne and Budget Speeches of 2004 fortuitously followed the awarding of the right to host the 2010 Olympics and Paralympics to Vancouver/Whistler and British Columbia. This remarkable communications opportunity prompted fulsome expressions of pride in the province's achievements – political and fiscal, as well as organizational. The 2004 Throne Speech proclaimed, "it is our time to shine in British Columbia, now and for many years to come. The groundwork for growth has been laid. The foundation for achievement has been built. The new era has begun."[11] British Columbia was now poised to reap the benefits of lower taxes, less red tape, and an enhanced investment climate.

The rhetoric of retrenchment was replaced by the unbridled optimism of the "Spirit of 2010." The steely eyed fiscal discipline that stripped funding from the BC Festival of the Arts, the BC Seniors Games, and the Athlete Assistance Program vanished in 2004 to reveal a bevy of new programs, such as LegaciesNow and ArtsNow. Although WomenNow failed to move beyond draft concept, the Throne Speech extolled the funding of seventy thousand child-care spaces, fifteen thousand more than in 2001. What had been wholly unsustainable only three years earlier had now been eclipsed. As the Throne Speech stated, "the hard work of the last two years has opened new promise for our province. It is bringing our children home."[12]

The self-laudatory tone continued in the 2004 Budget Speech: "Today marks a turning point in the history of British Columbia, a day that future generations will recall with pride ... We will balance the budget this year, next year and every year thereafter."[13] Budget 2004 included a brief, understated, and belated acknowledgment of political vulnerability arising from the bitter medicine imposed on social ministries: "We've monitored our progress, and we've made adjustments where necessary to ensure the best outcomes for our citizens. For example, last year, after a mid-term service plan review, we increased the budget for the Ministry of Children and Family Development." Even MHR, after shedding over $600 million from its budget in the previous three years, was now receiving an increase, "recognizing the changes in the makeup of the income assistance caseload."[14]

Critics were unimpressed by such triumphalism. Joy MacPhail slammed the pretense of happier times: "They seem to think that having crawled back to where they started in 2001 is progress. Getting back to where you started is not progress; it is failure."[15] Marc Lee of the CCPA argued that the budget was "balanced, but on a razor's edge," courtesy of $1.9 billion in cuts since 2001–02. He warned, "if there are any economic shocks – such as a repeat of last year's forest fires, or if planned changes to federal equalization go ahead – we'll be back in the red."[16]

The 2004 Throne and Budget Speeches declared victory in the war on overtaxation, government waste, and excessive regulation. Did they also signal that an ideal or optimal state had been achieved around smaller government? Most assuredly not, for as government coffers swelled between 2005 and late 2008 (the abbreviated Golden Decade), so too did reinvestment in health, education, and social services. Indeed, by February 2005 the government commitment to "build the best system of support in

Canada for persons with disabilities, special needs, children at risk, and seniors" stood among the five great goals for a golden decade.[17] Further, the government was now proudly extolling its multi-million-dollar investments in areas such as fuel cell development and aviation training that would have been chased from the core review and business subsidies committee rooms in 2001.

Was this newly discovered generosity a product of tax cut success? Not by Will McMartin's reckoning. As he notes, the revenues of four budget years demonstrate the painful truth that tax cuts had failed to live up to Campbell's billing. Although total revenues rose from $30.0 billion under the NDP to $32.6 billion under the Liberals, "nearly all of the increase is due to higher transfer payments from Ottawa." Corporation income tax revenue was slightly higher in 2004–05 than in 2000–01, but even after four years the yield from personal income taxes was 15 percent lower than before the 25 percent tax cut of 2001.[18] The government's new-found largesse reflected a pending election rather than tax cut success.

Lessons Learned about Political and Public Policy Change

The New Era offers lessons on both the direction and speed of political and public policy change. Campbell's mandate letters of 25 June 2001 quickly unleashed numerous processes that he believed would be mutually supportive. Tax cuts would stimulate the economy and underline the critical importance of core review. Core and budget target reviews would correct the NDP's profligate spending and reduce recourse to the taxpayer's wallet. Deregulation would cut unnecessary costs to industry, taxpayers, and government. Elimination of NDP waste, mismanagement, and business subsidies, symbolized by the Skeena Cellulose bailout and the fast ferries "fiasco," would save billions that could be redirected to enhanced public services. And the vaunted Waste Buster website would allow 4 million British Columbians to help "stamp out government waste," again allowing redeployment of taxpayer dollars to public services.[19]

The *New Era* narrative and its real-world performance were flawed in multiple ways. Most examples of purported NDP waste and mismanagement involved past capital rather than current operational expenditures. Their correction did not provide billions in savings to be harvested and redistributed to resource-deprived ministries. Similarly, the Waste Buster website uncovered remarkably little in the way of ongoing waste and none that might be redeployed in other public services, proving as futile in this respect as the elimination of business subsidies.

Deregulation was deemed a success by government because it exceeded its 33 percent goal. However, this success lay largely if not entirely in cleaning up the books – eliminating obsolete statutes and regulations that had never been formally repealed. Some observers would argue that the shift from the NDP's Forest Practices Code to greater industry self-regulation under the Forest and Range Practices Act saved millions of dollars. However, any savings (beyond those afforded to industry) from self-regulation only helped the Ministry of Forests achieve its 40 percent budget cut; there were no savings to pass on to other ministries. Regrettably, savings from deregulation – even in combination with the elimination of waste and business subsidies – could not even modestly shrink the immediate budgetary hole created by the tax cuts. These initiatives contributed to the New Era process burden but provided little or no relief from fiscal pressures.

Much of the New Era approach was grounded in New Public Management (NPM), whose measures can sometimes be contradictory, as Pollitt and Summa suggest. Although New Era measures and processes yielded some constructive results (most notably the products of devolution), overall the confluence and temporal intensity of processes inhibited rather than encouraged the innovative outcomes sought by government, particularly in connection with social policy. In many instances, the NPM tools that the New Era borrowed turned out to be mutually contradictory. The impairment of MCFD's regionalization and devolution processes by a 23 percent budget cut, along with a comparable staffing cut, was an obvious and compelling example. And the work of the External Panel threatened to undermine the devolution of the Safety Engineering Services Branch out of MCAWS and into an independent special-purpose authority.

Is NPM inherently contradictory as a public management philosophy? Or was it just the way NPM was implemented in British Columbia? On the basis of the New Era experience, I would suggest the latter. The efficacy of NPM tools was persistently undermined by their mode of employment. The haste to find immediate savings, to protect the tax cuts and the balanced budget, and to have everything at the same time moved NPM tools from useful to unconstructive. In interviews with the author, former officials complained that they were given too little time for careful policy analysis in areas as divergent as alternative service delivery ("just no time for proper assessment") and kith and kin agreements with First Nations ("rushed out the door without proper policy analysis").[20] The opportunity for positive results was too often imperilled by the demand for immediate results.

Core review could potentially have been a thoughtful and considered assessment of public value generated by government programs. Instead, it was a blunt and time-limited weapon to make government smaller – and to complement the drive for the balanced budget. As detailed in Chapter 5, elimination of services and programs was both the easiest and the preferred outcome of core review. Any program that did not deliver either incremental revenue or a *New Era* commitment was assumed to have a "termination" sign on it. The single-mindedness of core review was such that sometimes not even a *New Era* shield was sufficient defence. *New Era* promised to "increase efforts to protect and promote aboriginal languages," but core review's External Panel called for the elimination of the First Peoples' Heritage, Language and Culture Council, despite strong objections from MCAWS. Core review provided abundant confirmation of the adage that, if your only tool is a hammer, everything looks like a nail.[21]

Core review's goal of smaller government was undoubtedly reinforced by tax cuts and the subsequent burning platform, but the failure of the cuts to pay for themselves had implications beyond budgetary deficits. As Pollitt argues, austerity "increases the temptation to rush into some 'quick fix' without due diagnosis of the underlying problems."[22] Deep tax cuts demanded deep reductions in expenditure; the haste in assigning percentages to ministerial budget cuts precluded full and proper diagnosis of the results, setting in motion elements of the perfect storm that engulfed MCFD in 2003. The rush to achieve multiple and sometimes competing or contradictory objectives proved a prescription for failure in the New Era. Need it always be so?

Speed, Focus, and Process as Determinants of Public Policy Success

As discussed in Chapter 5, the Chrétien government's program review of the mid-1990s was widely regarded as "a political success."[23] On the basis of that experience, Jocelyne Bourgon, former clerk of the Privy Council, declares that governments "should speedily implement big reforms," unlike Christopher Pollitt, who suggests that they "need time to introduce, implement, and anchor reforms."[24] The optimal speed of reforms may well be linked to the area of public policy that is slated for reform. Les Foster argues convincingly that in social policy "major changes to complicated systems take time if they are to be implemented successfully" and that "such changes require additional resources, not a reduction in resources, at least until the changes have been effected."[25] MCFD's reforms proved incompatible with multiple and simultaneous process demands and resource attrition. On the other hand, the Ministry of Health Planning was successful in implementing complex organizational reforms in a remarkably short time, aided by a well-defined mission and an adequate budget (as detailed in Chapter 3).

The success of the Chrétien government's program review may reside as much with focus as with speed. Notably, the review did not attempt to cut taxes or to replace the Goods and Services Tax. Both would have consumed finite government energy and resources. Further, the complex nest of federal Indigenous programs remained untouched. Conversely, in the BC New Era, the extraordinary aspect of MCFD's experience was not that things fell apart in 2003, but rather that the ministry accomplished as much as it did given its constraints: budget and staffing cuts, regionalization, devolution, *New Era* commitments, 270-day plan deliverables, and wholesale executive changes. Would the 2001–02 regionalization of the BC health care system have succeeded had it faced simultaneous budget and staffing cuts?

As Pollitt and Bouckaert point out, governments can seldom have everything at the same time.[26] However, this was precisely what the Campbell government demanded of ministries in the New Era. As in Alberta, Ontario, and New Zealand, the siren song of "bigger, faster, deeper" convinced it that reform was a time-limited opportunity, thus unleashing a barrage of process.

Did policy transfer help the government to achieve its goals? Did ministries take full advantage of the premier's invitation to learn from the experience of other jurisdictions? Campbell certainly lit the path on policy transfer. His mandate letters of 25 June 2001 alone offered at least six new processes or institutions borrowed from elsewhere: core review, ministers of state, and mandate letters (from the federal realm), Government Caucus Committees and the Public Affairs Bureau (from Alberta), and deregulation (from NPM). Tax cuts (from NPM) and the Fiscal Review Panel (from Alberta) were out of the gate even before the mandate letters.

Chapters 6, 7, and 8 offer numerous examples of policy transfer in areas such as welfare reform, municipal powers, government services centres, devolutionary content and process, and child protection.[27] The experience of policy transfer in the New Era was shaped by the context in which the transfers were considered: core review and its strategic shifts, budget and staff cuts of up to 45 percent, plus 270-day plan deliverables. Staff displacement and compressed timelines seldom allowed for a thorough analysis of how well the policy had worked in the exporting jurisdiction. Analysis more often resembled last-minute gift shopping for a difficult recipient. Transfers were not coercive, but neither were they voluntary lesson drawing. Dolowitz and Marsh offer a mixed transfer category – voluntary "but driven by perceived necessity" – that would have broad application to the New Era.[28] Ministries did not enjoy the luxury of strategic, comparative assessment of programs and jurisdictions. Confronted by intractable problems, budget and staff cuts, and daunting timelines, they cast their nets widely and quickly in search of solutions.

The New Era's New Era?

The 2004 Throne Speech contained a curious passage, which stated that "the new era has begun."[29] The speech writers in the Premier's Office were undoubtedly deliberate in choosing this wording. So what are we to make of a lowercase "new era" in the midst of what I have called the New Era? Were the previous three years a hangover from the old era of the NDP, now rehabilitated and regenerated? If the answer is "yes," this conception is strikingly at odds with "the New Era full of promise and potential" in which the government would "cut personal income taxes and unleash the power of a thriving free enterprise economy."[30] Not a single word in the *New Era* document suggested that dislocation and sacrifice were essential preconditions for entry into the New Era. Were they?

British Columbia was neither the first nor the last jurisdiction that was obliged to or wished to achieve balanced budgets by trimming programs and expenditures. With or without tax cuts, the province was heading for a deficit in 2001, and austerity would not be an uncommon response. Further, given the frequent *New Era* promise of a dramatic tax cut, delivery of the same was unsurprising. Its timing and magnitude *were* surprising, particularly given cautionary advice from Finance and strong evidence of a weakening economy.

The tax cut was not only an example of prescription before diagnosis; it was also, as one former official argued, grounded in "ideologically based decision making rather than evidence-based decision making. Unfortunately, this reckless approach caused significant harm to vulnerable citizens, environmental protection, resource management, union relations, and government reputation."[31] The tragedy was not that the premier bet and lost, but that the vulnerable and disadvantaged paid so heavily for his engagement with the roulette wheel. For a province at the edge of economic recession, a smaller tax break would still have sent a bold signal to the world without producing the deep budget cuts that sacrificed the *New Era* social agenda.

Some neo-liberal elements of Gordon Campbell's ideology, such as his affection for tax cuts, persisted throughout his political career. Similarly, when confronted by economic downturn, he instinctively resorted to budget-cutting retrenchment. However, his ideological "collar and cuffs" did not always match. Campbell promised in the *New Era* document to "minimize undue government intervention in people's lives" but simultaneously offered more than two hundred expansive and costly commitments, many of which demanded larger – not smaller – government.[32] However, the New Era emphasis on tax cuts, smaller government, and retrenchment left little room for reformist zeal. Nor did Campbell demonstrate much interest in that direction. The New Era suggested that he would offer little more than unrepentant neo-liberalism.

Four years later, with the benefit of surplus budgets in the abbreviated Golden Decade (2005 to late 2008), and reinforced by the soaring aspirations of his Five Great Goals, Campbell embraced a more activist role for government, especially in the social and environmental realms. His reformist legacy was largely established during that period, including his leadership on Indigenous relations, on North America's first revenue-neutral carbon tax, and on the Great Bear Rainforest and other parks and protected areas.

Sadly, that legacy was and is tarnished by the continuing impact of New Era retrenchment. Drastic expenditure and staffing cuts hit resource ministries just as climate-driven fire and flood increasingly threatened the province.[33] Notwithstanding New Era deregulation, the Campbell years saw the number of responsibilities assigned to provincial land managers grow rapidly, while budgets for resource ministries shrank (as did the numbers of registered professional foresters and biologists employed within government).[34] As demonstrated in the case studies presented here, Campbell's pretense of doing more with less all too quickly surrendered to the reality of doing less with less.

New governments are confronted by a wide range of circumstances when they take power, and each will come equipped with a vast array of ideas, tools, and approaches that define its responses to economic, social, and political problems. Prescriptions will vary but must include a realistic assessment of the worst-case scenario should the tools not produce anticipated results. When a government attempts to do everything at the same time in an unpredictable economic environment, it risks inducing a host of side effects – from unintended consequences to cumulative impacts – that may undermine or confound its best-laid plans.

No political party, no matter how big its majority, wins the right to remake government and its programs in perpetuity. Reinventing government is not a time-limited venture; reforms that are rushed into place will ultimately be judged by succeeding governments and, if found wanting, will be repealed. The only permanent damage from rushed reforms is, alas, to the vulnerable and disadvantaged clients who rely on the targeted programs. If "life is what happens to you while you're busy making other plans," unanticipated and painful consequences are what happen to governments that push ideologically based and poorly diagnosed plans.[35]

Notes

Chapter 1: The New Era in Brief

Epigraph: Paul Simon, "Under African Skies," from *Graceland,* 1986.

1 BC Liberal Party, *A New Era for British Columbia: A Vision for Hope and Prosperity for the Next Decade and Beyond* (N.p.: BC Liberal Party, 2001), 2, 3. For clarity, *New Era* refers to the document cited here, whereas New Era, without italics, refers to the period 2001 to 2005.

2 BC Liberal Party, *New Era,* 2, but the commitments are repeated elsewhere in the document.

3 BC Liberal Party, *The Courage to Change* (N.p.: BC Liberal Party, 1996), 6, 13.

4 Frances Bula and Brian Kappler, "The Long Way Home: With a Commanding Lead in the Polls, Liberal Leader Gordon Campbell Is Days away from What Appears to Be His Destiny," *Calgary Herald,* 5 May 2001.

5 Frances Bula, "Hello Gordon: Is That You? Or the Other You?" *Vancouver Sun,* 28 April 2001.

6 The phrase "remake government" is drawn from a Vaughn Palmer interview with Campbell. Vaughn Palmer, "All Quiet on the BC Front," *National Post,* 20 December 2001.

7 Christopher Pollitt, "What Do We Know about Public Management Reform? Concepts, Models, and Some Approximate Guidelines" (paper presented at the "Towards a Comprehensive Reform of Public Governance" conference, Lisbon, 28–30 January 2013), 5.

8 Among them were most newspaper columnists and, more surprisingly, Martyn Brown, Campbell's chief-of-staff, who retrospectively described himself as "quite astounded" by the size and range of the decrease. Quoted in Doug Ward, "BC Liberals' 12 Years of Tax Shifts, Explained," *Tyee,* 6 May 2013.

9 BC Liberal Party, *New Era,* 2, 4, 5, 10, 11, 15, 33.

10 Vaughn Palmer, "Parsing Campbell's Tax-Cutting Promise," *Vancouver Sun,* 26 October 2000. For the 1996 promise, see BC Liberal Party, *Courage to Change,* page 4 of preface.

11 BC Liberal Party, *New Era,* 5 (emphasis in original). The same page of the document also prominently features a graph of Ontario tax cuts and revenue growth.

12 The $4.4 billion deficit comprised the 25 percent personal tax (estimated at $1.2 billion), reductions in corporate and machinery and equipment taxes (estimated at $800 million), plus market-based declining revenues on energy and commodities.

13 Growth was 0.6 percent in real GDP and -0.3 percent in GDP per capita. Michael Butler, "A Brief Examination of the British Columbia Government's Spending and Revenue Record," 18 April 2017, 17. This document, which was prepared for the Ministry of Finance, incorporates material that was released with the 2017 provincial budget on 21 February 2017.

14 "Burning platform" is used in a variety of ways in the literature on political and managerial change. I define it as a crisis that is either natural (for example, a deficit produced by a cyclical downturn) or, alternatively, engineered or inadvertently caused (for example, a deficit exacerbated by tax cuts).

15 BC Liberal Party, *New Era,* 21, 25. The estimated cost of the commitments was $2 billion. For example, *New Era* promised five thousand intermediate- and long-term units for the frail elderly in what became Independent Living BC. That commitment alone would consume a substantial portion of the estimated $2 billion. The cost of meeting "all patients' needs where they live and when they need it" would probably consume the entire amount if ever attempted. Ibid., 2. The New Era went in the opposite direction, with extensive hospital closures.

16 Ibid., 2, 26, 28.

17 See, for example, the "what we have done" lists provided in British Columbia, "2001/02 Annual Report: A New Era Update," https://www.bcbudget.gov.bc.ca/Annual_Reports/2001_2002/bcgovAR.pdf.

18 Christopher Pollitt and Geert Bouckaert, *Public Management Reform: A Comparative Analysis* (Oxford: Oxford University Press, 2011), 2.

19 *New Era* made just one specific tax cut promise – to provide the lowest tax rate of any province in Canada for the bottom two tax brackets, deliverable during the first term in office. BC Liberal Party, *New Era,* 5.

20 Simply tracking the content and flow of New Era processes is a challenging task. Among the documents attempting to achieve that goal was from the Premier's Office, "Cabinet Planning Session: The Next Six Months," 18 January 2002.

21 As detailed in Chapter 4, the 11 September 2001 attack on the World Trade Center and its aftermath extinguished any optimism that the tax cuts would pay for themselves, hopes that had already faded by that time.

22 See, for example, Norman Ruff, "Executive Dominance: Cabinet and the Office of the Premier in British Columbia," in *British Columbia Politics and Government,* ed. Michael Howlett, Dennis Pilon, and Tracy Summerville (Toronto: Emond Montgomery, 2010), 205–16; and Donald Savoie, *Governing from the Centre: The Concentration of Power in Canadian Politics* (Toronto: University of Toronto Press, 2004).

23 A neo-liberal by my definition is an advocate of smaller government, free markets, and less government intervention economically and socially. See, for example, J.R. Lacharite and Tracy Summerville, eds., *The Campbell Revolution? Power, Politics, and Policies in British Columbia* (Montreal and Kingston: McGill-Queen's University Press, 2017); and Katherine Teghtsoonian, "Social Policy in Neo-Liberal Times," in *British Columbia Politics,* ed. Michael Howlett, Dennis Pilon, and Tracy Summerville, 309–25.

24 Interactions occurred in meetings with the First Nations Leadership Council and the organizations that comprised it, in venues such as the First Citizens' Forum, and in processes such as negotiation of the Memorandum of Agreement on Regional Aboriginal Authorities. Annual First Citizens' Forums were a *New Era* commitment that was delivered by the Ministry of Community, Aboriginal and Women's Services. The negotiations around Regional Aboriginal Authorities were led by the Ministry of Children and Family Development.

25 Quoted in Vaughn Palmer, "Looney Tunes Times in the 'Renewal' Agenda," *Vancouver Sun,* 17 November 2001. The speech was surreptitiously recorded and leaked to the media.

26 Kevin Taft, *Shredding the Public Interest: Ralph Klein and 25 Years of One-Party Government* (Edmonton: University of Alberta Press, 1997), 25.

27 In response to a modest tax cut from the BC NDP government in 1998, Campbell argued that "drastic, bold action" was needed and that "he would have introduced a 10 or 15 percent tax break." Such measures, he said, "will spark economic growth, creating billions in revenues." Justine Hunter and Jim Beatty, "Small Tax Cuts Aimed at Sparking Economy," *Vancouver Sun,* 31 March 1998. With reference to

"two stage," see Norman Ruff, "An Ambivalent Electorate: A Review of the British Columbia General Election of 1996," *BC Studies* 110 (Summer 1996): 14.

28 BC Liberal Party, *New Era,* 5.

29 Rod Rhodes, *Everyday Life in the British Government* (Oxford: Oxford University Press, 2011), 7. "Absence" may overstate the case. Excellent participant-observer accounts can be found in Michael Barber, *An Instruction to Deliver: Tony Blair, Public Services and the Challenge of Achieving Targets* (London: Methuen, 2008); and Richard Crossman, *Richard Crossman: The Diaries of a Cabinet Minister* (London: Hamish, Hamilton and Jonathan Cape, 1975).

30 Rhodes, *Everyday Life,* 85, 163.

31 In a cabinet shuffle of late 2003, I moved to Sustainable Resource Management until the 2005 election. From 2005 to 2009, I was minister of health, happily at a time of surplus budgets and expansive agendas. After the 2009 election – and thrust once again into retrenchment after a four-year "Golden Decade" – I was minister of Aboriginal relations and reconciliation and finally minister of education before voluntarily leaving politics in 2013.

32 Deputies across government worked long and often stressful hours in the early years of the New Era. Community, Aboriginal and Women's Services (and I) enjoyed an excellent deputy in Bob de Faye.

33 David R. Cameron and Graham White, *Cycling into Saigon: The Conservative Transition in Ontario* (Vancouver: UBC Press, 2000), 45.

34 Martin Lodge and Derek Gill, "Toward a New Era of Administrative Reform? The Myth of Post-NPM in New Zealand," *Governance: An International Journal of Policy, Administration, and Institutions* 24, 1 (January 2011): 156.

35 Thea Vakil, "Changing Public Service Values: Limits of Fundamental Reform and Rhetoric" (PhD diss., University of Victoria, 2009), iii.

36 Rhodes, *Everyday Life,* 129.

37 Evert Lindquist, John Langford, and Thea Vakil, "Government Restructuring and the BC Public Service: Turmoil, Innovation, and Continuity in the 2000s," in *British Columbia Politics,* ed. Michael Howlett, Dennis Pilon, and Tracy Summerville, 239.

38 For example, Owen Lippert, *Change and Choice: A Policy Standard for British Columbia* (Vancouver: Fraser Institute, 1996), a document that makes the case for tax cuts.

39 For example, see Chapter 7; Seth Klein and Andrea Long, "A Bad Time to Be Poor: An Analysis of British Columbia's New Welfare Policies," Canadian Centre for Policy Alternatives, June 2003,

https://www.policyalternatives.ca/sites/default/files/uploads/
publications/BC_Office_Pubs/welfare.pdf; and Bruce Wallace, Seth
Klein, and Marge Reitsma-Street, "Denied Assistance: Closing the
Front Door on Welfare in BC," Canadian Centre for Policy Alternatives, 27 March 2006, https://www.policyalternatives.ca/sites/default/
files/uploads/publications/BC_Office_Pubs/bc_2006/denied_
assistance.pdf.

40 For examples, see Howlett, Pilon, and Summerville, *British Columbia
Politics;* Lacharite and Summerville, *The Campbell Revolution?;* and Rob
Shaw and Richard Zussman, *A Matter of Confidence: The Inside Story of
the Political Battle for BC* (Victoria: Heritage House, 2018). *BC Studies*
has published articles on the Campbell decade, such as Richard C.
McCandless, "Rate Suppression and Debt Transformation: The Political Use of BC Hydro, 2008–2014," *BC Studies* 191 (Autumn 2016):
9–33; and George Abbott, "The Precarious Politics of Shifting Direction: The Introduction of the Harmonized Sales Tax in British Columbia and Ontario," *BC Studies* 186 (Summer 2015): 125–48.

41 Jurisdictions may draw lessons from the policy of other jurisdictions
and may sometimes adopt elements of it (through policy transfer). An
extensive body of literature discusses such transfers, including Mark
Evans, "Policy Transfer in Critical Perspective," *Policy Studies* 30, 3
(June 2009): 243–68; Jonathan Boston et al., *Public Management: The
New Zealand Model* (Oxford: Oxford University Press, 1996), 2–27;
Richard Rose, "What Is Lesson-Drawing?" *Journal of Public Policy* 11,
1 (January 1991): 3–30; and David Dolowitz and David Marsh, "Learn-
ing from Abroad: The Role of Policy Transfer in Contemporary
Policy-Making," *Governance: An International Journal of Policy and
Administration* 13, 1 (January 2000): 5–23.

42 NPM literature is expansive, but among the sources used here are
Christopher Pollitt and Hilkka Summa, "Trajectories of Reform:
Public Management Change in Four Countries," *Public Management
and Money* 17, 1 (January–March 1997): 7–18; John Alford and Owen
Hughes, "Public Value Pragmatism as the Next Phase of Public
Management," *American Review of Public Administration* 38, 2 (June
2008): 130–45; Janine O'Flynn, "From New Public Management to
Public Value: Paradigmatic Change and Managerial Implications,"
Australian Journal of Public Administration 66, 3 (2007): 353–66; and
Patrick Dunleavy et al., "New Public Management Is Dead – Long
Live Digital-Era Governance," *Journal of Public Administration Research
and Theory* 16, 3 (September 2005): 467–89.

43 Written and performed by Robbie Robertson, "Somewhere Down the
Crazy River" was released in 1987. The title captures a sense of the
frenetic, sometimes bewildering, pace of the New Era.

Chapter 2: Roots of the Narrative

Epigraph: Roy Orbison, "The Only One," from *You Got It,* 1989.

1 The NDP won thirty-nine seats with 39.4 percent of the popular vote, the Liberals thirty-three seats with 41.8 percent of the vote, and Reform BC two seats with 9.3 percent of the vote.

2 BC Liberal Party, *New Era,* 11, 22–27. A reformist liberal in my definition embraces the notion of equality of opportunity through more extensive government intervention in the provision of public services, in contrast to the neo-liberal, who aims to minimize government.

3 Deborah Stone, *Policy Paradox: The Art of Political Decision Making* (New York: W.W. Norton, 2001), 138.

4 BC Liberal Party, *New Era,* 28.

5 Ibid., 29. I say "ironically" because one of the most unpleasant tasks facing the minister of health services in the New Era was closing rural hospitals.

6 Ruff, "An Ambivalent Electorate," 7; BC Liberal Party, *Courage to Change,* 9.

7 BC Liberal Party, *Courage to Change,* 9.

8 Cameron and White, *Cycling into Saigon,* 58.

9 Mike Harris speech, 27 June 1995, quoted in ibid., 183.

10 Ruff, "An Ambivalent Electorate," 7.

11 Palmer, "Parsing Campbell's Tax-Cutting." Clark was particularly effective in generating public apprehension over what programs might be lost because of the Liberals' 15 percent tax cut.

12 BC Liberal Party, *New Era,* 33. Weisgerber retired in 2001 from provincial politics; Brown became Campbell's long-term chief-of-staff.

13 In *New Era* language, the commitment became a referendum on "the principles that should guide BC's approach to treaty negotiations." Ibid., 27.

14 BC Reform's 1996 platform content was drawn from three sources. Tom McFeely, "Glen's Gambit, Gordon's Gain," *British Columbia Report,* 27 May 1996, 10–11; Ruff, "Ambivalent Electorate," 17; Doug Ward, "Accountability Top Issue for Opposition: The Reform and Liberal Leaders Both Start Their Campaigns with Pledges to Keep Their Word," *Vancouver Sun,* 2 May 1996.

15 BC Liberal Party, *Courage to Change,* 13. References to "smaller government" are on 1, 2, and 4–7.

16 Reform BC, *Voters' Warranty,* 1996, quoted in McFeely, "Glen's Gambit," 11.

17 BC Liberal Party, *New Era,* 9. In 2003, the Liberals reversed their promise regarding BC Rail. The verbal gymnastics are discussed in Chapter 5.

18 Will McMartin, "Fiscal Fictions," in *Liberalized: The Tyee Report on British Columbia under Gordon Campbell's Liberals,* ed. David Beers (Vancouver: New Star Books, 2005), 138. Note: *Liberalized* includes a second article from McMartin, "Conjuring a $5 Billion 'NDP' Deficit," which is also cited in this book. Page numbers cited overlap because the articles are in part presented in upper and lower panels on the same pages.

19 Chris Rudd, "Welfare Policy," in *New Zealand: Government and Politics,* 3rd ed., ed. Raymond Miller (Oxford: Oxford University Press, 2003), 435.

20 BC Liberal Party, *New Era,* 9, 13.

21 Campbell's comment on not tearing up agreements was made during a November 2000 interview with the Hospital Employees' Union newspaper the *Guardian.* HEU, "HEU Re-issues Campbell Interview on Tenth Anniversary of Publication," News Release, 5 November 2010. His statement on civil service layoffs is quoted in Les Leyne, "Voters Misled on Austerity Tactics," *Victoria Times-Colonist,* 18 January 2002.

22 BC Liberal Party, *New Era,* 5.

23 Reform Party of Canada, *63 Reasons,* 3, 4; BC Liberal Party, *New Era,* 4, 6–7, 30, 32.

24 Jennifer Smith, "Populist Democracy versus Faux Populist Democracy," in *Parliamentary Democracy in Crisis,* ed. Peter Russell and Lorne Sossin (Toronto: University of Toronto Press, 2009), 177.

25 Vaughn Palmer, "BC Liberals Play It Safe as Election Nears," *National Post,* 6 January 2001.

26 See, for example, British Columbia, *Debates* (15 July 1997), 5779.

27 Palmer, "BC Liberals Play It Safe."

28 Taft, *Shredding the Public Interest,* 25.

29 Quoted in Barry Cooper, *The Klein Achievement* (Toronto: University of Toronto Press, 1996), 75–76.

30 Taft, *Shredding the Public Interest,* 28; Cooper, *The Klein Achievement,* 76–77.

31 Quoted in Cooper, *The Klein Achievement,* 72.

32 Ibid., 73.

33 Provision in statute for ministers of state had existed in Canada since at least 1985.

34 In MCAWS, minister of state for community charter and minister of state for women's equality; in Health, minister of state for mental health and minister of state for intermediate, long term and home care; in MCFD, a minister of state for early childhood development; in MCSE, a minister of state for deregulation; and in the Premier's Office, a minister of state for intergovernmental relations.

35 Peter Aucoin, "The Design of Public Organizations for the 21st Century: Why Bureaucracy Will Survive in Public Management," *Canadian Public Administration* 40, 2 (Summer 2008): 300.

36 Gordon Campbell to George Abbott, 25 June 2001, 3.

37 Gordon Campbell to all ministers and ministers of state, 25 June 2001, 1. Ministers in the NDP government enjoyed more expansive staffing, most notably an executive assistant in their constituencies as well as in Victoria.

38 Aucoin, "The Design," 301.

39 British Columbia, *Debates* (22 August 2001), 754.

40 Ibid. (23 August 2001), 760.

41 Will McMartin, "Conjuring a $5 Billion 'NDP' Deficit," in Beers, *Liberalized,* 127.

42 Norman Spector, "There Is No Doubt: BC Has an Official Opposition," *Victoria Times-Colonist,* 8 June 2001.

43 McMartin, "Conjuring," 124. As examples, McMartin cites the NDP's engagement of Peat Marwick in 1991 and Social Credit's engagement of Clarkson Gordon in 1975.

44 Gordon Barefoot et al., "Report of the British Columbia Fiscal Review Panel," Victoria, 23 July 2001, letter of transmittal, 1–2, https://www2.gov.bc.ca/assets/gov/british-columbians-our-govern ments/government-finances/fiscal-review-panel-2001.pdf.

45 Cooper, *The Klein Achievement,* 77.

46 Campbell to Abbott, 25 June 2001, 1.

47 Ibid., 4 (emphasis in original). Mandate letters were made public by the premier on the date of their distribution.

48 Donald Savoie, "The Rise of Court Government in Canada," *Canadian Journal of Political Science* 32, 4 (December 1999): 655.

49 Peter Aucoin and Mark D. Jarvis, *Modernizing Government Accountability: A Framework for Reform* (Ottawa: Canada School of Public Service, 2005), 20.

50 Will McMartin, "Premier Shuts His Cabinet," *Tyee,* 14 December 2004.

51 Ruff, "Executive Dominance," 208.

52 Norman Ruff, "The West Annex: Executive Structure and Administrative Style in British Columbia," in *Executive Styles in Canada: Cabinet Structures and Leadership Practices in Canadian Government,* ed. Luc Bernier, Keith Brownsey, and Michael Howlett (Toronto: University of Toronto Press, 2005), 234.

53 Les Leyne, "It's Not a Cabinet, It's a Mutual Admiration Society," *Victoria Times-Colonist,* 15 December 2001.

54 Vaughn Palmer, "Campbell's 'Open' Cabinet Pure Infomercial," *Vancouver Sun,* 15 March 2003.

55 Taft, *Shredding the Public Interest,* 73–75.

56 Ibid., 75.

57 British Columbia, *Debates* (5 March 2002), 1487.

58 Campbell to Abbott, 25 June 2001, 2.

59 Quoted in Vaughn Palmer, "Government Spits Out 'Pablum' Proposal," *Vancouver Sun,* 14 November 2001.

60 British Columbia, *Debates* (23 August 2001), 765.

61 Vaughn Palmer, "Campbell Strangling the Communications Loop," *Vancouver Sun,* 27 November 2001. In June 2002, all 270 information officers were terminated as public service employees, after which 160 were rehired as Order-in-Council appointments.

62 Keith Baldrey, "Campbell Blamed for Defections," *Richmond News,* 18 December 2007.

63 One former official suggested that under the NDP, the Premier's Office budget was understated, with expenses being picked up by ministries. Respondent D, interview with the author, 21 September 2018.

64 British Columbia, *Debates* (22 August 2001), 739.

65 Vaughn Palmer, "Budget for Premier's Office Grows Seven-fold," *Vancouver Sun,* 3 August 2001.

66 Quoted in Naomi Klein, *The Shock Doctrine: The Rise of Disaster Capitalism* (Toronto: Alfred A. Knopf Canada, 2007), 7.

67 As noted in Chapter 1, *New Era* refers to the *New Era* document, whereas New Era refers to the period 2001 to 2005.

68 CBC, "NDP Calls Campbell's Tax Cut Desperate," CBC News, 28 October 2010, https://www.cbc.ca/news/canada/british-columbia/ndp-calls-campbell-s-tax-cut-desperate-1.915684. Campbell announced his plan to resign on 3 November, and cabinet chose not to act on the tax cut during the leadership transition.

69 Quoted in Klein, *The Shock Doctrine,* 7.

70 British Columbia, *Debates* (5 March 2002), 1517. For the complete quote, see page pages 81–82.

71 The author was a member of the Agenda and Priorities Committee in 2009, charged with finding cuts across the board. For an account of the HST saga, see Abbott, "The Precarious Politics," 125–48.

72 For example, the core review committee, and particularly Campbell as its chair, struggled with a redefinition of social housing, as provided by BC Housing (I was the minister responsible for BC Housing). Some committee members believed that a fortunate few exploited the

system while others were left out in the cold. One former official believed that this "recurring myth" encouraged "the destruction of social housing to create equity." Respondent C, interview with the author, 7 January 2019.

73 British Columbia, *Debates* (10 February 2004), 8444. The words are from the 2004 Throne Speech.

74 Crawford Kilian, "Gordon Campbell: The Forgotten Man," *Tyee,* 21 December 2017. Norman Spector described Campbell as "a policy wonk of considerable hubris." Norman Spector, "Gordon Campbell: A Not So 'Smooth and Orderly Transition,'" *Globe and Mail,* 10 November 2010. Both descriptions have merit.

75 J.R. Lacharite and Tracy Summerville, "Introduction: The Campbell Revolution?" in Lacharite and Summerville, *The Campbell Revolution?,* 5, 6.

76 Ibid., 9.

77 When the creation of safe-injection sites emerged as a prominent public issue in November of 2001, Campbell supported the controversial treatment option, as did I as minister responsible for the Vancouver Agreement. Frances Bula, "BC Supports Safe-Injection Sites," *Vancouver Sun,* 24 November 2001.

78 Kevin Ginnell, "Charting Gordon Campbell's Rise to the Top: The Pragmatic Mayor and the Politics of 'Efficiency,'" in Lacharite and Summerville, *The Campbell Revolution?,* 16.

79 Ibid., 25.

80 See Abbott, "The Precarious Politics," 125–48.

81 Cabinet minutes, 5 September 2001, 2. For the cabinet minutes, see "Exclusive: Campbell Cabinet Minutes – The First 100 Days," theBreaker.news, 1 September 2017, https://thebreaker.news/news/campbell-cabinet-minutes/. Reporter Bob Mackin obtained the minutes via a freedom-of-information request.

82 Quoted in Vaughn Palmer, "Beyond the Meanness," *National Post,* 6 January 1999. Nancy Campbell's comment was made in a get-to-know-your-leader video produced by the Liberal Party.

83 Philip Resnick, *The Politics of Resentment: British Columbia Regionalism and Canadian Unity* (Vancouver: UBC Press, 2000), 20.

84 Norman Ruff, "British Columbia and Canadian Federalism," in *The Reins of Power: Governing British Columbia,* ed. Terry Morley, Norman Ruff, and Walter Young (Vancouver: Douglas and McIntyre, 1983), 291.

85 Respondent C, interview with the author, 7 January 2019. For example, severe 2001 cuts to the Ministry of Forests (40 percent) and the

Ministry of Water, Land and Air Protection (45 percent) may have contributed to the challenge of responding to fire and flood in the decades ahead. George Abbott and Maureen Chapman, *Addressing the New Normal: 21st Century Disaster Management in British Columbia*, Report and findings of the BC Flood and Wildfire Review, 2018, 7–13, 116, https://www2.gov.bc.ca/assets/gov/public-safety-and-emergency -services/emergency-preparedness-response-recovery/embc/bc-flood -and-wildfire-review-addressing-the-new-normal-21st-century-disaster -management-in-bc-web.pdf.

86 Bula, "Hello Gordon." Bula's account even hints at some of the core values and beliefs that drove Campbell. "At another point," she recalled, "he recited a quote he has carefully memorized: 'Whatever you can do or dream you can do, begin it. Boldness has genius, power and magic in it.' When I asked where it was from, he turned anxious to help. Goethe, I think. Do you want me to find out? I can e-mail it to you. Just let me know." At moments when Campbell suspected others of nursing doubts – whether in caucus, cabinet, or party – Goethe and these inspirational words were apt to reappear as a tonic for failing political courage. One such moment is captured on page 69.

87 British Columbia, *Debates* (5 March 2002), 1517.

88 Bula, "Hello Gordon."

Chapter 3: Global Components and a Made-in-BC Solution

Epigraph: Eagles, "Hotel California," from *Hotel California*, 1977.

1 I feel confident in making this claim because I myself had never heard of New Public Management until 2013, when I embarked on doctoral studies.

2 Scholars disagree to some extent about the makeup of NPM. For a handy reference, see Gernod Gruening, "Origin and Theoretical Basis of New Public Management," *International Public Management Journal* 4 (2001): 2, which offers a table heading titled "Undisputed characteristics (identified by most observers)."

3 Philip Resnick, "Neo-Conservatism on the Periphery: The Lessons from BC," *BC Studies* 75 (Autumn 1987): 13.

4 Here I use "reform" in Irene Rubin's sense of the word: "Reform means change in a direction advocated by some groups or individuals. It does not necessarily mean improvement." Quoted in Pollitt and Bouckaert, *Public Management Reform*, 35.

5 Lacharite and Summerville, "Introduction: The Campbell Revolution?," 9.

6 Evans, "Policy Transfer," 253.

7 Lacharite and Summerville, "Introduction: The Campbell Revolution?," 7.

8 Teghtsoonian, "Social Policy," 315–18.

9 Abundant evidence supports Teghtsoonian's thesis. However, one former official suggests that the change of government signalled a shift in mindset more than an intensification: "Overnight in 2001, the public service had to adapt its discourse from 'social dividends' to 'return on investment' if they were to be understood by the new government." Respondent L, interview with the author, 24 February 2017.

10 Lacharite and Summerville, "Introduction: The Campbell Revolution?," 13.

11 Christopher Hood, "A Public Management for All Seasons?" *Public Administration* 69 (Spring 1991): 3 (emphasis in original).

12 Both the Community Charter and the devolution of the BC Safety Authority were products of the Ministry of Community, Aboriginal and Women's Services; they are described in detail in Chapter 6.

13 Alford and Hughes, "Public Value Pragmatism," 134.

14 Pollitt and Summa, "Trajectories of Reform," 7.

15 O'Flynn, "From New Public Management," 353.

16 Premier's Office, Internal directive to all deputies, "Deputy Minister Performance and Development Plan," 2002–03, 3.

17 Respondent C, correspondence with the author, 3 December 2018.

18 Gruening, "Origin and Theoretical Basis," 6.

19 Evert Lindquist and Ken Rasmussen, "Deputy Ministers and New Political Governance: From Neutral Competence to Promiscuous Partisans to a New Balance?" in *New Public Management to New Political Governance: Essays in Honour of Peter Aucoin,* ed. Herman Bakvis and Mark Jarvis (Montreal and Kingston: McGill-Queen's University Press, 2012), 187.

20 Ruff, "The West Annex," 239.

21 Quoted in Palmer, "Looney Tunes Times." The ninety-day agenda was a set of primarily legislative measures which the *New Era* platform promised to deliver within that time frame. Dobell's use of "looney" in relation to the ninety-day agenda was a comment on the pace of reform (which he characterized as "frantic") rather than on content of reform.

22 Dunleavy et al., "New Public Management Is Dead," 468.

23 Pollitt and Summa, "Trajectories of Reform," 12–13 (emphasis in original).

24 The Campbell cabinet included both a Ministry of Health Services and a Ministry of Health Planning, each with its own minister and

deputy minister. Both actively participated in creating the new regional model but with Health Planning as lead.

25 Ministry of Health Planning and Ministry of Health Services, "Core Services Review: Phase One," 12 December 2001, 15, http://www.llbc. leg.bc.ca/public/PubDocs/bcdocs2017_2/350124/health_planning_ dec12.pdf; Minister of Health Planning, "A New Era for Patient-Centred Care," PowerPoint presentation, 12 December 2001, 2.

26 The fifty-two authorities included eleven regional health boards, seven community health services societies, and thirty-four community health councils. Minister of Health Planning, "A New Era for Patient-Centred Care," 3, 4.

27 Ministry of Health Planning, "Government Restructures Delivery of Patient Care," News release, 12 December 2001. The regionalization model had been the object of extensive and sometimes intensive debate in closed cabinet. Public consultation was obviously very limited, unlike that of MCFD.

28 British Columbia, *Debates* (8 April 2002), 2589.

29 Ibid., 2600. The Provincial Health Services Authority remains in place today; an MCFD equivalent was never created.

30 See, for example, ibid. (24 March 2004), 9658–59, with Hogg's immediate successor Christy Clark; and ibid. (5 October 2004), 11415, with Clark's successor Stan Hagen, around regionalization.

31 The organizational structure for health service delivery – five regions and one pan-provincial tertiary authority – remains unchanged after nearly twenty years, a good start on success in a system that is prone to political rethinking. My description here deliberately simplifies the very complex challenge of transition from old to new regional models.

32 James A. Desveaux, Evert A. Lindquist, and Glen Toner, "Organizing for Policy Innovation in Public Bureaucracy: AIDS, Energy and Environmental Policy in Canada," *Canadian Journal of Political Science* 27, 3 (September 1994): 509.

33 British Columbia, *Debates* (30 July 2001), 134; Ministry of Health Planning, *2002/03 Annual Service Plan Report,* https://www.bcbudget. gov.bc.ca/Annual_Reports/2002_2003/hp/hp.pdf.

34 Respondent F, interview with the author, 10 January 2019. See Chapter 8 for full discussion.

35 Desveaux, Lindquist, and Toner, "Organizing for Policy Innovation," 493, 495–96.

36 Respondent F, correspondence with the author, 12 February 2019. In a 2006 report, Ted Hughes cited a 55 percent cut to the MCFD executive and the challenges arising from it.

37 The author, who was an Opposition Liberal MLA from 1996 to 2001, attended all caucus meetings whether he wanted to or not. Attendance was obligatory. The connection between New Zealand, Alberta, and subsequently British Columbia is discussed in Cooper, *The Klein Achievement,* 64–69.

38 Ibid., 65. Douglas was decidedly Friedmanesque on the pace of change, but he never acknowledged the connection, a sensible choice for a Labour government minister.

39 "Roger Douglas: Reflecting on the Fourth Labour Government," *New Zealand Herald,* 30 April 2004.

40 Quoted in Cooper, *The Klein Achievement,* 68.

41 Quoted in Palmer, "Looney Tunes Times."

42 "Cabinet Planning Session: The Next Six Months," Internal document, 18 January 2002, 1.

43 Quoted in Hall, "Policy Paradigms," 275.

44 Campbell to Abbott, 25 June 2001, 6.

45 Dolowitz and Marsh, "Learning from Abroad," 12.

46 Pollitt and Bouckaert, *Public Management Reform,* 4.

47 Evans, "Policy Transfer," 256.

48 Rose, "What Is Lesson-Drawing?," 5.

49 Cabinet minutes, 29 August 2001, 3, in "Exclusive," theBreaker.news. Fortunately, Management Services was not directed to seek investment advice from the latter.

50 British Columbia, *Debates* (31 March 2003), 5798. Similarly, as MCAWS contemplated the devolution of safety services, it looked at comparable devolved organizations created in Ontario and Alberta during the 1990s. See details in Chapters 5 and 6.

51 Evans, "Policy Transfer," 258.

52 During the period 2005–09, the British Columbia and New Zealand Ministries of Health engaged in a formal partnership to learn from one another based on remarkable similarities in demographics and health delivery systems.

53 Diane Stone, "Learning Lessons and Transferring Policy across Time, Space and Disciplines," *Politics* 19, 1 (1999): 51.

54 Ibid., 53; Hall, "Policy Paradigms," 289.

55 Dolowitz and Marsh, "Learning from Abroad," 5.

56 Colin Bennett, "Review Article: What Is Policy Convergence and What Causes It?" *British Journal of Political Science* 21, 2 (1991): 215.

57 Dolowitz and Marsh, "Learning from Abroad," 13.

58 Pollitt, "What Do We Know," 2.

59 MCAWS also brought in a social housing expert from Ontario. As debate on social housing ground on, MCAWS shrewdly repositioned

BC Housing as delivery agent for the *New Era*'s promised five thousand intermediate- and long-term-care units for the frail elderly.

60 Quoted in Alexandra Thornton and Galen Hendricks, "Kansas 'Real Live Experiment' in Trickle-Down Tax Cuts," Center for American Progress, 2 November 2017, https://www.americanprogress.org/issues/economy/reports/2017/11/02/441822/kansas-real-live-experiment-trickle-tax-cuts/.

61 Russell Berman, "You Better Learn Our Lesson," *Atlantic*, 11 October 2017, https://www.theatlantic.com/politics/archive/2017/10/tax-trump-kansas/542532/.

62 Howard Gleckman, "The Great Kansas Tax Cut Experiment Crashes and Burns," *Forbes*, 7 June 2017, https://www.forbes.com/sites/beltway/2017/06/07/the-great-kansas-tax-cut-experiment-crashes-and-burns/#17f9d5fb5508.

63 This sentence mimics one made by Campbell to Frances Bula in 2001. Quoted in Bula, "Hello Gordon."

Chapter 4: The Tax Cut

Epigraph: Traveling Wilburys, "Heading for the Light," from *Traveling Wilburys Vol. 1*, 1988.

1 Quoted in McMartin, "Fiscal Fictions," 153. This comment was part of Campbell's attempt to reassure his listeners of the genius of his tax policy, notwithstanding the harsh reality of the budget cuts that was emerging in October 2001. He attributed the quote to the German writer and poet Johann Wolfgang von Goethe, but there is some debate on this point. See Hyde Flippo, "A Well Known Quote Attributed to Goethe May Not Actually Be His," ThoughtCo., 24 June 2019, https://www.thoughtco.com/goethe-quote-may-not-be-his-4070881; and "What You Can Do, or Dream You Can, Begin It," Quote Investigator, 9 February 2016, https://quoteinvestigator.com/2016/02/09/boldness/.

2 Quoted in Craig McInnes, "Campbell Delivers on Dramatic Tax Cut," *Vancouver Sun*, 7 June 2001.

3 BC Liberal Party, *New Era*, 5, 8.

4 Campbell appointed the panel on 25 May 2001, during the interregnum before inauguration of the new government on 5 June 2001.

5 Quoted in Chad Skelton, "Campbell's Gamble: Will It Work? Critics Are Divided over Effects of Cuts," *Vancouver Sun*, 7 June 2001, 2.

6 Quoted in Will McMartin, "Remember the NDP's Supposed $5 Billion 'Structural Deficit,'" *Tyee*, 14 May 2005. Campbell provided a

similar comment on "the books" in October of 2000 to Palmer, "Parsing Campbell's Tax-Cutting."

7 Respondent J also commented, "Saying that taxes were cut and revenues increased does not mean that the tax cuts paid for themselves because the relevant metric is how much revenue would have been raised if taxes were not cut." Respondent J, correspondence with the author, 13 December 2018.

8 Barefoot et al., "Report of the British Columbia Fiscal Review Panel," i. The auditor general's summary concurs on this point.

9 Auditor General of British Columbia, "Monitoring the Government's Finances, Province of British Columbia 2001/2002," Victoria, January 2002, 30, https://www.bcauditor.com/sites/default/files/publica tions/2002/report4/report/monitoring-government%E2%80% 99s-finances.pdf.

10 British Columbia, *Debates* (30 July 2001), 132 (emphasis added).

11 Quoted in Ward, "BC Liberals' 12 Years," 2.

12 Les Leyne, "Tax Cuts Prove BC's Books Were in Good Shape," *Victoria Times-Colonist,* 9 June 2001.

13 Skelton, "Campbell's Gamble."

14 Ibid., 2.

15 Both Campbell and Clemens are quoted in ibid., 1.

16 Chris Sorensen, "Economist Expects BC Tax Cuts Will Boost Economy: He Says Cuts Will Pay for Themselves in Five Years," *Vancouver Sun,* 8 June 2001, 4.

17 Susan Danard, "Campbell Delivers on Tax Promise," *Victoria Times-Colonist,* 7 June 2001.

18 Ministry of Finance, "Government Honours Tax Cut Promise," News release and backgrounder, 6 June 2001. Annual savings by bracket showed that the two lowest brackets saved $236 and $430 annually versus $1,483 and $1,947 for the two highest brackets. See also Sylvia Fuller and Lindsay Stephens, "Cost Shift: How British Columbians Are Paying for Their Tax Cut," Canadian Centre for Policy Alternatives, 4 July 2002, 8, https://www.policyalternatives.ca/sites/default/ files/uploads/publications/BC_Office_Pubs/costshift.pdf.

19 Vaughn Palmer, "Patronage Cloud Obscures Tax Cut Sunshine," *Vancouver Sun,* 7 June 2001. As discussed below, Campbell claimed that including the higher brackets would deter "skilled" British Columbians from relocating to lower-taxed jurisdictions.

20 Cabinet minutes, 6 June 2001, in "Exclusive," theBreaker.news.

21 Appended to the tax cut press release were two pages of charts detailing the impact on each of the five tax brackets, as well as on comparative

provincial rates and on details of implementation. Ministry of Finance, "Government Honours Tax Cut."

22 An Ipsos-Reid poll conducted in early September 2001 showed that the approval rating for the Liberals stood at 62 percent, up 4 percent from election day. Campbell's personal approval rating was 70 percent. Jim Beatty, "Honeymoon Continues for Liberals: Gordon Campbell and His Party Have a Higher Approval Rating Than When They Were Elected," *Vancouver Sun*, 22 September 2001. The tax cuts were ostensibly still paying for themselves at that point.

23 Cabinet minutes, 27 June 2001, 2, in "Exclusive," theBreaker.news.

24 Quoted in Vaughn Palmer, "BC's Turnaround Delayed: Finance Minister's Optimistic Forecast Takes a Beating from Reality," *Edmonton Journal*, 28 August 2002. Collins delivered his line at the first Open Cabinet meeting.

25 Quoted in Bruce Bartlett, "The Laffer Curve, Part 1," *Tax Notes* 136, 3 (October 2012): 1207, https://papers.ssrn.com/sol3/papers.cfm?abstract_id=2155974.

26 Quoted in Skelton, "Campbell's Gamble."

27 BC Liberal Party, *New Era*, 10. The document claimed that more than 43,000 workers and employers had left the province since 1997, as had 469 businesses between 1994 and 1999.

28 Bruce Bartlett, "The Laffer Curve, Part 3," *Tax Notes* 137, 1 (October 2012): 76, http://www.taxhistory.org/thp/readings.nsf/ArtWeb/AAA36A918512355985257AC6006BC23F?OpenDocument.

29 BC Liberal Party, *New Era*, 2, 5.

30 Hunter and Beatty, "Small Tax Cuts." NDP finance minister Joy MacPhail's tax cut to individuals was about 1 percent but in combination with a variety of other tax breaks.

31 Jim Beatty, "Campbell Lays Out Plan to Restructure Government," *Vancouver Sun*, 19 April 1999.

32 British Columbia, *Debates* (14 March 2001), 17328.

33 Vaughn Palmer, "Tax Cut Tussle an Election 2001 Preview," *Vancouver Sun*, 22 November 2000.

34 André Blais, *Anatomy of a Liberal Victory: Making Sense of the Vote in the 2000 Canadian Election* (Peterborough: Broadview Press, 2002), 22.

35 The "getting government right" process was chaired by Marcel Massé, who was Treasury Board president at the time. His concluding report of 1997 was entitled "Getting Government Right: Governing for Canadians," Treasury Board of Canada, 20 February 1997, http://www.tbs-sct.gc.ca/report/gfc-gpc/gfc-gpc01-eng.asp.

36 Quoted in Vaughn Palmer, "A Critic Faces Some Slings and Arrows," *Vancouver Sun*, 12 January 2001.

37 Vaughn Palmer, "A Proposal to Make LNG and Site C Redundant," *Vancouver Sun,* 8 October 2015. Bond had weighed in on the energy controversies, prompting the retrospective commentary.

38 Quoted in McMartin, "Fiscal Fictions," 141.

39 Les Leyne, "Banker Bounced for Daring to Criticize the Liberals," *Victoria Times-Colonist,* 16 January 2001. From an economics perspective (courtesy of Brant Abbott of Queen's University), every change in tax policy is enacted in its own circumstances, making it difficult and perhaps impossible to tell the difference between effects that arise due to tax changes and effects that occur due to surrounding circumstances.

40 Ibid.

41 BC Liberal Party, *New Era,* 5 (emphasis in original). Faith in the infallibility of the Laffer curve may have been elevated by Lippert's *Change and Choice,* 6.

42 Quoted in Vaughn Palmer, "Liberal Non-economists Make Jobs Disappear," *Vancouver Sun,* 21 November 2001. Tax cuts actually cost close to $2 billion.

43 Quoted in Michael Smyth, "Economist Thinks Collins Smoking 'Funny Cigarettes,'" *Vancouver Province,* 10 January 2003.

44 British Columbia, *Debates* (30 July 2001), 132. As a consequence of diminishing BC exports, government revenues had declined $1.85 billion over the four-month period since 15 March 2001.

45 As noted above, provincial growth was 0.6 percent in real GDP and –0.3 percent in GDP per capita. Butler, "A Brief Examination," 17.

46 Palmer, "BC's Turnaround Delayed."

47 Quoted in Vaughn Palmer, "Liberal Scalpel Is Quietly Slicing Away," *Vancouver Sun,* 31 July 2001.

48 British Columbia, *Debates* (2 August 2001), 240.

49 Ibid. (30 July 2001), 132.

50 Of the $50 million, some $16 million came from child care, $7 million from communities, cooperatives and volunteers, $6 million from social housing (all under MCAWS), $9 million from environmental initiatives, and $8 million from labour market programs. Palmer, "Liberal Scalpel."

51 British Columbia, *Debates* (30 July 2001), 134.

52 Ken Dobell to deputies, 23 July 2001.

53 *The Common Sense Revolution* (page 3) promised a 30 percent tax cut over three years, but the *New Era*'s Ontario graph suggests the reductions were phased across five years. BC Liberal Party, *New Era,* 5.

54 Collins noted that most taxpayers would enjoy full benefit of the tax cut, effective 1 July 2001. British Columbia, *Debates* (8 August 2001), 325.

55 Ibid. (30 July 2001), 132.
56 Ontario, Ministry of Finance, and James M. Flaherty, *Ontario's Economic Outlook and Fiscal Review* (Toronto: Queen's Printer, 2001), 5.
57 Quoted in Vaughn Palmer, "Collins Cuts Back to 2.8 'Aluminum Smelters,'" *Vancouver Sun,* 5 September 2001.
58 Quoted in Vaughn Palmer, "Deficit Focuses Attention on Core Review," *Vancouver Sun,* 14 September 2001.
59 Quoted in Vaughn Palmer, "Yogic Flyer Collins Crashes Down to Earth," *Vancouver Sun,* 23 November 2001.
60 Palmer, "Deficit Focuses Attention."
61 Palmer, "A Proposal to Make LNG."
62 British Columbia, *Debates* (9 August 2001), 392.
63 Quoted in Palmer, "Liberal Non-economists."
64 British Columbia, *Debates* (5 March 2002), 1517 (emphasis added).
65 Quoted in Palmer, "Looney Tunes Times."
66 Pollitt, "What Do We Know," 7. See also Pollitt and Bouckaert, *Public Management Reform,* 27.
67 Respondent D, interview with the author, 16 November 2018.
68 Could the apparent faith in initial growth projections simply have been a smokescreen to mask an overt drive for budget cuts and smaller government? The author's long experience with Collins (including five years as his deputy House leader) suggests that his belief in the efficacy of tax cuts was genuine and that he would not have risked the potential embarrassment of a 3.8 percent growth prediction had he not believed it possible.
69 Quoted in McMartin, "Fiscal Fictions," 151.
70 Ministry of Finance, "Message for Use by Ministries," Message sheet, 18 September 2001, 1.
71 Vaughn Palmer, "A Liberal Era Far Less Cheery Than Envisioned," *Vancouver Sun,* 4 October 2001.
72 Vaughn Palmer, "Liberals' Big Changes Suffer a Reality Gap," *Vancouver Sun,* 30 October 2001.
73 British Columbia, *Debates* (12 February 2002), 1043.
74 Ibid., 1043–44.
75 Ibid. (12 February 2002), 1047. By contrast, the Throne Speech of July 2001, delivered a few months after the election, had proudly cited the 25 percent tax cut. Ibid. (24 July 2001), 41.
76 Together with Advanced Education, they comprised 70 percent of the provincial budget. According to Respondent N, correspondence with the author, 17 December 2018, Advanced Education was always placed in the same category as Education on budget cuts.

77 Those nine ministries were Agriculture; Competition, Science and Enterprise; Energy and Mines; Finance; Management Services; Provincial Revenue; Skills Development and Labour; Sustainable Resource Management; and the Premier's Office. As mentioned in Chapter 2, the budget for the Premier's Office was growing, not declining.

78 Respondent H, interview with the author, 27 January 2019.

79 British Columbia, *Debates* (12 February 2002), 1047, 1049.

80 Ibid., 1043, 1046.

81 Although many variables come into play, including timing of cuts, application to rate classes, and size of cut across those classes, a 25 percent decrease costing $1.2 billion will always have a far greater impact than one of 10 percent costing $480 million, particularly given the exemption of the larger ministries from budget reduction.

82 British Columbia, *Debates* (12 February 2002), 1043.

83 Ibid., 1046.

84 Ibid. (13 February 2002), 1064.

85 British Columbia, Ministry of Finance, "Budget 2002 in Brief," https://www.bcbudget.gov.bc.ca/2002/BudgetInBrief/default.htm.

86 British Columbia, *Debates* (19 February 2002), 1207, 1209.

87 Ministry of Finance, "Fact Sheet," appended to the news release "Government Honours Tax Cut Promise" of 6 June 2001. Newfoundland was second-highest at 48.6 percent, followed by Quebec at 48.2 percent, Prince Edward Island at 47.4 percent, Nova Scotia at 47.3 percent, New Brunswick at 46.8 percent, and Ontario and Manitoba at 46.4 percent each.

88 Statistics Canada, "Private and Public Investment Survey (Including Housing)," cited in British Columbia, "Confidential Cabinet Update: Economy and Fiscal Plan Status and Outlook," 14 July 2003, 15–16.

89 British Columbia, "Confidential Cabinet Update," 18, 36.

90 Peter Severinson, Jock Finlayson, and Ken Peacock, "A Decade by Decade Review of British Columbia's Economic Performance," Business Council of British Columbia online, 5 November 2012, 1–11, https://bcbc.com/reports-and-research/a-decade-by-decade-review -of-british-columbias-economic-performance. Investment in machinery and equipment was 4.59 percent in the 1990s and 3.52 percent in the 2000s, although the latter figure was higher than average in Canada, and the former figure lower than average. Some other indices, such as employment growth, were modestly better in the 2000s. Cause-and-effect assertions are indeed hard to prove.

91 British Columbia, *Debates* (12 March 2002), 1796 (Lynn Stephens).

92 Vaughn Palmer, "More Urgent Needs Threaten Core Review," *Vancouver Sun,* 18 September 2001.

93 Deputy Minister to the Premier and Cabinet Secretary to all deputies, "Fiscal Review," 23 July 2001 (emphasis added).

94 Quoted in Palmer, "Looney Tunes Times."

95 BC Ministry of Finance, "Message for Use by Ministries," 1–2.

96 Gary Collins to George Abbott, 18 February 2003, 2.

97 Respondent L, correspondence with the author, 26 March 2014 (emphasis in original).

98 Respondent H, interview with the author, 27 January 2019.

99 Respondent B, interview with the author, 4 January 2019.

100 Campbell to Abbott, 30 July 2001.

101 Boston et al., *Reshaping the State,* 11.

Chapter 5: Process Makes Perfect and the Drive to Survive

Epigraph: Beatles, "I'm So Tired," from the *White Album,* 1968.

1 In Gernod Gruening's list of NPM characteristics, "budget cuts" sits at the top. Gruening, "Origin and Theoretical Basis," 2.

2 Campbell to Abbott, 25 June 2001, 5, 6, 7 (emphasis in original).

3 Les Leyne, "Quest for Change: On Camera, Gordon Campbell Stays in His Box: Off Camera 'He's a Funny Guy. Quite a Smartass,'" *Victoria Times-Colonist,* 19 August 2001.

4 Campbell to Abbott, 25 June 2001, 8.

5 Vaughn Palmer, "A Peek inside the Core Review Revolution," *Vancouver Sun,* 27 October 2001; Palmer, "All Quiet."

6 Campbell to Abbott, 25 June 2001, 6.

7 Ibid. The process was officially known as the Core Services Review and Deregulation Task Force, but in practice the examination of core services and deregulation followed two parallel tracks.

8 Cabinet minutes, 29 August 2001, 2, in "Exclusive," theBreaker.news.

9 Vaughn Palmer, "More Urgent Needs."

10 British Columbia, Office of the Premier, "Overview of Streamlining or Eliminating Agencies, Boards and Commissions," handwritten date 9 May 2005, suggesting that the document is a retrospective review of core review, with an attached Appendix 2 titled "Core Review Questions," 1.

11 Campbell to all ministers, 31 July 2001, 1–3. The affordability test ensured that core review discussions were conducted in a climate of ambiguity and uncertainty. Declining energy prices in export markets, the softwood lumber dispute, the events of 9/11, and a general global economic downturn all contributed – along with over $2 billion in lost tax revenue – to the government's fiscal woes.

12 The federal program review was accompanied by modest tax increases rather than a tax cut.

13 Evert Lindquist, "Comprehensive Reform of Public Governance: Lessons from Canadian and Other Experiences" (paper presented at the "Towards a Comprehensive Public Governance" conference, Lisbon, 28 January 2013), 5–6.

14 Ibid., 7. The observation on Chrétien's responsibility for exempting Indigenous programs is from Savoie, *Governing from the Centre.*

15 Savoie, *Governing from the Centre,* 190–92.

16 Lindquist, "Comprehensive Reform," 7.

17 Campbell to all ministers, 31 July 2001, 1–4.

18 Premier's Office, "Core Services Review," undated, 2–3.

19 Office of the Premier, "Memorandum," 15 May 2002, 1–2.

20 British Columbia, Premier's Office to all ministers and deputies, "Core Review of Ministry Agencies, Boards and Commissions," 17 May 2002, 1–3.

21 Ibid., 1–2. Ministers first learned of the External Panel in this letter of 17 May 2002.

22 Ibid., 2.

23 As detailed below, during this period MCAWS and its Safety Engineering Services Branch were under pressure to serve up a one-third reduction in regulations, a daunting task in the area of technical safety, further exacerbated by staff and budget cuts.

24 MCAWS, "Briefing Note for Minister," 18 July 2002, 1.

25 Premier's Office, "Overview of Streamlining or Eliminating Agencies, Boards and Commissions – Role of the External Review Panel," 9 May 2005 (again reflecting a retrospective look at processes), Appendix 6, no page numbers.

26 Ibid.

27 Kevin Falcon to all ministers and deputies, "30-Day Deregulation Submissions," 30 October 2001, 1–2.

28 BC Regulatory Reform Office, "British Columbia Deregulation and Regulatory Reform Initiative: Mandate and Approach," 11 May 2005, 1.

29 Respondent A, interview with the author, 7 January 2019.

30 MCAWS, "Briefing Note for Minister," 9 July 2001, 1–2.

31 Campbell to Abbott, 25 June 2001, 7 (emphasis in original).

32 Campbell to Abbott, 13 February 2003, 1.

33 Vaughn Palmer, "Oh, They're the 'No-brainers' All Right," *Vancouver Sun,* 16 November 2001.

34 Vaughn Palmer, "Fudging Figures Helps to Cut Red Tape," *Vancouver Sun,* 6 May 2003.

35 Respondent A, interview with the author, 7 January 2019.

36 Respondent D, interview with the author, 3 January 2019.

37 Respondent B, correspondence with the author, 3 January 2019.

38 BC Regulatory Reform Office, "British Columbia Deregulation and Regulatory Reform," 2. The office delivered several seminars to enable that culture shift.

39 British Columbia, *Debates* (18 February 2003), 4865.

40 BC Liberal Party, *New Era,* 4, 8.

41 Deborah Stone, *Policy Paradox and Political Reason* (New York: Harper-Collins, 1988), 115.

42 British Columbia, *Debates* (30 July 2001), 134.

43 Respondent A, interview with the author, 7 December 2018.

44 Ministry of Management Services, "Waste Buster: Links to Submissions and Responses," February 2002, 1, http://www.wastebuster.gov.bc.ca:80/popt/sample.htm.

45 Vaughn Palmer, "Liberals Begin Their Era of No Subsidies," *Vancouver Sun,* 16 August 2001.

46 BC Liberal Party, *New Era,* 4, 10.

47 Ibid., 28.

48 MCSE, "Business Subsidies Eliminated to Revitalize Growth," News release, 16 January 2002.

49 Cited in Cooper, *The Klein Achievement,* 70.

50 Pollitt and Bouckaert, *Public Management Reform,* 98. Devolved agencies in Britain were known as "executive agencies," in Canada as "service" and "special operating" agencies.

51 Sandford Borins, "The New Public Management Is Here to Stay," *Canadian Public Administration* 38, 1 (Spring 1995): 125.

52 Aucoin, "The Design," 302.

53 Ibid., 303.

54 For example, an MCAWS ministerial briefing note argues that legislation "builds on the experiences of Alberta and Ontario." MCAWS, "Question and Answers: Safety Standards Act and Safety Authority Act," Spring 2003 Legislative Session, 2.

55 Aucoin, "The Design," 304.

56 I was the minister responsible for passage of the legislation that created the BC Safety Authority, which is now Technical Safety BC. I currently chair its board.

57 As minister of sustainable resource management, I was also responsible for passage of the legislation that created the Land Title and Survey Authority.

58 MCAWS, "Question and Answers," 3.

59 MCAWS, "MCAWS Fiscal 03/04 Budget Summary," 17 February 2003, 5.
60 Both Clark and Campbell are quoted in Leyne, "Voters Misled on Austerity."
61 Quoted in Michael Smyth, "Fat-Trimming Premier Brandishes a Hefty Axe," *Vancouver Province,* 28 September 2001.
62 Vaughn Palmer, "Review Panel Never Advised Such Deep Cuts," *Vancouver Sun,* 22 November 2001.
63 Quoted in Lindquist, Langford, and Vakil, "Government Restructuring," 227.
64 Kim Lunman, "Black Thursday Job Cuts Rock BC," *Globe and Mail,* 18 January 2002.
65 Quoted in Ian Bailey, "BC Government to Bring in Grief Counsellors for Laid-off Workers," *National Post,* 16 January 2002.
66 Palmer, "Liberal Non-economists."
67 Quoted in Bailey, "BC Government to Bring In."
68 Service provider to MLA George Abbott (Shuswap), 14 May 2002.
69 Lindquist, Langford, and Vakil, "Government Restructuring," 225.
70 Ben Parfitt, "Axed: A Decade of Cuts to BC's Forest Service," Canadian Centre for Policy Alternatives, December 2010, 4, https://www.policyalternatives.ca/sites/default/files/uploads/publications/BC%20Office/2010/12/CCPA_BTN_forest_service_web.pdf.
71 British Columbia, *Debates* (27 March 2002), 1099.
72 Respondent M, correspondence with the author, 10 December 2017.
73 Respondent B, correspondence with the author, 3 February 2016.
74 Respondent H, interview with the author, 27 January 2019.
75 Chris Tenove, "In the Hurtland," in Beers, *Liberalized,* 38, 46.
76 Evert Lindquist, "Recent Administrative Reform in Canada as Decentralization: Who Is Spreading What Around and to Whom and Why?" *Canadian Public Administration* 37, 3 (Fall 1994): 416.
77 British Columbia, *Debates* (12 March 2002), 1796 (Lynn Stephens).
78 Ibid. (24 March 2003), 5587.
79 Vaughn Palmer, "Liberal Cutters Run into Specific Resistance," *Vancouver Sun,* 15 November 2001. Proceedings of these committees were closed to the public but were sometimes leaked to the media.
80 Author's journal, 24 November 2001.
81 Author unknown but probably produced by the Premier's Office, "Towards a Coherent Social Policy Strategy for British Columbia," 4 July 2002, 1–2.
82 MCAWS, "Social Policy Strategy for Government," 27 June 2002, 1–2.

83 Chart attached to "Towards a Coherent Social," 4, 27.

84 Collins to Abbott, 18 February 2003, 2.

85 Respondent C, interview with the author, 5 June 2018.

86 "Cabinet Planning Session: The Next Six Months," Internal document, 18 January 2002, 1.

87 Premier's Office, "The Next Six Months: Deputy Ministers' Council," 22 January 2002, 1.

88 "Confidential Draft 270 Day Work Plan," Internal document, 18 January 2002, 2.

89 Premier's Office, "Six-Month Plan by Ministry," 4 February 2002, no page numbers. MCAWS had a similarly intimidating 270-day plan, as noted in Chapter 6.

90 Gordon Campbell, "State of the Province Address," 12 February 2003, 1, 3–4.

91 BC Liberal Party, *New Era*, 9.

92 Campbell, "State of the Province Address," 4.

93 Pollitt and Summa, "Trajectories of Reform," 9–10. The Ministry of Competition, Science and Enterprise nursed plans for privatization of government liquor stores, along the lines Alberta's retail liquor privatization. The initiative was abandoned in 2003.

94 George Abbott to Gordon Campbell, 15 June 2003, 1.

95 Ibid., 2.

96 Quoted in Les Leyne, "Campbell Eases Some of the Pain," *Victoria Times-Colonist,* 19 June 2003.

97 Office of the Premier, "Province Will Not Proceed with Lease of Coquihalla," News release, 23 July 2003.

98 Rose, "What Is Lesson-Drawing?," 27.

99 Office of the Premier, "Province Will Not Proceed."

Chapter 6: Community, Aboriginal and Women's Services

Epigraph: Bruce Cockburn, "Lovers in a Dangerous Time," from *Stealing Fire,* 1984.

1 Government of British Columbia, "Summary of Responsibilities: Community, Aboriginal and Women's Services, Minister of State for Community Charter, Minister of State for Women's Equality," undated, 3, https://web.archive.org/web/20010617232405/http://www.gov.bc.ca:80/bc.gov/popt/summary/. With seventy-seven Liberal MLAs, the demand for smaller government would not affect cabinet size.

2 I was MCAWS minister from 2001 to 2004, and the moniker in this case comes from the journals I kept at the time. Not everyone shared my sense of humour.

3 With similar irony, as MCAWS minister, I had the ill-fortune to announce the "freezing" (placing under review) of 700 of 1,702 units of approved social housing while simultaneously celebrating Affordable Housing Week. As one wag noted, "freezing" launched the "winter of our discount tent." Author's journal, 17 February 2002.

4 MCAWS, "Advice to Minister: Fiscal Update Cuts," 29 July 2001, 1–3.

5 For the full list of $50 million in cuts, see Palmer, "Liberal Scalpel."

6 George Abbott, "Mandate Review: First Presentation to the Core Review and Deregulation Task Force," 20 September 2001, 3.

7 BC Liberal Party, *New Era*, 25. The five thousand beds were ostensibly a Ministry of Health Services commitment, but under the new Independent Living BC program, the ministry was ill-equipped to deliver housing units for the frail elderly. BC Housing (as an agency within MCAWS) took on the challenge, a strategic marriage in the age of smaller government.

8 Pollitt and Bouckaert, *Public Management Reform*, 2.

9 Premier's Office, "Six-Month Plan by Ministry," 4 February 2002, no page numbers. GVSWDD was the Greater Vancouver Sewer, Water, and Drainage District.

10 Abbott, "Mandate Review," 8.

11 Ibid., 15.

12 These questions are drawn from my handwritten notes scribbled on my copy of the "Mandate Review" core review presentation.

13 George Abbott, "Ministry of Community, Aboriginal and Women's Services Core Services Review," 5 November 2001, 2. "Non-Core Functions-Eliminated" are listed on page 6 of the document.

14 In MCAWS, humour was a tool of survival. The author acknowledges the public servants who provided it.

15 The Premier's Office count of 730 ABCs included 191 boards of variance. However, for the purposes of calculating percentage of ABCs eliminated, the core review committee considered boards of variance as one entity (as noted in Chapter 5).

16 British Columbia, Premier's Office, "Core Review of Ministry Agencies," 1.

17 Judith Lavoie, "BC Spares Budget Cuts for Athletes," *Victoria Times-Colonist*, 4 July 2003.

18 BC Liberal Party, *New Era*, 13.

19 British Columbia, *Debates* (27 March 2003), 5701.

20 MCAWS, "Transferring of Management of Heritage Sites," 27 May 2003, 1, 3.

21 MCAWS, "Heritage Devolution Status Report," 1 October 2002, 21.

22 Quoted in Bill Horne, "Naked Defiance in Barkerville. Literally," in Beers, *Liberalized,* 43–44. Murray Bush, artist and activist, wrote the brochure.

23 BC Liberal Party, *New Era,* 4.

24 In sharp contrast, as noted on page 34, Alberta's Ministry of Municipal Affairs had its budget decreased by 47 percent, earning it the unenviable distinction of having the highest cut in Ralph Klein's overall 17 percent reduction in ministerial budgets.

25 See, for example, Gruening, "Origin and Theoretical Basis," 2.

26 British Columbia, *Debates* (21 August 2001), 679. Nebbeling was recounting the history of the charter as well as laying out the process to be undertaken before giving it statutory life.

27 BC Liberal Party, *New Era,* 4, 8.

28 British Columbia, *Debates* (29 April 2003), 6295.

29 Vaughn Palmer, "Pet Campbell Project Rife with Contention," *Vancouver Sun,* 29 November 2001.

30 News release, quoted in Vaughn Palmer, "Community Charter = Hang On to Your Wallet," *Vancouver Sun,* 12 March 2003.

31 Municipal institutions are within the constitutional authority of the provinces. I am indebted to Respondent A for insights with respect to the evolution of Community Charter components.

32 Respondent A, correspondence with the author, 3 December 2018.

33 Ibid.

34 Vaughn Palmer, "Business Wants Checks, Balances on Charter," *Vancouver Sun,* 3 April 2003.

35 Quoted in ibid.

36 British Columbia, *Debates* (3 November 2003), 7717.

37 Ibid. (17 November 2003), 7965. MLA Paul Nettleton (Prince George–Omineca) was also openly opposed. Ibid. (20 November 2003), 8099.

38 Ibid. (20 November 2003), 8094. Joy MacPhail cited letters from UBCM presidents Patricia Wallace and Frank Leonard. Ibid. (7 May and 7 November 2003), 8094–96.

39 Patrick J. Smith, "Local Government Legislative Reform in British Columbia: The Gordon Campbell Decade, 2001–11," in Lacharite and Summerville, *The Campbell Revolution?*, 220.

40 British Columbia, *Debates* (12 March 2002), 1836.

41 Ibid. (1 April 2003), 5850.

42 *New Era* twice promised a Domestic Violence Prevention Act on pages 26 and 31.

43 British Columbia, *Debates* (12 March 2002), 1821.

44 MCAWS, "Communications Plan: *Child Care BC Act* Amendments," 27 July 2001, 1, 6. See also Teghtsoonian, "Social Policy," 314.

45 BC Liberal Party, *New Era,* 26. The "funding to those who need it most" argument echoed the debate around social housing and the belief that some program recipients exploited the system.

46 British Columbia, *Debates* (21 August 2001), 665.

47 Ibid., 666.

48 Office of the Child, Youth and Family Advocate, "Rethink the Reductions: Children and Youth Need More," 2001 Annual Report, 32.

49 Ibid., 29.

50 Munroe payments referred to an arbitrated salary agreement for unionized child-care workers, which was reached under arbitrator Don Munroe in the latter years of the NDP government.

51 British Columbia, *Debates* (1 April 2003), 5875.

52 Ibid., 5846.

53 Ibid., 5852.

Chapter 7: Human Resources

Epigraph: George Gershwin, "Nice Work If You Can Get It," from *A Damsel in Distress,* 1937.

1 As previously noted, I use the word "reform" in the sense defined by Irene Rubin: "Reform means change in a direction advocated by some groups or individuals. It does not necessarily mean improvement." Quoted in Pollitt and Bouckaert, *Public Management Reform,* 35.

2 British Columbia, "Budget and Fiscal Plan – 2002/03 to 2004/05," Table 1.6: Expenditure by Ministry, 40, https://www.bcbudget.gov. bc.ca/2002/BudgetAndFiscalPlan/default.htm. The Canadian Centre for Policy Alternatives reported in 2003 that the cut had expanded to $609 million. Klein and Long, "A Bad Time to Be Poor," 4. In the spring of 2003, MHR Minister Murray Coell reported that his ministry's 2004–05 budget was now $1,220,593, a cut of more than $700 million. British Columbia, *Debates* (7 April 2003), 6046.

3 British Columbia, *Debates* (26 March 2002), 2167.

4 British Columbia, Ministry of Human Resources, "2001/02 Annual Report: A New Era Update," 6 (emphasis in original).

5 Ibid., 8.

6 Respondent G, interview with the author, 12 December 2018.

7 Rose, "What Is Lesson-Drawing?," 7.

8 British Columbia, *Debates* (26 March 2002), 2167.

9 Respondent G, interview with the author, 12 December 2018.

10 Judith Lavoie, "Find Work or Face the Music," *Victoria Times-Colonist,* 17 April 2002.

11 Respondent G, interview with the author, 12 December 2018.

12 One important exception here was "persons with persistent multiple barriers." Such individuals were not strong candidates for return to employment, and to its credit, MHR attempted to identify and protect them as broader processes unfolded. Respondent G, interview with the author, 12 December 2018.

13 British Columbia, *Debates* (26 March 2002), 2110.

14 MHR, "2001/02 Annual Report," 5.

15 B. Guy Peters, Jon Pierre, and Desmond S. King, "The Politics of Path Dependency: Political Conflict in Historical Institutionalism," *Journal of Politics* 67, 4 (November 2005): 1290.

16 Teghtsoonian, "Social Policy," 315.

17 Klein and Long, "A Bad Time to Be Poor," 5.

18 British Columbia, *Debates* (2 April 2002), 2384.

19 Judith Lavoie, "BC Government Asks for Proposals to Streamline Welfare, Job Programs," *Victoria Times-Colonist,* 28 December 2001.

20 British Columbia, *Debates* (7 April 2003), 6048 (Murray Coell).

21 Ibid. (2 April 2002), 2385.

22 Ibid. (26 March 2002), 2110–11.

23 Ibid. (2 April 2002), 2384.

24 The advocate's office was terminated in the core review process, along with Pallan himself after his last report.

25 Vaughn Palmer, "Welfare Scare Numbers Fell Far Wide of the Mark," *Vancouver Sun,* 7 February 2004.

26 Dolowitz and Marsh, *Learning from Abroad,* 8.

27 Peters, Pierre, and King, "The Politics of Path Dependency," 1290.

28 Ibid.

29 Wallace, Klein, and Reitsma-Street, "Denied Assistance," 7.

30 Chris Schafer and Jason Clemens, "Welfare Reform in British Columbia: A Report Card," Fraser Institute Occasional Paper, September 2002, 3–4, https://www.fraserinstitute.org/sites/default/files/Welfare ReforminBC.pdf.

31 Klein and Long, "A Bad Time to Be Poor," 5.

32 Schafer and Clemens, "Welfare Reform," 4. The single exception in British Columbia was an exemption for disability recipients.

33 Klein and Long, "A Bad Time to Be Poor," 5 (emphasis in original).

34 Judith Lavoie, "Jobs Ministry Shedding Hundreds of Positions," *Victoria Times-Colonist,* 14 November 2003. Klein and Long, "A Bad Time to Be Poor," 4, reported that thirty-six offices were closed.

35 British Columbia, *Debates* (12 February 2002), 1049.

36 Craig McInnes, "Province's Welfare Cuts Prompt Coell Censure Vote," *Victoria Times-Colonist,* 13 June 2002. Censure came from the BC Association of Social Workers.

37 Judith Lavoie, "Second Phase of BC Welfare Cuts Means Rent Money Reduction," *Trail Times,* 30 May 2002.

38 Previously, income assistance recipients who had dependent children were allowed to retain up to one hundred dollars of a family maintenance payment without a welfare payment reduction. Similarly, recipients could earn up to two hundred dollars per month from casual employment without penalty.

39 British Columbia, *Debates* (14 February 2002), 1105–6.

40 Ibid. (28 May 2002), 3662–63.

41 Judith Lavoie, "Dental-care Disaster Predicted," *Victoria Times-Colonist,* 8 July 2002. Some of those cutbacks were reversed within months after blowback from the Opposition, government caucus, and the media.

42 Barbara McLintock, "Female Trouble," in Beers, *Liberalized,* 26.

43 British Columbia, *Debates* (7 April 2003), 6047.

44 Judith Lavoie, "Government Yields on Questionnaire for the Mentally Ill," *Victoria Times-Colonist,* 22 November 2002.

45 Auditor General of British Columbia, "2003/2004: Report 6: Audit of the Government's Review of Eligibility for Disability Assistance," February 2004, 6, https://www.bcauditor.com/sites/default/files/publications/2004/report6/report/audit-government%E2%80%99s-review-eligibility-disability-assistance.pdf. The Opposition came into possession of an MHR communications plan that anticipated up to nine thousand clients were inappropriately receiving disability benefits. Judith Lavoie, "Thousands Targeted for Cut in Benefits," *Victoria Times-Colonist,* 14 March 2003.

46 Auditor General of British Columbia, "Auditor General Questions Government's Approach to Review of Eligibility for Disability Assistance," News release, 24 February 2004.

47 Auditor General of British Columbia, "2003/2004: Report 6," 7.

48 Respondent G, interview with the author, 12 December 2018.

49 British Columbia, *Debates* (13 February 2003), 4752.

50 Ibid. (2 March 2005), 12249. The minister in this case was Susan Brice, one of Coell's successors.

51 Klein and Long, "A Bad Time to be Poor," 4.

Chapter 8: Children and Family Development

Epigraph: Bernie Taupin and Elton John, "Sorry Seems to Be the Hardest Word," from *Blue Moves*, 1976.

1 For a flavour of the intense and frequent media and Opposition attention to child neglect and abuse tragedies, see Leslie Foster and Brian Wharf, eds., *People, Politics, and Child Welfare in British Columbia* (Vancouver: UBC Press, 2008). For a more sensational account, see William Rayner, *Scandal!! 130 Years of Damnable Deeds in Canada's Lotus Land* (Vancouver: Heritage House, 2001), 105–11.

2 BC Liberal Party, *New Era*, 2, 26, 28.

3 Ibid., 26.

4 British Columbia, *Debates* (9 August 2001), 378.

5 Early budget cut projections were issued in November and refined over time until they were formalized in Budget 2002. Hogg identified percentage cuts among the several ministerial departments (such as child protection, youth justice, and corporate services) in 2002 Estimates debates. See British Columbia, *Debates* (9 April 2002), 2661–62.

6 Leslie Foster, "Back to the Future," in Foster and Wharf, *People, Politics, and Child Welfare*, 188. In his dissertation, Hogg notes that Finance "required three budget reduction scenarios (at 20%, 35%, and 50%) ... After lengthy meetings with Treasury Board and over my objections, they selected a 23% budget reduction target." Gordon Hogg, "Creating Public Policy in a Complex Society: The Context, the Processes, the Decisions" (PhD diss., Simon Fraser University, 2015), 88.

7 Foster, "Back to the Future," 190. Treasury Board's perspective was unsurprisingly different, as noted below.

8 BC Liberal Party, *New Era*, 26. The advocate is incorrectly identified as the "Children, Youth and Family Advocate," and no date or published source for the quote are offered.

9 The MCFD workforce adjustment plan anticipated a 22 percent reduction over three fiscal years (or about 1,100 full-time equivalent positions). Ministry of Children and Family Development, "2001/02 Annual Report: A New Era Update," 7.

10 An insight provided by Respondent H, interview with the author, 27 January 2019.

11 Respondent F, interview with the author, 10 January 2019.

12 Leslie Foster and Brian Wharf, "Preface," in Foster and Wharf, *People, Politics, and Child Welfare*, xiii.

13 British Columbia, *Debates* (9 August 2001), 378.

14 Quoted in Judith Lavoie, "Ministry Cuts Youth Services," *Victoria Times-Colonist*, 23 October 2001.

15 An extensive analysis of the 2002 Throne Speech is provided in Chapter 4.

16 Quoted in Lavoie, "Ministry Cuts Youth Services."

17 Quoted in Judith Lavoie, "Kids' Minister Tries to Blunt Effect of Cuts," *Victoria Times-Colonist,* 29 November 2001.

18 Office of the Child, Youth and Family Advocate, "Rethink the Reductions," 28–29.

19 Ibid., 25–26. Calling out Campbell's failure to deliver on his promises must have provided a measure of satisfaction to Pallan, given that the *New Era* document includes a quote from the advocate describing the NDP government as "all talk and no action." BC Liberal Party, *New Era,* 26.

20 Foster, "Back to the Future," 187.

21 British Columbia, Ministry of Children and Family Development, "Core Services Review," undated but presented at Open Cabinet, 7 November 2001.

22 Quoted in Judith Lavoie, "Troubled Children at Heart of Storm," *Victoria Times-Colonist,* 16 March 2003.

23 Quoted in Lavoie, "Kids' Minister Tries."

24 British Columbia, *Debates* (8 April 2002), 2598.

25 Ibid., 2599–600.

26 Hogg, "Creating Public Policy," 91–98.

27 BC Liberal Party, *New Era,* 26.

28 British Columbia, *Debates* (8 April 2002), 1954 (Hogg in Estimates debate). Kith and kin agreements involved placement of a child in the home of a relative versus placement, post-apprehension by the state, in the home of an unrelated foster parent.

29 Respondent F, interview with the author, 10 February 2019.

30 Respondent F, correspondence with the author, 12 December 2018.

31 Deryck Thomson, "Foreword," in Foster and Wharf, *People, Politics, and Child Welfare,* xii.

32 The concerns and suspicions of critics were effectively summarized by Joy MacPhail, in British Columbia, *Debates* (24 March 2003), 5587: "The fact of the matter is that communities are struggling unbelievably, but they know they don't have any choice except to move in this direction not of the model but of making massive cuts while moving in this direction."

33 Respondent F, interview with the author, 10 January 2019.

34 British Columbia, *Debates* (8 April 2002), 2599.

35 Ibid. (9 April 2002), 2658.

36 Ibid. (8 April 2002), 2602.

37 Ibid. (9 April 2002), 2656. Hogg also mentioned a meeting with the Western Australia Disabilities Commission. Ibid. (10 April 2002), 2733.

38 Ibid. (8 April 2002), 2602–3. Of the ten thousand children in care, 40 percent were Indigenous, even though Indigenous people formed only 8 percent of the BC population.

39 Ibid. (24 March 2003), 5588. The only answer that Hogg could offer was continued identification and adoption of best practices. He mentioned New Zealand's program of foster care through kin care within extended families, little utilized to date in British Columbia.

40 Ibid., 5593. MacPhail did not identify either the name of the report or its authors.

41 Ibid. (13 February 2002), 1071. The NDP saw the elimination of these two offices as the silencing of critics. Other avenues for challenging government policy were also weakened, as independent officers of the legislature – such as the ombudsperson and the auditor general – were dealing with heavy budget cuts to their offices.

42 British Columbia, *Debates* (24 March 2003), 5587.

43 Quoted in Lavoie, "Troubled Children."

44 British Columbia, *Debates* (31 March 2003), 5821. For another example of Hogg on exogenous learning, see ibid. (24 March 2003), 5590.

45 Ibid. (25 March 2003), 5605–7.

46 Ibid. (31 March 2003), 5793.

47 Ibid. (24 March 2003), 5572.

48 Foster, "Back to the Future," 190–91.

49 "Receivership" was the word that one former public servant attached to the relationship between MCFD and Treasury Board. Respondent L, interview with the author, 12 September 2018. It involved a meeting with Treasury Board every two weeks for an update on budget, and any revisions to the budget target plan required a "change order" approval from the board.

50 Quoted in Vaughn Palmer, "Ministry Gets Hired Help to Meet Budget Targets," *Vancouver Sun,* 13 May 2003.

51 Judith Lavoie, "Cash-poor Children's Ministry Needs Budget Top Up," *Victoria Times-Colonist,* 8 May 2003.

52 For example, MCFD was accused of cutting $30 million in funding for children with special needs. British Columbia, *Debates* (7 May 2003), 6555.

53 Quoted in Judith Lavoie, "Disabled at Risk as Cuts Affect Changes, Group Says," *Victoria Times-Colonist,* 15 May 2003.

54 Quoted in Les Leyne, "Deep Cuts Were Politically Unworkable," *Victoria Times-Colonist,* 21 June 2003.

55 Jim Fisher of the South Island Child and Family Development Planning Group, quoted in Lavoie, "Cash-poor Children's Ministry."

56 British Columbia, *Debates* (6 May 2003), 6525–26.

57 Ibid. (12 May 2003), 6661.

58 Ibid., 6663.

59 Ibid. (13 May 2003), 6730. A September 2003 report by former deputy Doug Allen and Sage Group Management Consultants mentioned that "a three-member panel of experts appointed by government" was assisting the interim authority and the ministry in the continuing process of devolution and regionalization. The experts were probably from the management consulting firm BearingPoint (formerly KPMG) engaged in May 2003 by Treasury Board. See Palmer, "Ministry Gets Hired Help."

60 British Columbia, *Debates* (13 May 2003), 6731.

61 Quoted in Les Leyne, "Children's Ministry Is Behaving Badly," *Victoria Times-Colonist,* 8 May 2003.

62 Quoted in Lavoie, "Cash-poor Children's Ministry."

63 Quoted in Judith Lavoie, "Beleaguered Ministry Gets Budget Lift," *Victoria Times-Colonist,* 9 June 2003.

64 Quoted in Leyne, "Campbell Eases Some of the Pain."

65 Quoted in Lavoie, "Beleaguered Ministry." Notably, in an interview over fifteen years later, Respondent F reiterated (unprompted) that the document did not list what MCFD "intended to do" but rather that it was a way to get Collins's attention. Interview with the author, 10 January 2019.

66 Foster, "Back to the Future," 191. Similarly, in 2001, Vaughn Palmer reported the appointment of a new deputy minister and "wholesale change at the executive level," including replacement of three fired assistant deputy ministers. Vaughn Palmer, "Blood Flows as NDP Legacy Is Wiped Out," *National Post,* 11 August 2001.

67 Foster, "Back to the Future," 191, 198.

68 Gordon Hogg, interview with the author, 20 January 2019.

69 Judith Lavoie quoted figures from Deputy Minister Chris Haynes. Judith Lavoie, "Children's Ministry Staff Cuts End 525 BC Jobs," *Victoria Times-Colonist,* 15 October 2003.

70 Judith Lavoie, "Family Ministry Reels over $70-million Cut," *Victoria Times-Colonist,* 26 June 2003. According to Respondent F, consolidation of often small community-based service providers was highly controversial and staunchly resisted by MLAs. Interview with the author, 10 January 2019.

71 This followed investigative reporting by Sean Holman of *Public Eye* in articles published in the *Victoria Times-Colonist* and the *Vancouver Sun.*

72 British Columbia, *Debates* (29 March 2004), 9799 (Jenny Kwan).

73 Ibid., 9798.

74 Ibid. (24 March 2004), 9652.

75 Ibid. (5 October 2004), 11410.

76 Ibid. (8 February 2005), 11729; for the Budget 2005 speech, see ibid. (15 February 2005), 11894.

77 Respondent F, correspondence with the author, 12 December 2018.

78 An account of this controversy can be found in Foster, "Back to the Future," 199–200.

79 Robert Matas, "A Native Toddler's Final Day," *Globe and Mail,* 29 October 2005.

80 Foster, "Back to the Future," 200. After the children's commissioner was eliminated, the Coroner's Office took on this task.

81 Ted Hughes, *BC Children and Youth Review: An Independent Review of BC's Child Protection System, April 7, 2006,* 3–4, https://cwrp.ca/sites/default/files/publications/en/BC-HuguesReviewReport.pdf. The lack of training cited directly contradicted *New Era* promises noted early in this chapter.

82 Quoted in Dirk Meissner, "BC's Child Protection System Stretched beyond Limits, Judge Wants Reform," *Nelson Daily News,* 10 April 2006.

83 Pollitt, "What Do We Know," 8.

84 All quotes in this paragraph are from Miro Cernetig, "Liberals 'Took the Knife Too Far,' Child Death Investigator Says," *Vancouver Sun,* 8 April 2006.

85 British Columbia, *Debates* (16 November 2005), 1852. He made no reference to the role of budget cuts.

86 Quoted in Vaughn Palmer, "Will Campbell Apologize for Child Protection Findings? Well, No," *Kamloops Daily News,* 26 April 2006.

87 British Columbia, *Debates* (31 March 2003), 5793.

88 John Kingdon, *Agendas, Alternatives, and Public Policies,* 2nd ed. (Boston: Longman's, 1997), 177–78.

Chapter 9: Lessons Learned from the New Era

Epigraph: Jim Cuddy and Blue Rodeo, "Bad Timing," from *Five Days in July,* 1993.

1 The Murray aphorism was heard during the New Era and was also very much in play as Campbell reached his decision to support harmonization of taxes in 2009. See Abbott, "The Precarious Politics," 125–48.

2 Cabinet minutes, 27 June 2001, 2, in "Exclusive," theBreaker.news.

3 Statistics Canada, "Private and Public Investment Survey," 15–16.

4 Severinson, Finlayson, and Peacock, "A Decade by Decade Review," 1–11.

5 Seth Klein, "Reckless and Unnecessary: CCPA's Analysis, Facts and Figures for Understanding and Challenging BC's January 17 Budget and Job Cuts," Canadian Centre for Policy Alternatives, 21 January 2002, 3.

6 British Columbia, *Debates* (1 April 2003), 5852.

7 Ibid. (8 April 2002), 2602.

8 Ibid. (31 March 2003), 5793.

9 Office of the Child, Youth and Family Advocate, "Rethink the Reductions," 35.

10 Klein and Long, "A Bad Time to Be Poor," 5.

11 British Columbia, *Debates* (10 February 2004), 8444.

12 Ibid., 8449.

13 Ibid. (17 February 2004), 8607.

14 Ibid., 8610.

15 Ibid., 8613.

16 Marc Lee, "Balanced Budget for BC – But on a Razor's Edge," Canadian Centre for Policy Alternatives news release, 17 February 2004, 1, https://www.policyalternatives.ca/newsroom/news-releases/balanced -budget-bc-razors-edge.

17 British Columbia, Office of the Premier, "Throne Speech Sets Out Great Goals for a Golden Decade," News release, 8 February 2005.

18 McMartin, "Fiscal Fictions," 169, tables provided on 166–67.

19 BC Liberal Party, *New Era*, 4, 8.

20 Respondent D, interview with the author, 3 January 2019; Respondent F, interview with the author, 10 January 2019.

21 Variations of this saying are attributed to Abraham Kaplan (1964) and Abraham Maslow (1966). Google offers many excellent explanations of it.

22 Pollitt, "What Do We Know," 7.

23 Lindquist, "Comprehensive Reform," 7.

24 Quoted in ibid., 12.

25 Foster, "Back to the Future," 208.

26 Pollitt and Bouckaert, *Public Management Reform*, 2.

27 Following are the sources for various policy transfers, with the impetus for each noted in parentheses. MCAWS: government agents' offices/Service BC (core review), from Australia, Ontario, and New Brunswick; devolution of Safety Engineering and Services Branch to

BCSA (core review), from Alberta and Ontario; Community Charter broad powers model (*New Era*), from Alberta and Ontario. MHR: welfare reform (budget), from Alberta, Ontario, and some US states; term limits on welfare collection (budget), from the United States; liens on homes owned by welfare recipients (budget), from Manitoba and Ontario; disability to include mental illness (budget), from other provinces. MCFD: community-level child protection reforms (budget), from Manitoba and Ontario; school-based programs (budget), from twenty models throughout the world.

28 Dolowitz and Marsh, "Learning from Abroad," 13.

29 British Columbia, *Debates* (10 February 2004), 8444.

30 BC Liberal Party, *New Era,* 1.

31 Respondent B, interview with the author, 3 January 2019.

32 BC Liberal Party, *New Era,* 11.

33 The 2003 wildfires at Kelowna and Barriere prompted the commissioning of a report by former Manitoba premier Gary Filmon. Titled "Firestorm 2003 Provincial Review," it was delivered in 2004. The record-breaking 2017 fire and flood season prompted another review, Abbott and Chapman, *Addressing the New Normal,* which was delivered in 2018 along with a report by the BC Auditor General, *Managing Climate Change Risk: An Independent Audit.* The latter reports highlighted the gap in planning, preparedness, and prevention since 2003. See also the discussion of workforce adjustment in Chapter 5.

34 Ralph Archibald et al., "Trends in Renewable Resource Management in British Columbia," *Journal of Ecosystems and Management* 13, 3 (2013): 4–7. This article is authored by four former senior BC public servants – Archibald, Don S. Eastman, Rick Ellis, and Brian Nyberg.

35 John Lennon, "Beautiful Boy (Darling Boy)," from *Double Fantasy,* by John Lennon and Yoko Ono, Geffen Records, 1980.

Bibliography

Abbott, George. "The Precarious Politics of Shifting Direction: The Introduction of the Harmonized Sales Tax in British Columbia and Ontario." *BC Studies* 186 (Summer 2015): 125–48.

Abbott, George, and Maureen Chapman. *Addressing the New Normal: 21st Century Disaster Management in British Columbia.* Report and findings of the BC Flood and Wildfire Review, 2018. https://www2.gov.bc.ca/assets/gov/public-safety-and-emergency-services/emergency-preparedness-response-recovery/embc/bc-flood-and-wildfire-review-addressing-the-new-normal-21st-century-disaster-management-in-bc-web.pdf.

Alford, John, and Owen Hughes. "Public Value Pragmatism as the Next Phase of Public Management." *American Review of Public Administration* 38, 2 (June 2008): 130–45.

Archibald, Ralph, Don S. Eastman, Rick Ellis, and Brian Nyberg. "Trends in Renewable Resource Management in British Columbia." *Journal of Ecosystems and Management* 13, 3 (2013): 1–20.

Aucoin, Peter. "The Design of Public Organizations for the 21st Century: Why Bureaucracy Will Survive in Public Management." *Canadian Public Administration* 40, 2 (Summer 2008): 290–306.

Aucoin, Peter, and Mark D. Jarvis. *Modernizing Government Accountability: A Framework for Reform.* Ottawa: Canada School of Public Service, 2005.

Auditor General of British Columbia. "Monitoring the Government's Finances, Province of British Columbia, 2001/2002." Victoria, January 2002. https://www.bcauditor.com/sites/default/files/publications/2002/report4/report/monitoring-government%E2%80%99s-finances.pdf.

–. "2003/2004: Report 6: Audit of the Government's Review of Eligibility for Disability Assistance." February 2004. https://www.bcauditor.com/sites/default/files/publications/2004/report6/report/audit-government%E2%80%99s-review-eligibility-disability-assistance.pdf.

Bailey, Ian. "BC Government to Bring in Grief Counsellors for Laid-off Workers." *National Post,* 16 January 2002.

Baldrey, Keith. "Campbell Blamed for Defections." *Richmond News,* 18 December 2007.

Barefoot, Gordon, Linda Coady, John Cowperthwaite, Tim Duholke, Hugh Gordon, Mary MacGregor, and Stephen Thomson. "Report of the British Columbia Fiscal Review Panel." Victoria, 23 July 2001. https://www2.gov.bc.ca/assets/gov/british-columbians-our-governments/government-finances/fiscal-review-panel-2001.pdf.

Bartlett, Bruce. "The Laffer Curve, Part 1." *Tax Notes* 136, 3 (October 2012): 299–301. https://papers.ssrn.com/sol3/papers.cfm?abstract_id=2155974.

–. "The Laffer Curve, Part 3." *Tax Notes* 137, 1 (October 2012): 74–76. http://www.taxhistory.org/thp/readings.nsf/ArtWeb/AAA36A918512355985257AC6006BC23F?OpenDocument.

BC Liberal Party. *The Courage to Change.* N.p.: BC Liberal Party, 1996.

–. *A New Era for British Columbia: A Vision for Hope and Prosperity for the Next Decade and Beyond.* N.p.: BC Liberal Party, 2001.

Beatty, Jim. "Campbell Lays Out Plan to Restructure Government." *Vancouver Sun,* 19 April 1999.

–. "Honeymoon Continues for Liberals: Gordon Campbell and His Party Have a Higher Approval Rating Than When They Were Elected." *Vancouver Sun,* 22 September 2001.

Bennett, Colin. "Review Article: What Is Policy Convergence and What Causes It?" *British Journal of Political Science* 21, 2 (1991): 215–33.

Berman, Russell. "You Better Learn Our Lesson." *Atlantic,* 11 October 2017. https://www.theatlantic.com/politics/archive/2017/10/tax-trump-kansas/542532/.

Blais, André. *Anatomy of a Liberal Victory: Making Sense of the Vote in the 2000 Canadian Election.* Peterborough: Broadview Press, 2002.

Borins, Sandford. "The New Public Management Is Here to Stay." *Canadian Public Administration* 38, 1 (Spring 1995): 122–32.

Boston, Jonathan, John Martin, June Pallot, and Pat Walsh. *Public Management: The New Zealand Model.* Oxford: Oxford University Press, 1996.

–, eds. *Reshaping the State: New Zealand's Bureaucratic Revolution.* Oxford: Oxford University Press, 1991.

–. "Budget and Fiscal Plan — 2002/03 to 2004/05." Table 1.6: Expenditure by Ministry, 40. https://www.bcbudget.gov.bc.ca/2002/BudgetAndFiscalPlan/default.htm.

British Columbia. "2001/02 Annual Report: A New Era Update." https://www.bcbudget.gov.bc.ca/Annual_Reports/2001_2002/bcgovAR.pdf.

British Columbia, Ministry of Children and Family Development. "Core Services Review." Presented at Open Cabinet, 7 November 2001.

–. "2001/02 Annual Report: A New Era Update."

British Columbia, Ministry of Finance. "Budget 2002 in Brief." https://www.bcbudget.gov.bc.ca/2002/BudgetInBrief/default.htm.

–. "Government Honours Tax Cut Promise." News release and backgrounder, 6 June 2001.

British Columbia, Ministry of Human Resources. "2001/02 Annual Report: A New Era Update."

British Columbia, Premier's Office. "Core Review Actions to Be Implemented, by Ministry." An internal document from 2001.

–. "2001/02 Annual Report: A New Era Update." https://www.bcbudget.gov.bc.ca/Annual_Reports/2001_2002/premier.pdf.

British Columbia, Premier's Office to all ministers and deputies. "Core Review of Ministry Agencies, Boards and Commissions." 17 May 2002.

Bula, Frances. "BC Supports Safe-Injection Sites." *Vancouver Sun,* 24 November 2001.

–. "Hello Gordon: Is That You? Or the Other You?" *Vancouver Sun,* 28 April 2001.

Bula, Frances, and Brian Kappler. "The Long Way Home: With a Commanding Lead in the Polls, Liberal Leader Gordon Campbell Is Days away from What Appears to Be His Destiny." *Calgary Herald,* 5 May 2001.

Butler, Michael. "A Brief Examination of the British Columbia Government's Spending and Revenue Record." Report produced for the BC Ministry of Finance. 18 April 2017.

Cameron, David R., and Graham White. *Cycling into Saigon: The Conservative Transition in Ontario.* Vancouver: UBC Press, 2000.

CBC. "NDP Calls Campbell's Tax Cut Desperate." CBC News, 28 October 2010. https://www.cbc.ca/news/canada/british-columbia/ndp-calls-campbell-s-tax-cut-desperate-1.915684.

Cernetig, Miro. "Liberals 'Took the Knife Too Far,' Child Death Investigator Says." *Vancouver Sun,* 8 April 2006.

Cohen, Michael D., James G. March, and Johan P. Olsen. "A Garbage Can Model of Organizational Choice." *Administrative Science Quarterly* 17, 1 (March 1972): 1–25.

Cooper, Barry. *The Klein Achievement.* Toronto: University of Toronto Press, 1996.

Danard, Susan. "Campbell Delivers on Tax Promise." *Victoria Times-Colonist,* 7 June 2001.

Desveaux, James A., Evert A. Lindquist, and Glen Toner. "Organizing for Policy Innovation in Public Bureaucracy: AIDS, Energy and Environmental Policy in Canada." *Canadian Journal of Political Science* 27, 3 (September 1994): 493–528.

Dolowitz, David, and David Marsh. "Learning from Abroad: The Role of Policy Transfer in Contemporary Policy-Making." *Governance: An International Journal of Policy and Administration* 13, 1 (January 2000): 5–23.

Dunleavy, Patrick, Helen Margetts, Simon Bostow, and Jane Tinkler. "New Public Management Is Dead – Long Live Digital-Era Governance." *Journal of Public Administration Research and Theory* 16, 3 (September 2005): 467–94.

Evans, Mark. "Policy Transfer in Critical Perspective." *Policy Studies* 30, 3 (June 2009): 243–68.

Foster, Leslie, and Brian Wharf, eds. *People, Politics, and Child Welfare in British Columbia.* Vancouver: UBC Press, 2008.

Fuller, Sylvia, and Lindsay Stephens. "Cost Shift: How British Columbians Are Paying for Their Tax Cut." Canadian Centre for Policy Alternatives, 4 July 2002. https://www.policyalternatives.ca/sites/default/files/uploads/publications/BC_Office_Pubs/costshift.pdf.

Ginnell, Kevin. "Charting Gordon Campbell's Rise to the Top: The Pragmatic Mayor and the Politics of 'Efficiency.'" In *The Campbell Revolution? Power, Politics, and Policies in British Columbia,* edited by J.R. Lacharite and Tracy Summerville, 15–36. Montreal and Kingston: McGill-Queen's University Press, 2017.

Gleckman, Howard. "The Great Kansas Tax Cut Experiment Crashes and Burns." *Forbes,* 7 June 2017. https://www.forbes.com/sites/beltway/2017/06/07/the-great-kansas-tax-cut-experiment-crashes-and-burns/#17f9d5fb5508.

Gruening, Gernod. "Origin and Theoretical Basis of New Public Management." *International Public Management Journal* 4 (2001): 1–25.

Hall, Peter A. "Policy Paradigms, Social Learning, and the State: The Case of Economic Policymaking in Britain." *Comparative Politics* 25, 3 (April 1993): 275–96.

Hogg, Gordon. "Creating Public Policy in a Complex Society: The Context, the Processes, the Decisions." PhD diss., Simon Fraser University, 2015.

Hood, Christopher. "A Public Management for All Seasons?" *Public Administration* 69 (Spring 1991): 3–19.

Horne, Bill. "Naked Defiance in Barkerville. Literally." In *Liberalized: The Tyee Report on British Columbia under Gordon Campbell's Leadership,* edited by David Beers, 40–44. Vancouver: New Star Books, 2005.

Howlett, Michael, Dennis Pilon, and Tracy Summerville, eds. *British Columbia Politics and Government.* Toronto: Emond Montgomery, 2010.

Hughes, Ted. *BC Children and Youth Review: An Independent Review of BC's Child Protection System,* April 7, 2006. https://cwrp.ca/sites/default/files/publications/en/BC-HuguesReviewReport.pdf.

Hunter, Justine, and Jim Beatty. "Small Tax Cuts Aimed at Sparking Economy." *Vancouver Sun,* 31 March 1998.

Kilian, Crawford. "Gordon Campbell: The Forgotten Man." *Tyee,* 21 December 2017.

Kingdon, John. *Agendas, Alternatives, and Public Policies.* 2nd ed. Boston: Longman's, 1997.

Klein, Naomi. *The Shock Doctrine: The Rise of Disaster Capitalism.* Toronto: Alfred A. Knopf Canada, 2007.

Klein, Seth. "Reckless and Unnecessary: CCPA's Analysis, Facts and Figures for Understanding and Challenging BC's January 17 Budget and Job Cuts." Canadian Centre for Policy Alternatives, 21 January 2002.

Klein, Seth, and Andrea Long. "A Bad Time to Be Poor: An Analysis of British Columbia's New Welfare Policies." Canadian Centre for Policy Alternatives, June 2003. https://www.policyalternatives.ca/sites/default/files/uploads/publications/BC_Office_Pubs/welfare.pdf.

Lacharite, J.R., and Tracy Summerville, eds. *The Campbell Revolution? Power, Politics, and Policies in British Columbia.* Montreal and Kingston: McGill-Queen's University Press, 2017.

Lavoie, Judith. "BC Government Asks for Proposals to Streamline Welfare, Job Programs." *Victoria Times-Colonist,* 28 December 2001.

–. "BC Spares Budget Cuts for Athletes." *Victoria Times-Colonist,* 4 July 2003.

–. "Beleaguered Ministry Gets Budget Lift." *Victoria Times-Colonist,* 9 June 2003.

–. "Cash-poor Children's Ministry Needs Budget Top Up." *Victoria Times-Colonist,* 8 May 2003.

–. "Child and Family's Move to Regions Stalled by Cuts." *Victoria Times-Colonist,* 6 September 2003.

–. "Children's Ministry Staff Cuts End 525 BC Jobs." *Victoria Times-Colonist,* 15 October 2003.

–. "Dental-care Disaster Predicted." *Victoria Times-Colonist,* 8 July 2002.

–. "Disabled at Risk as Cuts Affect Changes, Group Says." *Victoria Times-Colonist,* 15 May 2003.

–. "Family Ministry Reels over $70-million Cut." *Victoria Times-Colonist,* 26 June 2003.

–. "Find Work or Face the Music." *Victoria Times-Colonist,* 17 April 2002.

–. "Government Yields on Questionnaire for the Mentally Ill." *Victoria Times-Colonist,* 22 November 2002.

–. "Jobs Ministry Shedding Hundreds of Positions." *Victoria Times-Colonist,* 14 November 2003.

–. "Kids' Minister Tries to Blunt Effect of Cuts." *Victoria Times-Colonist,* 29 November 2001.

–. "Ministry Cuts Youth Services." *Victoria Times-Colonist,* 23 October 2001.

–. "Second Phase of BC Welfare Cuts Means Rent Money Reduction." *Trail Times,* 30 May 2002.

–. "Thousands Targeted for Cut in Benefits." *Victoria Times-Colonist,* 14 March 2003.

–. "Troubled Children at Heart of Storm." *Victoria Times-Colonist,* 16 March 2003.

Lee, Marc. "Balanced Budget for BC – But on a Razor's Edge." Canadian Centre for Policy Alternatives news release, 17 February 2004. https://www.policyalternatives.ca/newsroom/news-releases/balanced -budget-bc-razors-edge.

Leyne, Les. "Banker Bounced for Daring to Criticize the Liberals." *Victoria Times-Colonist,* 16 January 2001.

–. "Campbell Eases Some of the Pain." *Victoria Times-Colonist,* 19 June 2003.

–. "Children's Ministry Is Behaving Badly." *Victoria Times-Colonist,* 8 May 2003.

–. "Deep Cuts Were Politically Unworkable." *Victoria Times-Colonist,* 21 June 2003.

–. "It's Not a Cabinet, It's a Mutual Admiration Society." *Victoria Times-Colonist,* 15 December 2001.

–. "Quest for Change: On Camera, Gordon Campbell Stays in His Box: Off Camera 'He's a Funny Guy. Quite a Smartass.'" *Victoria Times-Colonist,* 19 August 2001.

–. "Tax Cuts Prove BC's Books Were in Good Shape." *Victoria Times-Colonist,* 9 June 2001.

Lindquist, Evert. "Comprehensive Reform of Public Governance: Lessons from Canadian and Other Experiences." Paper presented at the "Towards a Comprehensive Public Governance" conference, Lisbon, 28 January 2013.

–. "Recent Administrative Reform in Canada as Decentralization: Who Is Spreading What Around and to Whom and Why?" *Canadian Public Administration* 37, 3 (Fall 1994): 416–30.

Lindquist, Evert, John Langford, and Thea Vakil. "Government Restructuring and the BC Public Service: Turmoil, Innovation, and Continuity in the 2000s." In *British Columbia Politics and Government,* ed. Michael Howlett, Dennis Pilon, and Tracy Summerville, 217–44. Toronto: Emond Montgomery, 2010.

Lindquist, Evert, and Ken Rasmussen. "Deputy Ministers and New Political Governance: From Neutral Competence to Promiscuous Partisans to a New Balance?" In *New Public Management to New Political Governance:*

Essays in Honour of Peter Aucoin, edited by Herman Bakvis and Mark Jarvis, 179–203. Montreal and Kingston: McGill-Queen's University Press, 2012.

Lippert, Owen. *Change and Choice: A Policy Standard for British Columbia.* Vancouver: Fraser Institute, 1996.

Lodge, Martin, and Derek Gill. "Toward a New Era of Administrative Reform? The Myth of Post-NPM in New Zealand." *Governance: An International Journal of Policy, Administration, and Institutions* 24, 1 (January 2011): 141–66.

Lunman, Kim. "Black Thursday Job Cuts Rock BC." *Globe and Mail,* 18 January 2002.

Massé, Marcel. "Getting Government Right: Governing for Canadians." Treasury Board of Canada, 20 February 1997. http://www.tbs-sct.gc.ca/report/gfc-gpc/gfc-gpc01-eng.asp.

Matas, Robert. "A Native Toddler's Final Day." *Globe and Mail,* 29 October 2005.

McFeely, Tom. "Glen's Gambit, Gordon's Gain." *British Columbia Report,* 27 May 1996.

McInnes, Craig. "Campbell Delivers on Dramatic Tax Cut." *Vancouver Sun,* 7 June 2001.

–. "Province's Welfare Cuts Prompt Coell Censure Vote." *Victoria Times-Colonist,* 13 June 2002.

McLintock, Barbara. "Female Trouble." In *Liberalized: The Tyee Report on British Columbia under Gordon Campbell's Leadership,* edited by David Beers, 17–37. Vancouver: New Star Books, 2005.

McMartin, Will. "Conjuring a $5 Billion 'NDP' Deficit." In *Liberalized: The Tyee Report on British Columbia under Gordon Campbell's Leadership,* edited by David Beers, 124–44. Vancouver: New Star Books, 2005.

–. "Fiscal Fictions." In *Liberalized: The Tyee Report on British Columbia under Gordon Campbell's Leadership,* edited by David Beers, 119–71. Vancouver: New Star Books, 2005.

–. "Premier Shuts His Cabinet." *Tyee,* 14 December 2004.

–. "Remember the NDP's Supposed $5 Billion 'Structural Deficit.'" *Tyee,* 14 May 2005.

Meissner, Dirk. "BC's Child Protection System Stretched beyond Limits, Judge Wants Reform." *Nelson Daily News,* 10 April 2006.

Ministry of Health Planning. *2002/03 Annual Service Plan Report.* https://www.bcbudget.gov.bc.ca/Annual_Reports/2002_2003/hp/hp.pdf.

Mucciaroni, Gary. "The Garbage Can Model and the Study of Policy Making: A Critique." *Polity* 24, 3 (Spring 1992): 459–82.

Office of the Child, Youth and Family Advocate. "Rethink the Reductions: Children and Youth Need More." 2001 Annual Report.

O'Flynn, Janine. "From New Public Management to Public Value: Paradigmatic Change and Managerial Implications." *Australian Journal of Public Administration* 66, 3 (2007): 353–66.

Ontario, Ministry of Finance, and James M. Flaherty. *Ontario's Economic Outlook and Fiscal Review*. Toronto: Queen's Printer, 2001.

Ontario Progressive Conservative Party. *The Common Sense Revolution*. N.p.: Ontario Progressive Conservative Party, 1995.

Osborne, David T. "Reinventing Government." *Leadership Abstracts* 6, 1 (January 1993): 2–3.

Palmer, Vaughn. "All Quiet on the BC Front." *National Post*, 21 December 2001.

–. "BC Liberals Play It Safe as Election Nears." *National Post*, 6 January 2001.

–. "BC's Turnaround Delayed: Finance Minister's Optimistic Forecast Takes a Beating from Reality." *Edmonton Journal*, 28 August 2002.

–. "Beyond the Meanness." *National Post*, 6 January 1999.

–. "Blood Flows as NDP Legacy Is Wiped Out." *National Post*, 11 August 2001.

–. "Budget for Premier's Office Grows Seven-fold." *Vancouver Sun*, 3 August 2001.

–. "Business Wants Checks, Balances on Charter." *Vancouver Sun*, 3 April 2003.

–. "Campbell Strangling the Communications Loop." *Vancouver Sun*, 27 November 2001.

–. "Campbell's 'Open' Cabinet Pure Infomercial." *Vancouver Sun*, 15 March 2003.

–. "Collins Cuts Back to 2.8 'Aluminum Smelters.'" *Vancouver Sun*, 5 September 2001.

–. "Community Charter = Hang On to Your Wallet." *Vancouver Sun*, 12 March 2003.

–. "A Critic Faces Some Slings and Arrows." *Vancouver Sun*, 12 January 2001.

–. "Deficit Focuses Attention on Core Review." *Vancouver Sun*, 14 September 2001.

–. "Fudging Figures Helps to Cut Red Tape." *Vancouver Sun*, 6 May 2003.

–. "Government Spits Out 'Pablum' Proposal." *Vancouver Sun*, 14 November 2001.

–. "Liberal Cutters Run into Specific Resistance." *Vancouver Sun*, 15 November 2001.

–. "A Liberal Era Far Less Cheery than Envisioned." *Vancouver Sun*, 4 October 2001.

–. "Liberal Non-economists Make Jobs Disappear." *Vancouver Sun*, 21 November 2001.

–. "Liberal Scalpel Is Quietly Slicing Away." *Vancouver Sun,* 31 July 2001.

–. "Liberals Begin Their Era of No Subsidies." *Vancouver Sun,* 16 August 2001.

–. "Liberals' Big Changes Suffer a Reality Gap." *Vancouver Sun,* 30 October 2001.

–. "Looney Tunes Times in the 'Renewal' Agenda." *Vancouver Sun,* 17 November 2001.

–. "Ministry Gets Hired Help to Meet Budget Targets." *Vancouver Sun,* 13 May 2003.

–. "More Urgent Needs Threaten Core Review." *Vancouver Sun,* 18 September 2001.

–. "Oh, They're the 'No-brainers' All Right." *Vancouver Sun,* 16 November 2001.

–. "Parsing Campbell's Tax-Cutting Promise." *Vancouver Sun,* 26 October 2000.

–. "Patronage Cloud Obscures Tax Cut Sunshine." *Vancouver Sun,* 7 June 2001.

–. "A Peek inside the Core Review Revolution." *Vancouver Sun,* 27 October 2001.

–. "Pet Campbell Project Rife with Contention." *Vancouver Sun,* 29 November 2001.

–. "A Proposal to Make LNG and Site C Redundant." *Vancouver Sun,* 8 October 2015.

–. "Review Panel Never Advised Such Deep Cuts." *Vancouver Sun,* 22 November 2001.

–. "Tax Cut Tussle an Election 2001 Preview." *Vancouver Sun,* 22 November 2000.

–. "Welfare Scare Numbers Fell Far Wide of the Mark." *Vancouver Sun,* 7 February 2004.

–. "Will Campbell Apologize for Child Protection Findings? Well, No." *Kamloops Daily News,* 26 April 2006.

–. "Yogic Flyer Collins Crashes Down to Earth." *Vancouver Sun,* 23 November 2001.

Parfitt, Ben. "Axed: A Decade of Cuts to BC's Forest Service." Canadian Centre for Policy Alternatives, December 2010. https://www.policyalternatives.ca/sites/default/files/uploads/publications/BC%20Office/2010/12/CCPA_BTN_forest_service_web.pdf.

Patten, Steve. "Preston Manning's Populism: Constructing the Common Sense of the Common People." *Studies in Political Economy* 50 (Summer 1996): 96–125.

Peters, B. Guy, Jon Pierre, and Desmond S. King. "The Politics of Path Dependency: Political Conflict in Historical Institutionalism." *Journal of Politics* 67, 4 (November 2005): 1275–300.

Pollitt, Christopher. "What Do We Know about Public Management Reform? Concepts, Models, and Some Approximate Guidelines." Paper presented at the "Towards a Comprehensive Reform of Public Governance" conference, Lisbon, 28–30 January 2013.

Pollitt, Christopher, and Geert Bouckaert. *Public Management Reform: A Comparative Analysis.* Oxford: Oxford University Press, 2011.

Pollitt, Christopher, and Hilkka Summa. "Trajectories of Reform: Public Management Change in Four Countries." *Public Management and Money* 17, 1 (January–March 1997): 7–18.

Reform Party of Canada. *63 Reasons to Support the Reform Party of Canada.* Calgary: Reform Party of Canada, 1995. https://www.poltext.org/sites/poltext.org/files/plateformesV2/Canada/CAN_PL_1995_RP_en.pdf.

Resnick, Philip. "Neo-Conservatism on the Periphery: The Lessons from BC." *BC Studies* 75 (Autumn 1987): 3–23.

–. *The Politics of Resentment: British Columbia Regionalism and Canadian Unity.* Vancouver: UBC Press, 2000.

Rhodes, Rod. *Everyday Life in the British Government.* Oxford: Oxford University Press, 2011.

Rose, Richard. "What Is Lesson-Drawing?" *Journal of Public Policy* 11, 1 (January 1991): 3–30.

Rudd, Chris. "Welfare Policy." In *New Zealand: Government and Politics,* 3rd ed., edited by Raymond Miller, 432–42. Oxford: Oxford University Press, 2003.

Ruff, Norman. "An Ambivalent Electorate: A Review of the British Columbia General Election of 1996." *BC Studies* 110 (Summer 1996): 5–24.

–. "British Columbia and Canadian Federalism." In *The Reins of Power: Governing British Columbia,* edited by Terry Morley, Norman Ruff, and Walter Young, 271–304. Vancouver: Douglas and McIntyre, 1983.

–. "Executive Dominance: Cabinet and the Office of the Premier in British Columbia." In *British Columbia Politics and Government,* edited by Michael Howlett, Dennis Pilon, and Tracy Summerville, 205–16. Toronto: Emond Montgomery, 2010.

–. "The West Annex: Executive Structure and Administrative Style in British Columbia." In *Executive Styles in Canada: Cabinet Structures and Leadership Practices in Canadian Government,* edited by Luc Bernier, Keith Brownsey, and Michael Howlett, 225–42. Toronto: University of Toronto Press, 2005.

Sabatier, Paul, and Christopher Weible. *Theories of the Policy Process.* 2nd ed. Boulder: Westview Press, 2007.

Savoie, Donald. *Governing from the Centre: The Concentration of Power in Canadian Politics*. Toronto: University of Toronto Press, 2004.

–. "The Rise of Court Government in Canada." *Canadian Journal of Political Science* 32, 4 (December 1999): 635–64.

Schafer, Chris, and Jason Clemens. "Welfare Reform in British Columbia: A Report Card." Fraser Institute Occasional Paper, September 2002. https://www.fraserinstitute.org/sites/default/files/WelfareReformin BC.pdf.

Severinson, Peter, Jock Finlayson, and Ken Peacock. "A Decade by Decade Review of British Columbia's Economic Performance." Business Council of British Columbia, 5 November 2012. https://bcbc.com/reports -and-research/a-decade-by-decade-review-of-british-columbias-economic -performance.

Shaw, Rob, and Richard Zussman. *A Matter of Confidence: The Inside Story of the Political Battle for BC*. Victoria: Heritage House, 2018.

Skelton, Chad. "Campbell's Gamble: Will It Work? Critics Are Divided over Effects of Cuts," *Vancouver Sun*, 7 June 2001.

Smith, Jennifer. "Populist Democracy versus Faux Populist Democracy." In *Parliamentary Democracy in Crisis*, edited by Peter Russell and Lorne Sossin, 175–88. Toronto: University of Toronto Press, 2009.

Smith, Patrick J. "Local Government Legislative Reform in British Columbia: The Gordon Campbell Decade, 2001–11." In *The Campbell Revolution? Power, Politics, and Policies in British Columbia*, edited by J.R. Lacharite and Tracy Summerville, 210–30. Montreal and Kingston: McGill-Queen's University Press, 2017.

Smyth, Michael. "Economist Thinks Collins Smoking 'Funny Cigarettes.'" *Vancouver Province*, 10 January 2003.

–. "Fat-Trimming Premier Brandishes a Hefty Axe." *Vancouver Province*, 28 September 2001.

Sorensen, Chris. "Economist Expects BC Tax Cuts Will Boost Economy: He Says Cuts Will Pay for Themselves in Five Years." *Vancouver Sun*, 8 June 2001.

Spector, Norman. "Gordon Campbell: A Not So 'Smooth and Orderly Transition.'" *Victoria Times-Colonist*, 8 June 2001.

–. "There Is No Doubt: BC Has an Official Opposition." *Victoria Times-Colonist*, 8 June 2001.

Steinmo, Sven, Kathleen Thelen, and Frank Longstreth. *Structuring Politics: Historical Institutionalism in Comparative Analysis*. Cambridge: Cambridge University Press, 1992.

Stone, Deborah. *Policy Paradox: The Art of Political Decision Making*. New York: W.W. Norton, rev. ed., 2001.

–. *Policy Paradox and Political Reason.* New York: HarperCollins, 1988.

Stone, Diane. "Learning Lessons and Transferring Policy across Time, Space and Disciplines." *Politics* 19, 1 (1999): 51–59.

Taft, Kevin. *Shredding the Public Interest: Ralph Klein and 25 Years of One-Party Government.* Edmonton: University of Alberta Press, 1997.

Teghtsoonian, Katherine. "Social Policy in Neo-Liberal Times." In *British Columbia Politics and Government,* edited by Michael Howlett, Dennis Pilon, and Tracy Summerville, 309–25. Toronto: Emond Montgomery, 2010.

Tenove, Chris. "In the Hurtland." In *Liberalized: The Tyee Report on British Columbia under Gordon Campbell's Leadership,* edited by David Beers, 38–70. Vancouver: New Star Books, 2005.

Thornton, Alexandra, and Galen Hendricks. "Kansas 'Real Live Experiment' in Trickle-Down Tax Cuts." Center for American Progress, 2 November 2017. https://www.americanprogress.org/issues/economy/reports/2017/11/02/441822/kansas-real-live-experiment-trickle-tax-cuts/.

Vakil, Thea. "Changing Public Service Values: Limits of Fundamental Reform and Rhetoric." PhD diss., University of Victoria, 2009.

Wallace, Bruce, Seth Klein, and Marge Reitsma-Street. "Denied Assistance: Closing the Front Door on Welfare in BC." Canadian Centre for Policy Alternatives, 27 March 2006. https://www.policyalternatives.ca/sites/default/files/uploads/publications/BC_Office_Pubs/bc_2006/denied_assistance.pdf.

Ward, Doug. "Accountability Top Issue for Opposition: The Reform and Liberal Leaders Both Start Their Campaigns with Pledges to Keep Their Word." *Vancouver Sun,* 2 May 1996.

–. "BC Liberals' 12 Years of Tax Shifts, Explained." *Tyee,* 6 May 2013.

Index

Note: "(t)" following a page number indicates a table

A New Era for British Columbia
(commitments document): about,
5, 194*nn*1–2, 202*n*67; child, youth,
and family advocate, 225*n*19;
child protection, 159, 177; child-
care funding, 140, 221*n*45; vs
Common Sense Revolution
(Ontario), 79, 211*n*53; vs *Courage
to Change* document, 28–32;
criticisms of NDP, 28, 225*n*19;
deregulation, 103; document
display, 9; domestic violence, 139,
220*n*42; economic vs social
agenda, 10, 15, 45, 49; election
platform (2001), 26; employer
migration, 74, 210*n*27; flaws, 187;
fulfillment of, 9, 21, 195*n*17;
heritage resources, 133; local
government, 135; ninety-day
agenda, 56, 205*n*21; referendum
(treaties), 30, 199*n*13; Reform BC
policy, 30; "smaller government"
phrase, 31; social programs,
126–27, 159–60; social workers,
176; spending promises, 9, 88,
195*n*15; tax cuts, 7–10, 69, 76,

86–87, 194*n*8, 195*n*11, 195*n*19,
211*n*41; vision, 27–28, 32; waste
website, 105. *See also* New Era
Abbott, Minister George M.
(Community, Aboriginal and
Women's Services [MCAWS]):
about, 11, 15–18, 197*n*31,
202*nn*71–72; Agenda and
Priorities Committee (2009),
202*n*71; BC Safety Authority,
216*n*56; black humour, 125,
130–31, 134, 218*n*2, 219*n*3, 219*n*14;
caucus meeting attendance,
207*n*37; core review, 129, 219*n*12;
Land Title and Survey Authority,
216*n*57; New Public Management
(NPM), 204*n*1; oath of
confidentiality, 19; research
methodology, 18–23; safe-
injection sites, 47, 203*n*77; social
housing, 202*n*72, 219*n*3
Aboriginal Health Association, 116
abortion policy, 34, 47
ActNow BC program, 46
Advisory Council on
Multiculturalism, 102

humour, 125, 130–31, 134, 218*n*2,
219*n*3, 219*n*14

income assistance (single parents),
141, 154–56, 163, 166, 183, 185, 223*n*38
income tax. *See* tax cuts policy
Independent Living BC, 195*n*15,
219*n*7
Indigenous peoples: agreements, 47,
188; children in care, 226*n*38;
federal program review, 98; kith
and kin agreements, 188; languages
preservation, 128, 132; settler
relations, 12–13, 47, 49, 192, 196*n*24;
treaties, 12–13, 30, 199*n*13
Industrial Development Incentive
Act (1985), 106
infrastructure spending, 32, 119, 121
Interim Authority for Community
Living BC, 165, 170–71, 172, 173–74.
See also Community Living BC
investments, 74, 77, 89, 180, 184
Ipsos-Reid polls, 210*n*22

Jarvis, Mark, 41
Job Access Loan program
(Wisconsin, USA), 151–52
justice system, 112, 113

Kamloops, 111, 120
Kansas (tax cuts policy), 65–66
Kehler, John, 174
Kelowna, 111
Kelowna Accord (2005), 49
Khaldun, Ibn, 73
Kilian, Crawford, 46
King, Desmond, 147, 150
Kingdon, John, 177
kith and kin agreements (children
in care), 165, 175, 188, 225*n*28,
226*n*39

Klein, Naomi, 43
Klein, Ralph (Alberta premier), 13,
23, 39–40. *See also* Alberta
government
Klein, Seth, 151, 152, 182
Kwan, Jenny (NDP MLA), 81, 147,
148, 149, 155, 173

labour agreements, 32, 200*n*21
Lacharite, J.R., 46–47, 53
Laffer curve (economic graph), 74,
76, 211*n*41
Land Title and Survey Authority,
54, 109, 216*n*57
Lange, David (New Zealand
government), 52, 56, 61, 119
Langford, John, 17
Lavoie, Judith, 154, 155, 172, 223*n*41
Law Courts Education Society of
BC, 102
Lee, Marc, 185
Lee, MLA Richard, 141
LegaciesNow, 184
Legal Aid Office closure, 113, 115
Lekstrom, Blair MLA, 137
Leyne, Les, 41, 71, 76, 95, 211*n*39
Liberal Party (BC Liberals). *See*
British Columbia Liberal Party
(BC Liberals)
Liberal Party of Canada, 75,
97(t)–99, 210*n*35, 215*n*12
Lillooet (public service layoffs), 113
Lindquist, Evert, 17, 58, 59, 98, 113
liquor stores (privatization), 41,
218*n*93
local government: broad powers
model, 135–36; budget
responsibilities, 166, 225*n*32;
Community Charter, 134–38;
constitutional authority, 135,
220*n*31